THE REGIONS AND THE EUROPEAN COMMUNITY: THE REGIONAL RESPONSE TO THE SINGLE MARKET IN THE UNDERDEVELOPED AREAS

THE REGIONS AND THE EUROPEAN COMMUNITY

The Regional Response to the Single Market in the Underdeveloped Areas

edited by

ROBERT LEONARDI

FRANK CASS

First published in 1993 in Great Britain by
FRANK CASS & CO. LTD.
Gainsborough House, Gainsborough Road,
London E11 1RS, England

and in the United States of America by
FRANK CASS
c/o International Specialized Book Services, Inc.
5602 N.E. Hassalo Street
Portland, Oregon 97213

British Library Cataloguing in Publication Data

Regions and the European Community:
Regional Response to the Single Market in
the Underdeveloped Areas. – (Special
Issues of "Regional Politics & Policy"
Series, ISSN 0959-2318; Vol. 2, No. 1)
I. Leonardi, Robert II. Series
337.1

ISBN 0 7146 3460 3

Library of Congress Cataloging-in-Publication Data

The Regions and the European Community : the regional response to the single market in the underdeveloped areas / edited by Robert Leonardi.
p. cm.
Articles originally published in Regional politics & policy, v. 2, no. 1, Spring 1992.
Includes bibliographical references.
ISBN 0-7146-3460-3
1. European Economic Community. 2. Europe 1992. 3. European Economic Community countries—Economic conditions—Regional disparities. I. Leonardi, Robert, 1945–
HC241.2.R433 1992
337.1'42—dc20 92-28756
CIP

This group of Studies first appeared in a Special Issue on 'The Regions and the European Community: The Regional Response to the Single Market in the Underdeveloped Areas' in *Regional Politics & Policy* Vol. 2, Nos. 1 & 2, published by Frank Cass & Co. Ltd.

Typeset by Regent Typesetting, London

Contents

Notes on the Contributors

Robert Leonardi is Jean Monnet Lecturer at the London School of Economics. He has conducted a number of studies for the European Commission and various regional governments on the role of regional political institutions in the pursuit of economic development.

Jürgen R. Grote is a Ph.D. candidate at the European University Institute Florence, Italy, and is completing a dissertation on networking and small and medium-sized business representation in the European Community.

Giuliano Bianchi is a senior official in the Department of Planning, Tuscan Regional Government and an Adjunct Lecturer at the University of Siena.

Carmel Coyle is Research Associate at the Centre for European Economic and Public Affairs, University College Dublin, Ireland.

Richard Sinnott is Director of the Centre for European Economic and Public Affairs, University College Dublin, Ireland.

Susannah Verney is Research Fellow (Unit on South-East Europe) at the University of Bradford, and teaches Greek politics in Athens.

Fouli Papageorgiou is a planning consultant in Greece working on regional and local development projects.

Walter C. Opello, Jr. is Professor of Political Science at the State University of New York, Oswego. He has just completed a book on public administration in Portugal.

Francesc Morata is Assistant Professor in the Department of Political Science at the Autonomous University of Barcelona. He has conducted extensive work on the impact of the EC on Spanish regions.

Shari Garmise is a Ph.D. candidate at the London School of Economics, and is currently working on a dissertation looking at the role of subnational government policies toward the stimulation of endogenous economic development.

The Role of Sub-National Institutions in European Integration

ROBERT LEONARDI

I. INTRODUCTION

The articles in this volume represent the outcome of the project, 'The European Community, Regions, and European Integration: A Comparative Study of Policy Sectors in Preparing for 1992', financed by the European Commission and conducted under the auspices of the European University Institute's European Policy Unit.[1] The project was directed by the author and initiated in December 1988. Fieldwork was terminated in February 1990, and the final report was submitted to the Commission in September 1990. Based on the mandate given to the project at the 26–27 February 1989 meeting in Palermo of European Community (EC) ministers,[2] the project undertook to: (1) survey elite opinion at the sub-national level on the perceived consequences and attitudes toward the creation of a single market, (2) analyse the regional impact of Community sectoral policies, (3) conduct an intensive investigation of the structure and implementation of the Integrated Mediterranean Programmes (IMPs), and (4) conceptualize the possibilities of creating regional networks to take advantage of the provisions of Article 10 in the 1988 European Regional Development Fund (ERDF) regulation providing for joint policy-making and implementation structures for border regions. Interviews with political and interest group leaders were conducted in the seven countries of the European Community containing 'less developed', Objective 1 areas.[3]

The survey of sub-national political and economic elites constitutes the first large-scale comparative study ever conducted of local political systems and the activities of sub-national institutions within the context of the EC. The project also represented the first time that the issue of the goals of stimulating economic growth and social development was treated from an institutional perspective based on the hypothesis that:

> the development of peripheral areas in the Community is as much a question of capital investments in economic and social infrastructures as one of developing adequate institutional structures, pro-

cedures, and networks for the purpose of engaging in effective policy making and implementation at the sub-national level.

The results of the research work conducted in each country and policy sector (for example, IMPs and sectoral policies) will be discussed in separate articles in the context of each individual country's experience with regional forms of sub-national government. In the conclusions an attempt will be made to place the national responses in comparative perspective and discuss the implications of the Maastricht summit for the role of regional institutions in the realization of the single market and the achievement of EMU. Each article has been prepared by the researcher(s) responsible for the conduct of the interviews in the field or the survey of a particular policy area. Thus, the current volume constitutes a unique survey of: regional institutions and policy processes in the Community's Objective 1 areas, attitudes and evaluations of sub-national political and interest group elites toward their own regional economy and society and the prospect of creating a single European market by 1993, and alternative approaches that can be used by the Community in structuring its support for regional economic and social development once the current phase of the structural fund approach – that is, special types of intervention by the Community to alleviate structural problems in less-developed regional economies – is exhausted and a new structure is created to take its place.

Before introducing the country-by-country analysis, it is necessary to provide some background information on how the project was launched and lay out the conceptual framework that underpins the common research design. The Community's recent focus on institutions at the sub-national level as part of its evolving regional policy is characteristic of how the EC operates in a gradual, piecemeal fashion, and how the dynamics of European integration have the power of drawing into the policy-making and implementation process institutions and forces that have for a long time remained on the periphery of the integration movement.[4]

II. THE PALERMO CONFERENCE MANDATE

On 26–27 February 1988 the representatives responsible for European Community affairs of the 12 member states along with representatives of the European Parliament and Commission met in Palermo at the invitation of the Italian Minister for EC affairs, Professor Antonio LaPergola. The main item on the agenda for the meeting was the discussion of the role that inter-regional co-operation could play in the full realization of the Single European Act. In his introductory statement, LaPergola observed that the member states and the Community could, through the use of inter-regional co-operative agreements, make real gains in the pursuit of the two basic goals of the Single European Act: the realization of the internal market and the achievement of economic and social cohesion.

The argument presented by LaPergola and other member state representatives was that through inter-regional agreements the Community could bring into play a series of forces – sub-national government units, economic groups, cultural organizations, and individual interests with strong territorial roots – that would stimulate the multiplication of activities in the economic and social spheres and accelerate the achievement of cohesion. Belief that sub-national forces could play a positive role in the achievement of cohesion was encouraged by the view that the dynamic of European integration had profoundly change after the passage of the Single European Act. It was argued that prior to 1985 the dynamic of European integration was dominated by the member states or, more accurately, the national organs of member states. Member state dominance rested on the acceptance of the 1966 'Luxembourg compromise' that guaranteed each member state a *de jure* veto and, therefore, placed it in a position to jealously guard its power and authority *within* its own borders.

This state of affairs, though, was profoundly undermined and rendered obsolete by the ramifications of the Single European Act and the agreement to create a single market by 1 January 1993. In the Single European Act member states not only gave up control of their external borders to the EC, but they also agreed to transfer to Brussels significant portions of their policy-making powers in specific sectors. One of the sectors that has achieved significant prominence since the ratification of the Single European Act has been regional policy. The Single European Act provided regional policy a specific Treaty basis and awarded the Community ascendancy on the matter. National governments receiving assistance from the Community through the Structural Funds had now to clear their regional development plans with the Community to make sure that national policies were in line with the goals of cohesion and the rules and requirements of the single market. In the context of the new Treaty commitments, national governments could no longer exclude sub-national institutions, groups, or forces from becoming actively engaged in the European integration process and, more importantly, becoming direct interlocutors with the European Community.

In Palermo LaPergola observed that the achievement of cohesion had to be understood as

> a process concerning primarily the restoring of balance to situations with differing levels of development; it could not take place effectively without the full involvement of society and the active participation of the bodies operating in society to promote economic development, social welfare and the quality of life.

He concluded that in the present context of an increasingly integrated Europe the process of cohesion could only be furthered by a vigorous, pro-active role on the part of Community institutions 'to seek out, encourage and co-ordinate all the forces which in the cultural, institutional and economic spheres act spontaneously or, given a stimulus, may be prompted to act in line with that objective'.[5]

In the message sent by the President of the Commission, Jacques Delors, the importance of the new regional dimension was highlighted. Delors noted that, given the changes already implemented in the reorganization of the Structural Funds,[6] the Community was prepared to 'give the greatest support to such local or regional initiatives with the greatest effect for investment or employment'. The implications of the Delors' message was that the regions would be recognized as 'active partners' in the promotion and implementation of EC regional policies in the operationalization of the principle of 'subsidiarity' reflected in the Act.

The innovation introduced by LaPergola was the observation that if regions were to become primary actors in the pursuit of the goal of economic and social development in the Community existing national laws, customs, and administrative rules could not function as obstacles to their interaction. Within the EC context regions had to be free to come together in formal as well as informal bases to discuss common problems and, if necessary, to propose common solutions to these problems. In fact, La Pergola argued that sub-national institutions and the '*forces vives*' of regional society should be encouraged and stimulated by the Community through financial assistance to pool their institutional resources and ideas for the tackling of mutual problems. According to LaPergola, the institutions capable of exercising a vanguard role in the pursuit of inter-regional co-operation were universities and research institutes, public and private enterprises, and regional and local authorities. However, for these entities to engage in co-operative, inter-regional activities on a transnational basis, certain modifications would have to be made in Community and national legislation.

LaPergola stated that Community and national laws should be changed to allow: (1) Community rules to determine the forms to be taken by co-operative ventures, identify their main functions, and make them an integral part of Community policy-making, (2) member states to make provisions permitting partners from other Community countries to co-operate with groups operating within their own national boundaries, (3) the formulation of measures providing economic incentives for inter-regional co-operative ventures, (4) provisions for direct Community participation in setting up these operations, and (5) in cases of projects of particular significance, the Community could 'set up ... bodies coming under Community law and entirely governed by such law in accordance with the possibility outlined in Article 130 of the Single European Act.'[7]

The models for inter-regional co-operation proposed at the meeting were Europrogrammes[8] for the promotion of university scientific research, Euroconsortia[9] bringing together public and private enterprise with forces at the university and local authority level, and Euroagencies[10] for the distribution of services in a territorial context defined by the Community and/or member-state(s). A number of these ideas have been implemented in the 1990–91 period (for example, INTERREG, OUVERTURE, etc.) as part of the network creation process undertaken as part of the Article 10 provisions of the 1988 ERDF regulation.

Emile Nöel, president of the European University Institute, was asked to illustrate the proposed research activities of the Institute in the field of European integration. He presented the outlines of a research project that was currently under discussion at the Institute on the role of regional institutions in the accelerated movement toward the creation of a single market and the reform of Community institutions.

At the conclusion of the meeting, a communiqué was issued which found all members in agreement that inter-regional co-operation should be encouraged and promoted through flexible structures adapted to the diverse national institutional settings and that the European University Institute was the suitable institution to conduct – in collaboration with the member states and Community institutions – the study on the topic of inter-regional co-operation along the lines illustrated by Noel in his presentation.

III. THE RESEARCH ASSIGNMENT

The proposal setting out the European University's research assignment identified five basic components that needed to be studied in order to create a Community policy instrument for the purpose of promoting inter-regional co-operation:[11]

(1) the conduct of surveys among 'private' actors – for example, entrepreneurs, financial institutions, sectoral associations, trade unions, etc. – or 'the vital socio-economic forces' that ultimately would

determine the success or failure of development initiatives in peripheral areas;

(2) the conduct of surveys among 'institutional actors' – that is, regional governmental bodies, development boards, inter-regional authorities or agencies already in place for the management of specific problems and frontier areas;

(3) a conceptualization of the ideas launched at the Palermo meeting and the formulation of potential experiments – or 'pilot projects' – for inter-regional co-operation in a number of sectors vital to the future development of Objective 1 areas;

(4) an analysis of the regional impact of Community sectoral policies to verify whether sectoral programmes were cancelling out the efforts aimed at regional development promoted by the three structural funds; and

(5) an analysis of the objectives, structure, and implementation of the Integrated Mediterranean Programmes which in 1988 represented the Community's most advanced model of the integrated and multi-year approach to the formulation of policies aimed at attacking the root causes of underdevelopment in a significant part of the regions along the northern shores of the Mediterranean.

Thus, the Commission's mandate was to focus the research project on the role of institutions and socio-economic forces in tackling the problems of Objective 1 areas, but it was also recognized that during various phases of the research project attention would be given to inter-regional co-operation involving non-Objective 1 regions.[12] As was evident in the discussions that took place during the Palermo conference, the Community and member states placed a fundamental importance on the prospect of developing inter-regional co-operation or 'trans-regional networks' – that is, regional co-operation among political, economic, and social forces in various parts of the Community – in the formulation of common solutions to problems. LaPergola had made it clear in the introductory statement that his conception of regional co-operation was not limited to the establishment of informal networks for the exchange of information on individual problems and solutions but rather was the building block for more permanent structures that could assume the form of institutionalized programmes and agencies. Basically, the LaPergola notion of networking was rooted in the conception of the transformation of informal networks into more formal relations and even into institutions as the pressure to adjust to the post-1992 reality of the single market made itself felt at the sub-national level.

IV. THE STRUCTURE OF SUB-NATIONAL INSTITUTIONS IN THE COMMUNITY

It should be noted that at the present time sub-national institutional structures differ radically from one country to another. In just the Objective 1 areas covered by this study, a wide variety of institutional forms exist. Some member states (Italy, Spain, and France) have a full structure of regional government that is organized at the sub-regional level through provinces or departments and communes and villages while others have highly centralized governmental structures and very weak sub-national governmental entities (Greece and Ireland). Portugal falls in between these two groups because it has decentralized power to two (Azores and Madeira) of its seven regions, but the other five (Algarve, Norte, Alentejo, Lisboa e Val de Tejo, and Centro) are still waiting for a devolution of power from the national to the regional level of government. The United Kingdom, on the other hand, has during the reign of the Conservative Party moved toward a greater centralization of power to the national government with the abolition of the planning regions and the county councils.

Table 1 contains a description of the variety and number of sub-national governmental institutions present in Objective 1 member states. The seven countries listed in the Table have significantly different institutions and experiences in developing linkages with other levels of government and socio-economic groups in their immediate surroundings. In addition, a number of member states (Greece, Portugal, UK, Ireland) are involved in an active debate on the reform of their sub-national structures in light of the increased pressure being applied by the Community to decentralize the administration of policies and resources. In experimenting with the Integrated Development Operations (IDOs) and Integrated Mediterranean Programmes (IMPs), the Community has used its influence to encourage the adoption of administrative changes in the implementation of Community programmes.[13]

The experience of the last twenty years shows that the process of European integration *has* had an impact on the direction and content of sub-national governmental reform. This is evident in the fact that the regions have become one of the privileged links between, on one hand, the national government and, on the other, the European Community in the formulation and administration of sectoral policies – for example, agricultural, social, and regional policy. Secondly, the regions have assumed a variety of functions that are intimately linked to the determination of economic outcomes at the regional level. Keeping in mind

TABLE 1
STRUCTURE OF SUBNATIONAL GOVERNMENTS IN OBJECTIVE 1 COUNTRIES

Country	Regional	Intermediate	Local
Ireland	–	County Councils 26	85 City/borough: 6 boroughs 49 districts 30 municipalities
Portugal	2 Regions Azores/ Madeira 5 Plng.Reg.	Municipalities 305	Frequesias 4183
Spain	17 Regions	Provinces 50	Cities 8,027
France	Regions 22	Departments 100	Communes 36,627
U.K.	3 offices Wales, Scotland N. Ireland	Counties 66 + 6 in N. Ireland	City/borough 481 districts +10000 Parishes +800 Community Councils
Italy	20 regions	Provinces 102	Communes 8,074
Greece	13 ad. regions	Pref. councils 55	Communes 5,999

Source: Fondation pour la Gestion des Villes et des Collectivités Territoriales, 'Forces et Faiblesses des Collectivités Locales Europeennes Avant 1993' (Paris: 1988), mimeo, Tables 3 and 4.

these developments, it is clear that participation by sub-national governments in economic and social policy-making can no longer be seen as characteristic of only federal systems. In both *decentralized* unitary systems (such as Spain, France, and Italy) and federal systems (Germany), decision-making powers are shared among various levels of government. In analysing the way that European Community policies are handled at the sub-national level in the seven countries of our study we see that complex forms of inter-governmental policy-making and administrative structures are common in both unitary and federal systems. The pressure to formulate effective policies for the use of the substantial amount of funds put at the disposal of sub-national governments by the Community has produced hybrid forms of policy-making responsibilities and implementation structures that have substantially neutralized the classic distinction between policy-making and implementation in federal *vis-à-vis* regional state structures.

In classic regionalist systems the responsibility for decision-making and financial allocations is shared in both practice and form by the two levels of government. In the case of the Italian regions or the Dutch municipalities, the ultimate power lies with the national government to legitimize decisions taken by the sub-national governmental body. Effective decision-making in policy areas is, in fact, allocated to the sub-national governmental level by the centre in its desire to off-load to lower governmental levels the administrative work in delivering essential governmental services.

In contrast, in an ideal federalist structure the sub-national entity is formally empowered by the constitution to exercise exclusive rights to decide and implement policy in specific areas. This is the case in many federal systems such as the Federal Republic of Germany or the states in the US system. However, empirical experience and studies suggest that the reality does not easily fit into the abstract representation of an ideal model of federalism. The functioning of federal systems that exist in Germany and Belgium or, for that matter, those in the United States, Canada, Switzerland, Austria, and Australia demonstrate that policies in the field of economic growth, education, professional education, taxation, etc. are not made exclusively at one level of the system or hermetically sealed off from other levels when it comes to administration. Rather, policy-making responsibilities and administration are shared between two or more levels of policy-making. The implications of shared responsibilities, even in situations where constitutionally powers are divided, is that units of government must co-operate in the management of policy areas.

Motivations for inter-governmental co-operation in the management of policies can be found in the inability of sub-national levels of government in most federal systems to finance their activities exclusively through their own taxing powers and the need for co-operation in dealing with supranational authorities. One of the reasons for the inability of sub-national units to depend on self-financing has been the significant accumulation of responsibilities in the provision of socio-economic services without an adequate decentralization of taxing powers. As a consequence, mixed forms of financing – for example, revenue sharing – have become a common feature of inter-governmental relations in both regional as well as federal state systems.

The emergence of significant inter-governmental bargaining and co-operation is to be found in a variety of Community member states when it comes to formulating the positions of national representatives in Community deliberations. In fact, in the recent changes to the Belgian legislation (as had already been the case in Germany) national authorities are obliged to seek the views of the responsible sub-national representatives before entering into negotiations at the Community level concerning areas attributed to the regions by the constitutional reforms.[13]

In evaluating the potential role of regions in members states in the process of establishing networks on a trans-regional basis, it must be remembered that regional governments can no longer be conceived as only intermediate levels of government interacting with the national government or local government. European regions now have to establish and maintain ties, administer policies, and lobby in an active fashion the European Community in order to obtain additional funds to pursue crucial economic and social policies; they have become important actors in the socio-economic development process at the regional level; and they have exercised fundamental powers with regard to the delivery of social services over the regional territory through the intermediation of sub-regional governmental bodies. All of these activities are not attributes of only atypical or temporary actions of the more advanced and experimentally-oriented regional bodies. They have become the defining elements of a new model of sub-national governmental activity.[14]

What exists at the present time is an empirical reality of regional and local government that lacks a proper institutional framework that can take into account its potential for activity and use this potential in a creative manner to achieve the goals of social and economic cohesion.[15]

To understand why trans-regional co-operation is necessary in the post-1992 Community, the role that the regions and other levels of sub-national government play in social and economic policy-making and administration needs to be highlighted. The four areas that are of critical importance in the functioning of sub-national units in the context of the accelerating pace of economic development and social change that is sweeping over Europe are:

(1) the ability of the sub-national units to 'receive', 'internalize' through internal decision-making mechanisms, and 'respond' to requests for change through the formulation of public policies, institutional instrumentation, and innovative processes for administrating policies that originate from other levels of government, individual citizens, or organized groups in society;
(2) the number and quality of policy areas and the efficiency of sub-national governmental institutions in penetrating the surrounding environment for the purpose of distributing the goods and services that are produced by regional decision-making;

(3) the norms and values of the political and administrative elite and the surrounding society in structuring demands and opportunities for the production and distribution of goods and services (that is, collective versus individual goods); and
(4) the linkage network that connects the sub-national unit at the present time in an internal, ongoing relationship with other parts of the governmental system and surrounding society and which can in the future be projected into a European dimension.

The reader will find in the following articles an analysis of the current structures of sub-national government, the national debate on structural reforms, and the impact that the single market will have on national and regional trends as seen by local and regional elites. Each article is based on an extensive survey of sub-national elites; in many cases the respondents are drawn from samples of politicians directly involved in the management of public policies and representatives of private organizations preparing their organizations for the rendezvous with Europe. Taken as a whole, the country surveys and the two chapters on Community sectoral policies represent an analysis of where the Community, member states, and their sub-national structure are in formulating a reasoned response to the challenges posed by the creation of the single market and where the Community will be heading as the full implications of the Maastricht Treaty are debated and realized.

NOTES

1. The project was financed by the Commission of the European Community under grant number 88–88001. The views expressed here and in the other articles in the volume are those of the authors and do not necessarily reflect those of the European Community. This special issue of *Regional Politics and Policy* represents an abridged and updated version of the final report that was submitted to the European Community.
2. The meeting was attended by the national ministers for EC affairs of the twelve member states, two EC commissioners, and two vice-presidents of the European Parliament. The author participated in the meeting as a member of the European University Institute delegation. The results of the meeting are contained in the 'Conclusions' of the meeting prepared by the Italian Ministry for European Community Affairs.
3. These include the entire countries of Ireland, Portugal, and Greece, two-thirds of Spain, one-half of Italy – that is, the Mezzogiorno – , and the island of Corsica in France and Northern Ireland in the UK. According to the ranking system developed in the Single European Act, these were designated 'Objective 1' areas – that is, those areas in the Community with the highest priority for the allocation of funds for the promotion of social and economic development.
4. Since the launching of the single market programme, a policy 'vortex' has been set into motion that is pulling into the preparation of the rendezvous with 1993 by the Community an expanding number of new economic and political actors. That 'vortex effect' can be seen as constituting the dynamic of European integration.

5. Minister Antonio LaPergola, 'Inter-Regional Co-Operation: A Means to Full Implementation of the Single Act', Meeting of Ministers of the European Community, Palermo, 26–27 Feb. 1988, p. 1.
6. The three structural funds are: The European Agricultural Guarantee and Guidance Fund-Guidance (EAGGF-Guidance), European Social Fund (ESF), and European Regional Development Fund (ERDF). See Philip Lowe, 'The Reform of the Community's Structural Funds', *Common Market Law Review*, Vol. 25, No. 3 (1988) , pp. 503–21.
7. LaPergola, p. 5. The paragraph cited in Article 130o of the Single European Act states: 'The Community may set up joint undertakings or any other structure necessary for the efficient execution of programmes of Community research, technological development and demonstration.'
8. The statement defined Europrogrammes as 'typical forms of inter-university co-operation bringing "European thinking" to bear in the education of teaching staff and students and in the promotion of scientific research', ibid., p. 6.
9. The statement described Euroconsortia in the following manner: 'Consortia involving universities and enterprises, in which a key part should also be played by local authorities, can do a job of economic and social development throughout the area covered, with transfers of experience from one country to another and positive results in particular for less-developed or declining areas.'
10. Euroagencies were supposed to 'take the form of bodies combining research institutions, local authorities and public and private enterprises in the management and distribution of services in a framework confined to the Community and Member States concerned. The service provided by a Euroagency should play a key role as an instrument making for the long-term development of a varied network of economic activities in the region covered, with all-round knock-on effects in the specific regional setting', ibid., p. 7.
11. In fact, the decision to promote transregional cooperation had already been taken and was to enter into the 1988 regulation reforming the ERDF (European Regional Development Fund).
12. The project made a basic distinction between 'interregional' and 'transregional' cooperation. The former was used to refer to co-operation among regions within one nation-state while the latter to co-operation among regions in different nation-states. Trans-regional co-operation was, therefore, applied to both transfrontier border co-operation between/among regions on opposite sides of an international border as well as to co-operation among regions not sharing a contiguous border.
13. See the discussion contained in the articles on the IMP programmes by Fouli Papageorgiou and Susannah Verney and Giuliano Bianchi in this volume.
13. See the paper presented by Yves Lejeune, 'Belgian Regionalism and EC Integration: A Dilemma?' at the IPSA-SOG meeting on 'Relations Between Levels of Government: Looking Toward 1992', Montpellier, 5–7 April 1990.
14. See Robert Leonardi and Raffaella Y. Nanetti (eds.), *The Regions and European Integration: The Case of Emilia-Romagna* (London: Pinter Publishers, 1990) and Robert D. Putnam, Robert Leonardi and Raffaella Y. Nanetti, *Governance and the Civic Community: Regional Politics in Italy* (Princeton, NJ: Princeton University Press, 1992).
15. One of the more interesting aspects of comparative work on sub-national institutions inside and outside of Europe is the extraordinary similarities in the pattern of responses to social welfare and economic growth formulated by local and regional governments. In a number of cases, what one observes taking place in Europe is also underway in other institutional and political settings in North America and Asia. Take, for example, the two most striking innovations experienced by sub-national government in Europe during the last two decades: 'institution building' and 'local government as a vital economic actor'. Today, we see European sub-national governments facing a changing reality that closely parallels developments noted by scholars of Canadian federalism in the 1960s: the growth in the size, power, and scope of provincial governments in

response to the exigencies associated with the evolution of the welfare state and growing concern of sub-national governments with issues of economic development. The concept was labelled by Canadian scholars as 'province building'. See Edwin R. Black and Alan C. Caims, 'A Different Perspective on Canadian Federalism', *Canadian Public Administration*, 9 (1966), pp. 27–46 for the first discussion of the concept. In a recent survey of the literature R.A. Young, Philippe Faucher, and André Blois in 'The Concept of Province Building: A Critique', *Canadian Journal of Political Science* 23 (1984), pp. 783–818, discuss the process of province building in a manner that closely parallels what has been happening at the sub-national level in Europe in the 1970s and 1980s: 'Provincial bureaucracies have grown enormously in size and competence; not only are they essential tools of provincial politicians, but their own interests also favor expanded, activist states. Increased revenues and new capabilities of policy-making and co-ordination have enabled surer management of socio-economic change. Hence, provincial states have grown in capacity to serve provincial interests – or to shape them' (p. 784).

Diseconomies in Space: Traditional Sectoral Policies of the EC, the European Technology Community and their Effects on Regional Disparities

JÜRGEN R. GROTE

This article is not concerned with either the history or the effectiveness of transnational regional policies by the European Communities. It rather tries to assess the effects and consequences of traditional and more recent sectoral EC policies for the performance of regional economies and argues that classic redistributive measures will no longer suffice to neutralize and cancel out the negative territorial externalities of the former. Traditional financial transfers to peripheral regions might not be as Sharpe suggests 'the price that rationality ... pays to democracy, or economics to altruism ... but quite the contrary ... the price payed by the core to the peripheral region for peripheralising it' [*Sharpe, 1984: 58*].

Hence, the interest here is on those policies undertaken by the Community which are co-responsible for and amplify peripherality. With the help of a small number of critical studies undertaken in this field (especially Molle and Cappellin [*1988*]; Cappellin [*1988*]), some of the territorial externalities of EC policies in agriculture, industrial policy, energy, transport, social policy, trade and monetary policy and services are discussed briefly. The regional impact of a wide range of intersectoral Community initiatives in the fields of technological innovation, telecommunications and R&D are then made the subjects of more detailed analysis.

Two demands are submitted as an appropriate response against a further widening of existing development gaps. The first concerns a reform in the structural-institutional environment of sectoral policies and includes such issues as a more systematic regional impact assessment (RIA) of sectoral policies[1] and an improved internal coordination of the latter across the different directorates of the Commission.[2] More importantly, suggestions are being submitted for a proper European regional policy that, in going beyond the wishful thinking about a 'Europe of the

---

This article is a substantially shortened version of a report submitted to DG XVI of the EC Commission in August 1990.

Regions',[3] would contribute to a more equal factor endowment of regions with social and organizational assets and resources (intangible software infrastructure) rather than merely dealing with the provision of traditional physical (tangible or hardware) infrastructure. Finally, the opportunity space is evaluated which the Commission possesses for instigating the institutional reforms being required for achieving this by means of coercive strategies[4] which would compel both national governments and relevant actors at the regional level to contribute to a number of non-economic capacities and public goods whose supply, otherwise, would continue to remain in short supply.

The second demand is linked to the first and concerns a form of structural intervention and Community-wide regulation which would go beyond merely redistributive measures and financial assistance which are predominantly being used for providing regions with traditional 'hard infrastructure' such as transport networks, water and energy supply and so forth. The latter type of policy might actually have helped to generate the problems it was intended to solve.[5]

Both of these demands are at odds with purely economistic visions of the kind recently being advanced by Cecchini against sectoral policy evaluation in general.[6] They subscribe, rather, to alternative positions available within the services of the Commission which view regional and sectoral forecasts as a vital condition for the achievement of economic and social cohesion.[7] The ultimate aim of the suggestions presented here would lie in the establishment of an internal 'regulatory budget' [*Majone, 1989*] within the services of the Commission where each sectoral initiative is checked in terms of costs and benefits accruing to the targets of regulation, that is, to individual regions of the Community and to the enterprises populating them. That the following remarks on traditional sectoral policies by the EC and on more recent EC initiatives in the high-tech domain exclusively highlight the negative effects and externalities of both of the former, does not imply that they have been altogether detrimental to the interests of regions in general. They have, however, not substantially reduced existing disparities and, in many cases, even contributed to their widening. The EC's initiatives in the high-tech domain tend to support especially the existence of uneven developments in a pattern which is likely to weaken the prospects for economic and social cohesion after the coming into force of the internal market.

I. TERRITORIAL EFFECTS OF COMMUNITY POLICIES IN TRADITIONAL DOMAINS AND SECTORS

The probably most evident example for spatial diseconomies triggered off by sectoral policy intervention of the EC is the Community's Agricultural Policy (CAP). It still absorbs the most relevant part of the budget (74 per cent in 1985 with slight decreases since the passing of the SEA) and thereby reduces the possibility to undertake alternative policies in other and more relevant sectors. The CAP receives significantly more attention than is warranted by total share in value added (four per cent of GNP [*CEC, 1984c; 1985*] and in employment contributed by agriculture.[8] More importantly, CAP's contribution to a widening of regional development gaps is significant, especially as a result of two factors.

First, it benefits most substantially those regions whose output is greatest [*RICAP study, CEC, 1981*], whereby output rates, in most cases, coincide with productivity rates of agricultural work. The bulk of the EC's output is produced in the more favoured areas of the North which receive up to 24 times more from the EAGGF Guarantee Section expenditure per annual work unit [*CEC, 1987b*] than the less favoured regions of the South (all of Greece, most of Spain, Portugal and Italy, and parts of Southern France). These latter areas rank low or very low on both labour productivity and output. The regional objectives of the CAP have never been very clear during the initial phases of Community activity in this sector [*Strijker and Veer, 1988*]. Article 39.2 of the Rome Treaty makes only marginal reference to potential regional disparities and possible counteraction to be taken and a distinct regional element was not introduced into the CAP before 1975,[9] the same year in which the launching of the ERDF opened up potential ways for a better balance between structural and spatial elements in agricultural policy.

Second, the distribution of EC monies in agriculture is also determined by the fact that most farmers are embedded in a service environment being provided by downstream and upstream industries which are interrelated among themselves (marketing of farm products, service firms, government-controlled research institutes, veterinary and quality control services). Inter-regional competition for fund allocation, hence, is ultimately determined by the commercial and contractual bonds between farmers on the one hand, and private service firms, industry and government on the other. Both the relative power of these agro-industrial complexes and the size of individual farms are highest in the core regions of the EC between Copenhagen and Paris, Hannover and London, parts of the Po valley also being included. Vested interests of this kind will surely oppose and try to block positive Community policies in favour of a more balanced growth of agriculture and of a relative reduction in the leverage of the CAP in the interest of promoting alternative policy domains.

As to the industrial policy of the Community, activities of transnational authorities in this domain have mainly been concerned with the restructuring of declining industries. Although substantial regional disequilibria have emerged in the provision of regions with services [*Illeris, 1989: 3*], until now, the Community has primarily focused on the manufacturing sector [*Molle, 1988: 47*]. Neither growth industries nor services formed part of EC initiatives until very recently when the launching of the European Technology Community and of the First Framework Programme for Cooperative R&D started to involve various Directorate Generals of the Commission in one way or the other being co-responsible for parts of this cross-sectoral venture.

As in the case of the CAP, the Rome Treaty is not very explicit with regard to the regional impact of industrial policies and the high concentration of both declining and growth industries in specific territories of the Community. Following the Treaty's basic philosophy, a sound competition was expected to suffice for regulating the market without a need for governments to fix prices or quantities of particular products. At least since the mid-1970s, when it became apparent that the centre of gravity of industrial policy approaches had to change and when the restructuring issue achieved more prominence on the agenda of the Community, 'coping with the losers and spotting the winners to replace them increasingly came to dominate industrial policy thinking' [*Swan, 1983: 178*]. The current phase is characterized by a de-coupling of these two principles. 'Coping with the losers' is being delegated to those services being responsible for social, regional and small firm policy (DGs 5, 16 and 22, 23), not least because in the realm of restructuring declining industrial sectors, unlike that of agriculture, there is nothing to compare with the powerful financial resources of the ERDF. 'Spotting the winners', on the other hand, has come to mean providing a limited group of leading European multinationals with a liberalized transnational regulatory framework and with significant financial assistance especially in the high-tech domain.

These tasks are now jointly assumed by the services of the DG for telecommunications, information industries and innovation (DG 13) and that responsible for industry and the internal market (DG 3). Competition rules are widely relaxed for trans-border co-operative ventures (block exemption) and the European Parliament recently asked whether the schemes coming under the roof of the EC's Technology Framework Programme should actually continue to be limited to so called 'pre-competitive' collaboration. Parliament is demanding a modification of the Treaties which would allow for an extension of the eligibility criteria for the schemes coming under the Framework Programme also to product-oriented research.[10] If the Community were to follow these demands, the creation of a proper industrial policy of the MITI-type would be a very probable outcome.[11] Concerns for the territorial impact of this new type of EC high-tech policy are either neglected and supressed or externalized to other branches of the Commission with the resulting effects of considerable co-ordination problems and fierce internal struggles over competences and responsiblities. Since the top priority in the Community is the full implementation of the White Paper (that is, dismantling the material and technical barriers to transborder business activities and abolition of domestic protectionism in procurement markets), it is unlikely that those fractions of the Commission dealing with problems of either size (DG 4 and 23) or spatial location (DGs 16 and 22) of industrial groupings and economic activity will be able to improve their relative power positions within the institution under current conditions.

The term 'Community energy policy' is of recent vintage and in its review 'Energy and Europe', the Commission refers to the year 1967, when the executive institutions of the three Communities merged, as that of the first 'Community energy action'. The notion was first diffused publicly in 1980, when the Community committed itself to energy objectives to be realized by 1990. The proposal was approved and, given a minimum of political support by the member states, concerned all of the main problems of energy policy. More recently, the Commisssion has included energy considerations in its actions of regional policy with a view to support economic development in the less favoured regions, or to help adjust potential energy supply to energy requirements. The most important initiative in this context is the Valoren Programme[12] whose main objective is to strengthen the economic base in the regions concerned by improving the conditions of local energy supply.

The underlying idea of the programme is to make such regions less sensitive to disturbances in the traditional energy markets, in particular oil. Generally, as regards the territorial impact in the conditions of energy supply, no author has yet attempted to assess this problem. The study 'Energy 2000', however, clearly concludes that Italy, Ireland and Greece are, together with Portugal and Spain, the member states with the structurally most unfavourable energy situation. They are the same countries which have the most underdeveloped regions and which are particularly vulnerable to disturbances in energy supply while, at the same time, in the UK, Germany, France and Belgium the situation is characterized by a contraction of the coal industry. Generally, the possibilities of the Commission to undertake action in this field are rather limited and programmes such as Valoren are not likely to change very much in this respect. It is also hard to predict whether Community energy policy action will concentrate on Northern European industrial regions in severe decline or whether it will switch to the developing regions of the South.

Before the ERDF reforms took off, almost three quarters of the Structural Funds had been spent on physical or hard infrastructures, that is, mainly on transport.[13] Important as the incorporation of peripheral regions into a comprehensive transport network may be, at least three points can be made which raise some doubts about the effectiveness of EC initiatives in this sector. First, the improvement of transport infrastructure may also be harmful to the regions concerned. The opening up of transport and export opportunities for a peripheral region is also likely to promote out-migration of labour[14] and to expose that region to imports from other territories. If the peripheral economy is initially weak, improvements in transport may serve to expose those weaknesses to outside competition and may destroy a 'protection of distance' [*Aberle, 1979; Oettle, 1979, Voigt, 1979*]. Also, Community legislation on working conditions in transport industries may raise those costs which are directly attributable to distance and so weaken the competitive position of the periphery.[15] Second, few EC regions possess such a deficient transport system that major regional resources are lying untapped. Some argue that the role of transport is now marginal to regional development [*Bonnafous, 1979*] and others maintain that computer networks have much more profound implications for the development prospects of peripheral or otherwise less-favoured regions than transport structures [*Hepworth, 1986; Bukis, 1985*]. Considering the foregoing, it is very likely that the quality of 'regional information environments' will emerge as the main factor differentiating one region from another. Third, as in the case of industrial policy for declining industries, regional policy budget lines are far more important in terms of direct Community spending[16] than the limited expenditure under transport policy.

Since the objectives of the ERDF and of the transport funds are different, there has been little integration of spending in either schemes or areas. Transport fund expenditure did not particularly consider the needs of less favoured regions and its appropriations were rather equally apportioned between the core and periphery. Attempts of the Commission since the early 1970s to create a more coordinated European transport policy[17] and to increase its own capacities in this respect have been rather unsuccessful although a resolution was passed in 1976, and finally adopted by the Council, which suggested that a fraction of the total transport budget should be reserved and allocated for infrastructural projects of Community interest. Overall, problems surrounding the role of transport policy in regional development suggest that Community policies did relatively little to help the development of disadvantaged regions and, even more so, they may have worked in the opposite direction.

Various empirical studies have attempted to clarify how Community trade policy and figures for import and export affect employment on the national level.[18] The, so far, only available study on the regional impacts of trade policy by Kirschen *et al.* [*CEC, 1984b*] provides much evidence for negative territorial externalities of Community trade policy in terms of a worsening of the economic situation in backward regions. Also, outdated accounting variables being used and a lack of data available at that level make a precise quantification of integration effects at a sub-national scale a very difficult task. Yet, Kirschen *et al.*, who 'examine how the patterns of regional development within the European Community are affected by policies regarding the Community's trade with the rest of the world' [*ibid: 1*], come to similar conclusions as the RICAP study of the Community with respect to agricultural trade: the Community protected its markets for agricultural products and, hence, helped many peripheral regions. The final impact, however, was much greater in several better-off regions in the northern parts of the Community.

With regard to the territorial effects of EC monetary policy, a common currency and a European Monetary Union, there is generally much pessimism among observers. The tendency for capital and labour to move to the central and more developed regions may be accentuated by monetary union as a result of the fact that wages in the peripheral low productivity areas may be increased to those of the high productivity areas while differences in productivity remain unchanged – a prospect which would lead to subsequent out-migration of capital from these areas and to further decline. Yet, as to initiatives which would forbid the encouragement of such moves, most authors remain rather vague in their policy deliberations and, quite conveniently, shift solutions to this problem to other services of the Commission which come increasingly to perform the function of a dumping ground for all kinds of negative externalities without actually being equipped for that task: 'a vigorous regional policy as an integral part of monetary unification in the EC'.[19] Given that irrevocably fixed exchange rates would, other things being equal, unavoidably produce severe problems of inflation and unemployment in particular regions, the objective of economic cohesion presents the Community with a serious, and so far unresolved, dilemma.

This is also acknowledged by the report of the Delors Committee on Economic and Monetary Union of 18 April 1989. The report admits that further monetary and economic integration might, without compensatory measures, exacerbate regional disequilibria. Just as the document quoted above, it recommends as part of its proposed solution to the disparities that are expected as a result of convergence, common (regional and social) policies to enhance the process of resource allocation in those economic sectors and geographical areas where the working of the market forces needed to be reinforced or complemented (paragraph 27).[20] Hence, again a recommendation which shifts the solution to negative externalities produced within a given policy domain to other institutional compartments which are badly endowed for coping with a task of this magnitude. The doubling of the Structural Funds, in this context, appears to be nothing more than a literal side-payment to those states expecting to experience greatest difficulty in adjusting to the conditions of monetary integration, with the removal of protective devices those conditions entail.

Before drawing attention to the territorial effects of more recent Community policies in the field of high-tech, two other domains shall shortly be discussed. The service sector and social policies lend themselves particularly well for emphasizing the problems the Community has to face with respect to both a better internal coordination of its activities across different sectors and to the territorial effects of these sectoral activities. Services are of interest to the scholar of negative externalities of transnational sectoral policy especially for two reasons.

First, the sector continues to be a non-issue for EC authorities [*Molle, 1983: 18; 1988: 47; Illeris, 1989: 3*], be it from the viewpoint of a potentially new policy specifically dealing with this area – an objective actually made mandatory by existing market failures ocurring in this domain or be it in terms of more traditional counter-measures to be taken within the realm of regional policies. Second, the service sector cannot be discussed seperately without considering the Information Technology (IT) domain and the Community's recent initiatives in joint R&D [*CEC, 1984d; 1987a*].

Given the strategic importance the sector possesses in terms of value added and employment, the reluctance of the Community to develop a consistent strategy for services in order to create conditions for a more balanced factor endowment of the regions is astounding. At current market prices, the share of manufactured products in gross-value added in the Community (EUR 6) has declined from 33 per cent in 1960 to about 26 per cent in 1983. This declining pattern is mirrored by the corresponding share of market services, which expanded from 36 per cent to over 43 per cent. The share of non-market services also grew steadily from 11 to 15 per cent. With regard to employment figures, the share accounted for by market and non-market services (EUR 6) rose from 48 to 59 per cent. In some countries, these figures are approaching 70 per cent [*Molle, 1983:*

18; Vanhoven and Klaassen, 1987: xviii]. Especially the new telecommunications services – and notably the value-added 'telecarried' services 'will have a major impact on the future tradeability of services and on the location of economic activities' [*Ungerer and Costello, 1988: 98*].

By the early 1990s, telecommunications will have grown into one of the largest industrial sectors. Interestingly, despite the expected 'distance-shrinking' effects of innovative developments in transport and telecommunication which could, potentially, 'relax the need for most service activities to locate close to their customers' [*Illeris, 1989: 68*] and, subsequently, lead to the advantage of agglomeration in big cities to diminish, the exact opposite is more likely to happen [*Goddard et al., 1985: 225*]. Because functional polarization is accompanied by social polarization,[21] with knowledge-intensive jobs that require advanced qualifications being located in the key areas while a less-qualified and frequently female workforce tends to be employed part-time in the peripheral zones, the distance-shrinking effect actually turns out to favour central positions even more than was the case before the introduction of innovative technologies. Clear moves towards service decentralization in the member states of the Community exclusively occur in countries such as Belgium, the Netherlands, Denmark and Germany, while France, Ireland and Portugal tend to further strengthen already existing service concentrations in their growth poles [*Illeris, 1989: 137–84*]. Moreover, it appears that type-1 services[22] are over-represented in particular tourist areas of the Mediterranean while high-quality services are much better distributed in the Northern countries. EC policies tend to reinforce the existing pattern, since 'the vast majority of projects financed by the Community are in Central and Northern Europe in centres of excellence' [*CEC, 1987a*]. Non-policy-making in the service sector, hence, is coupled to substantial efforts in adjacent policy domains which, ultimately, might lead to irreversible variances in regional factor endowment. Generally, the regulatory competences which the Community has acquired in these latter domains tend to be spent to the benefit of centrally located, and to the detriment of less developed, regions and 'the regulatory framework chosen to govern the liberalization of the exchange of services ... will have extremely different effects at regional level' [*ibid: 21*].

To complete this 'tour de force' through domains where the negative externalities of traditional transnational policies are likely to have most serious effects, let us finally turn to the social policies of the European Community. The distinction which has been recommended in the introduction, namely that between traditional redistributive policies carried out by those services of the Commission that are in charge of 'coping with the losers' on the one hand, and more positive and direct regulatory interventions into the sectors which actually cause and determine the emergence of regional disequilibria on the other hand, appears to be most evident in a field which has come to be called the 'social dimension of the internal market'. Yet, traditional EC social policy, being predominantly of a redistributive character, does not add up to the creation of something which could legitimately be attributed the label of a social dimension. Social policy and the operations of the European Social Fund, even when looked at from the more narrow and redistributive perspective, are clearly biased towards regions in industrial decline and disregard those belonging to the group of Objective 1 regions [*Steinle, 1988*].

This has been the case at least until the late 1970s when the Commission started to work towards an increased coherence and coordination of its policies in this domain, reorienting ESF operations so that more regions than before are now eligible for Fund application.[23] Authors do not completely agree, however, on the problem of regional effects of the Fund. While Vanhoven and Klaassen [*1987: 443*] maintain that 'the Fund is a very valuable complement to the ERDF', Cappellin [*1988: 107*] attributes only minor importance for regional development to its operations. The often observed lack of effective additionality of Community measures to existing domestic policies in the social policy domain [*Steinle, 1988*] is not likely to change even if completely new guidelines for ESF intervention would be adopted.[24] The Commission itself relates the higher geographical spread of ESF operations, relative to those of the ERDF, to principally different logics underlying the two instruments, the ESF's tasks being functional and those of the ERDF being territorial in character.[25]

In the light of the above observations, it seems that the ESF's effects hardly precipitate in benefits to less developed regions. Attempts at assessing its territorial impact are generally rather disappointing. While a Belgian report laments that 'it is difficult to quantify the impact of the ESF in terms of jobs created' and its German counterpart regrets that 'the inaugural effect of the Social Fund on measures taken within the framework of labour market policy in the FRG cannot be measured precisely', the French and other national reports completely dismiss the argument [*CEC, 1984a: 19–20*].

The foregoing remarks, however, exclusively concern the reductionist version of discussing the social dimension in redistributive terms. The distinction having been suggested in the introduction between 'hard' physical – schools, training centres, etc. – and 'soft' institutional resources – the organizational capability and willingness of regional actors to provide for broad-based skills, social peace, etc. – is nowhere as apparent as in the current discussion of the social dimension of the internal market. Redistributive policies in the social policy domain which aim at an endowment of regions with 'hard' devices such as the building of training centres and the provision of qualified personnel able to run these centres, are severely contrained by existing budgetary appropriations for that domain and by the relatively marginal effects they had in the past with regard to a diminution of disequilibria in the socio-economic factor endowment of regions.

Some system engineering is required, therefore, to identify those social and organizational capacities at the regional level which directly influence the productive sphere of firms and economic performance of regions, in order to arrange institutional assets in such a way that each region would be granted comparable start-up conditions in politico-administrative terms before embarking on interregional co-operation and competition.

> A social dimension defined in 'redistributive-political' terms is not of great interest to the scholar. It is rather a matter of horse-trading in the political market. For non-politicians and outside observers, whether they want it bigger or smaller depends at best on paradigmatic prejudice (economists being customarily for 'efficiency', sociologists 'for equity') and political taste ... This is different, however, where the social dimension of an economy is seen as serving a productive and not just a redistributive purpose [*Streeck, 1989: 3–4*].

Policy recommendations viewing the social dimension as serving a productive purpose would essentially converge around the demands which were raised above in the introduction. Thus, the Community would have to instigate the building up of institutional assets and resources at the regional level which enable the most relevant actors at that level to provide for a range of non-economic production inputs[26] which, by helping to solve many problems related to market and hierarchy failure, have made leading European regions so successful [*Grabher, 1990; 1991; Anderson, 1988; 1991; Cooke and Morgan, 1990; Holland, 1990; Garmise and Grote, 1990; Grote, 1992a; 1992b*].

In other words, a social dimension would have to be incorporated in a proper European regional policy. Joint action of this type which, ideally, could be operated by a new 'super-DG' into which the administrative branches of the directorates dealing with regional policy, social policy, structural funds and small and medium-sized enterprises (DGs 5, 16, 22 and 23) would have to be merged, could then contribute to the generation of a kind of 'software infrastructure', the supply or absence of which probably determine the relative performances of regional economies more than 'hard' devices of the traditional type. 'Soft' resources possess two dimensions, a technological and a social-organizational one. The first relates to the capacities of regional entrepreneurs to adopt flexible automation strategies and restructure the assets internal to their firms, while the second, largely determining the former, requires the existence of social networks and co-operative attitudes between public authorities and organized private actors at the regional level as the most appropriate instruments for coping with market and hierarchy failure.

The problem with these resources is that, as a result of the effective properties they possess, they tend to be in short supply. Individual actors at the regional level, in part tempted by immediate benefits and short-sighted hyper-rationality, in part by opportunism and 'free-riding', are not likely to contribute to their provision on a voluntary basis, as long as a centrally-positioned authority does not assume the role of an external enforcement agency capable of instigating their supply by some form of coercion. The Community, it is argued here, is bound to face this task in the future, even if this does not correspond to the short-term interests of its individual members to maintain their sovereignty and 'go it alone'.

In any case, 'software infrastructures' typically prosper in regional economies characterized by a high degree of institutional saturation. To the most important of them belong training and the provision of general as opposed to workplace-specific skills. Yet, present Community policies, despite the increasing attention they pay to training measures and the qualification of the workforce [*CEC, 1988b: 46*], continue to treat training, retraining and employment in isolation, as disparate parts of labour market policies which possess little affiliation to regional policy objectives [*Steinle, 1988*]. Attempts to provide for other 'soft' resources, namely ones addressing the problems of social peace and cooperative labour relations, have of course a track record at the Community level.

It is questionable, however, whether the social dialogue between EC-level employers' and workers' associations will succeed if exclusively following a sectoral logic [*Grote, 1987; Buda and Vogel, 1989; Ebbinghaus and Visser, 1992*]. The Dialogue lacks any element which would make social partner concertation operational for purposes of regional development, thus raising the question whether its 'regionalization' would not represent a more viable option, especially if taking account of the obstacles to collective action by organized business and labour at the transnational sectoral and intersectoral levels [*Greenwood et al., 1992*]. Provided a pertinent geographical level with sufficient institutional saturation and regulatory capacity can be defined[27] where concertation

TABLE 1
SCHEMATIC VIEW OF IMPACTS BY POLICY AREA AND TYPE OF REGION

Effect	Metropolitan		Intermediate		Agricultural/ peripheral		Old industrial	
Policy Area	N	S	N	S	N	S	N	S
Agriculture	0	0	+	0	0	-	0	0
Industry	-	0	+	+	0	0	-	-
Energy	0	-	0	-	-	-	0	0
Transport/Telecm.	+	0	+	-	0	-	0	0
Social/Employmt.	?	?	?	?	?	?	?	?
Trade	0	0	0	0	0	0	0	0
Macro/Monetary	+	0	+	0	0	-	0	0

Source: Molle and Cappellin [*1988*].

has a chance to thrive, organized collective action 'might meet the needs of economic development better than direct intervention by public authorities itself' [*EPRU, 1989: 7/1*].[28]

By way of concluding this section, the need should be emphasized again that any policy aimed at combatting a further widening of regional development gaps would have to go beyond purely redistributive measures and include those structural-institutional and productive-socio-political elements which have been outlined above for the case of social policy, albeit possessing validity also for other domains. If the Community were to continue on the traditional lines of dispersed and uncoordinated sectoral policies and if regional policies were to continue to be restricted to financial allocations predominantly fuelled into the provision of 'hardware', then the territorial consequences of such an approach in the future would hardly differ substantially from those of the past. The largely self-evident results of the picture drawn by Molle and Cappellin [*1988*], presented in Table 1, demonstrate negative (–), positive (+) and neutral (0) effects of past sectoral EC policies by policy area, type of region and the latter's location (North and South).

II. THE EUROPEAN TECHNOLOGY COMMUNITY

What was once merely seen as a strategic option advanced by some leading member states of the Community, namely the establishment of a Community of two speeds, has meanwhile become reality. The features assumed by the European Technology Community (ETC) during its brief history of only five years [*Wäldchen, 1988: 50*] demonstrate that large territories of the EC, entire countries included, do not only not form part of this exclusive club[29] but, moreover, are likely to stay out for a long period to come. Data on the territorial distribution and size of firms participating in either specific schemes of the Second Framework Programme for Cooperative R&D[30] or in parts of the Eureka Programme,[31] demonstrate extraordinary concentration rates.

As was been mentioned in the previous section, positive Community initiatives in the industrial policy domain are now more than ever dominated by activities aimed at enhancing the EC's high tech potential. The sustained focus of Community policies on R&D and other knowledge-intensive industries is, of course, understandable.[32] What is less understandable is that the intersectoral character of these policies has rarely been acknowledged and, also, that little is being done to fight the whole array of resulting negative externalities which precipitate both territorially in regions and functionally in related policy domains.[33]

Most initiatives of the Community in the high-tech domain, with the exclusion, of course, of programmes such as 'Star',[34] tend to widen already existing gaps in the technological factor endowment of regions. These gaps are already wider than those dividing less developed and advanced areas in overall economic terms. Disparities will increase even more than before as technology advances, and they are likely to become a persistent and permanent feature of future economic progress in the Community, slowing down the overall pace of economic development.

A Stride report (Science and Technology for Regional Innovation and Development in Europe) produced by the National Board for Science and Technology in Dublin [*CEC, 1987c*], for the first time quantifies high tech disparities at a regional level. GDP and GERD (Gross Expenditure on R&D) figures per capita in the Southern member states and Ireland show that the ratio in the level of R&D intensity at the national level across the Community oscillates between 1:12 and, considering private investment intensity (BERD or Business Expenditure on R&D), between 1:28. A group of Mediterranean countries, accounting for about 40 per cent of the Community population, arrives at a meagre share of not more than 10 per cent of R&D activity in the EC [*ibid.: v*]. At the sub-national level, disparities appear to be more pronounced:

> Many regions have almost zero R&D capacity. Their technology level can be a factor of 100 times lower than that of more developed core regions ... The scale of the technology gap is estimated at 7 billion ECU per annum. This indicates the level of additional annual investment which less favoured member states would require in R&D to reach average Community levels [*ibid.*].

The economic gap, which for so long has been formally recognized by the Community through its regional and other structural policies, is a factor of between three and ten times smaller than the R&D gap for these countries. The question arises, therefore, as to whether the technology gap should not also be explicitly recognized within Community policy. In any case, 'a gap of this magnitude suggests that solutions will be long-term' [*ibid.*]. Official EC documents recognize the extent of these problems. Yet, as regards positive strategic proposals for counteraction to be taken, one looks in vain for suggestions going beyond verbal and mere obligatory exercises in favour of economic and social cohesion which do seem to belong to a set of standard rituals of many official publications since the signing of the SEA (Article 130A).

One well-informed and most comprehensive study on telecommunications in Europe [*Ungerer and Costello, 1988*] dedicates not more than one and a half pages (of a total of 260) to an investigation of potential territorial impacts of EC policy in that sector. Apart from a brief description of existing problems, the authors refer to a Council Resolution of 30 June 1988 which suggests the Star Programme as the most appropriate tool for coping with these problems [*ibid.: 253*], and demand that 'a fundamental pre-condition for a Community-wide market in 1992 is the full integration of the less favoured regions of the Community into the economic mainstream of Europe' [*ibid.: 158–60*].

It remains to be seen, however, whether the purely deregulatory and market-driven solution submitted by the authors will actually contribute to more balanced growth.[35] Deregulating the domestic procurement markets for telecommunications and high technology products is certainly necessary if competitiveness is to be re-established on international markets. The question is in whose interest should this primarily be done and to what extent is this going to result in forms of transnational re-regulation. Stevers [*1990: 65*] observes that the main initiatives in favour of deregulation were actually taken by the

> big European [equipment] industries. They stressed the importance of bigger home markets and congruent national regulation. The more technocratic decision-making at the EC level promised ... to be more successful than decision-making at the national level ... [where] distributive equity considerations ... are likely to carry more weight.

The deal struck between national governments and big business when the foundations for the Technology Community were hammered out consisted in business being prepared to support government in a reconstitution of eroding national sovereignty over economic policy at the supranational level if government was prepared to concede that a future European political economy was to be significantly less subject to institutional regulation [*Streeck, 1989: 6*]. While the increasing withdrawal of member states from past patterns of 'dirigisme' would have opened opportunities for the issuing of a vast array of transnational regulatory rules by the EC benefiting its entire territory, the opposite occurred and the Commission, by way of its 'block exemption' from EC competition rules and the unconditional transfer of substantial resources to a small group of European multinational corporations, almost completely abstained from imposing binding norms on enterprises which agreed to participate in Community-guided co-operative ventures. The resulting effects of these deals, that is, the characteristics of different industry-led schemes for technological and R&D co-operation, are remarkable both in terms of spatial and corporate concentration.[36]

III. THE SPATIAL CONCENTRATION OF COMMUNITY R&D SCHEMES

Several studies have been carried out by the International Union of Local Authorities (IULA) in order 'to verify whether or not Community policies in R&D (via programmes as, for example, Brite, Race, etc.) really contribute to economic and social cohesion in the Community' [*Saublens, 1988: 2*]. The results of this work fully confirm what has been argued so far: Community policy in the IT, in the telecom and in other related high tech sectors does not only do little to offset existing disparities but actually contributes to a significant widening of these gaps. Figure 1 presents data on the rate of participation of companies and research institutes of four Southern member states – Spain's and Italy's Objective 1 regions presented separately[37] – plus Ireland in four R&D schemes of the EC's Framework Programme.

Although only countries with minor shares in the four schemes have been included, significant differences emerge with regard to the participation of, for example, Italian and Greek enterprises. While Italian firms participate in 89 Esprit projects, enterprises from the country's South are represented by only seven participants, and the overall number of Greek participants does not exceed 20 firms. If including enterprises from all member states, the picture would change dramatically: French and UK firms have the highest share in terms of participation in the schemes, the former leading in the case of Brite (63 participants) and Sprint (29 participants), the latter in Esprit (164 particpants) and Comett (83 participants). In relation to the UK, Italy obtains 54.3 and Portugal 7.9 points in Esprit while the ratio of the nine Spanish Objective 1

FIGURE 1
ABSOLUTE PARTICIPATION RATE OF FIRMS FROM MEMBER STATES WITH OBJECTIVE 1 REGIONS IN 4 EUROPEAN R&D PROGRAMMES

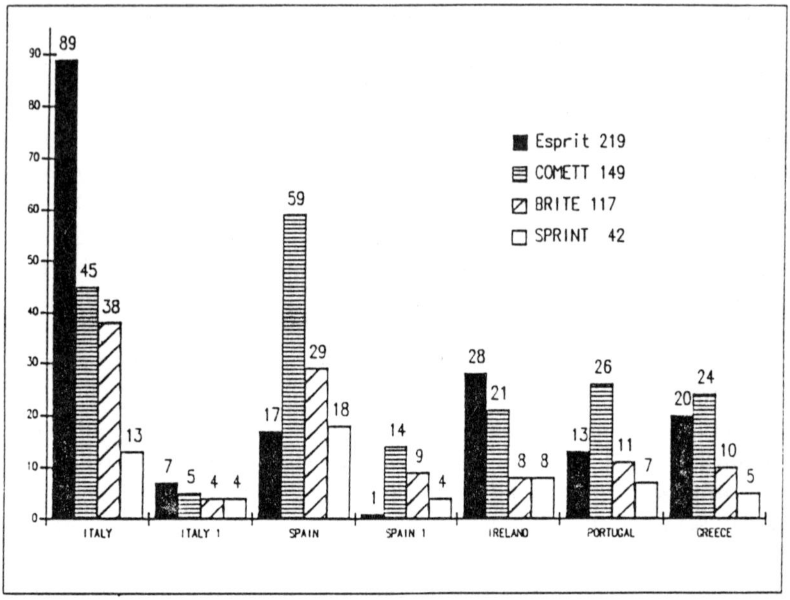

Source: Saublens [*1988*] (author's elaboration).

regions drops to 0.6. The maximum number of Greek, Irish and Portuguese firms participating in either of the four schemes does not exceed 28. Another important feature of the four programmes is the strong geographical concentration of participating firms in a small number of regions and, within these regions, in a limited number of sub-regional agglomeration areas such as provinces, departments and 'Regierungsbezirke'. Most French participants have their headquarters in the Ile-de-France and, specifically, the Paris area, followed by Rhône–Alpes and Provence–Côte d'Azur, while the biggest number of British firms tends to come from the South East, especially the Greater London area, and from East Anglia. The same applies to Italy (Milan, Pisa, Rome) and Spain (Barcelona, Madrid).

With respect to an overall number of 50 different DG XII-managed co-operation programmes, average participation rates per Community country figure at 135 projects in 1986 and 112 projects in 1987. Average participation of countries with Objective 1 regions for the two years oscillates between 16 and 37. A comparison of financial allocations from the Structural Funds with those coming under co-operative R&D programmes also reveals little complementarity between the actions. Community interventions in the high tech domain (DG 12) are proportionally more relevant for countries benefiting in only modest terms from Structural Fund allocations (DGs 16 and 22). Germany receives only four per cent of the total contributions of the Structural Funds but gets 22 per cent of the total contributions of the R&D programmes while Spain, which receives 16.5 per cent from the former source, gets only one per cent from the latter. What has been argued above, namely that traditional redistributive measures basically being used for providing less-developed regions with hard infrastructure do not outweigh the negative effects of the Community's high-tech policy, is corroborated by the findings of the IULA study. 'Keeping in mind that in the majority of the structurally backward regions ERDF interventions are essentially transport infrastructure investments, the disparities of the fallout of the R&D financing efforts might intensify more strongly the development gaps between the Community regions' [*Saublens, 1988: 10*].

A recent study of a more comprehensive set of Community programmes[38] carried out by the same organization, points to the territorial concentration of project participants in the large metropolitan growth poles of seven member states. As demonstrated by Figure 2, almost half of the French participants (42.5 per cent) of the 15 co-operation projects under investigation have their headquarters in Ile-de-France, with 16.7 per cent directly being located in the Paris area. While in France, the UK and Germany[39] the contribution of leading provinces to the participation rate of leading regions ranges between 30 and 50 per cent, thus indicating a still quite acceptable distribution of participants across the regional territory; the picture changes the more one goes South. The share of Lazio, for example, in total Italian participation is 21.6 per cent, while the Rome area alone accounts for 20.9 per cent. The figures for Greece and Portugal show that considerably more than 50 per cent of the participating firms are located in the respective national capital of these countries.

With regard to Portugal, the high share of Lisbon-based enterprises leaves almost nothing for regions like Algarve (one participant) or Norte (four participants). The same applies to Athens in Greece where Thessalia and the Peloponnese are left with four participants each, while Macedonia and Ipeiros together have only two participants (that is, roughly three per cent of the national total). In general, going beyond the limited data presented here, it appears that 50 to 75 per cent of the firms from one of the 99 regions studied are hosted by the leading town or metropolitan growth pole of the respective region. In less developed and

FIGURE 2

SHARE OF LEADING REGION AND LEADING DEPARTMENT PER COUNTRY IN 15 EUROPEAN HIGH-TECH COOPERATION PROGRAMMES (%)

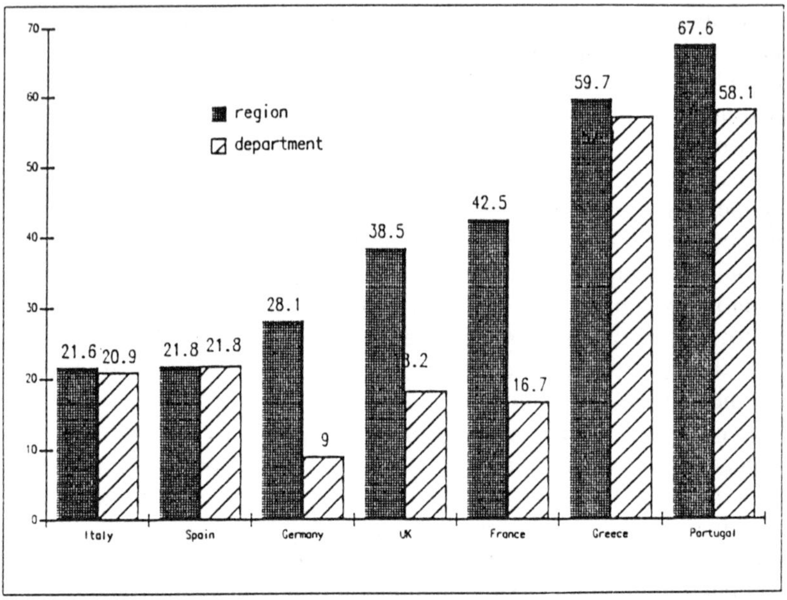

Source: Saublens [*1989*] (author's elaboration).

peripheral zones, this figure reaches 100 per cent (Basilicata, Molise, Northern Ireland, Normandie, Algarve, etc.). With the above information in mind, it might be interesting to consider the extent to which territorial concentration, alone contributing to considerable increases in regional disparities across the regions of the Community, is matched by concentration in size and corporate power of participating firms.

IV. THE CORPORATE STRUCTURE OF THE EC'S R&D NETWORK

The development of a European Technology Community is largely due to the activities of the big 12 leading European multinationals [*Buda/Vogel, 1989, Mytelka and Delapierre, 1987; Shearman, 1989*] whose representatives have, since 1979, formed the European Business Roundtable, and to those of a second group of firms (the Gyllenhammer group), including many non-IT manufacturers like Volvo and other European car producers. The 'declaration of common intent' of 20 June 1985 (see Peterson

[*1990: 12*]) issued by Philips, Siemens, GEC and Thompson in response to the Community's effort to counterbalance US offers to European partners to participate in the Strategic Defense Initiative (SDI), finally paved the way for the creation of the European Research Cooperation Agency (Eureka). For various reasons, large firms are not only systematically favoured in the capacity to steer and shape the predominantly industry-led schemes of the Technology Framework Programme but, actually, operate large parts of it without much interference by public institutions.[40] These reasons relate to the critical nature of technical information as a source of power, to the oligopolistic structure of markets, to the political momentum at the Community level to restore competitiveness versus Japan and the US, to the institutional self-interest of the Commission to enlarge its influence and opportunity space for action and, finally, to the EC's democratic deficit and the insulation of technology scheme decision-making structures from normal channels of democratic accountability [*ibid.: 7*]. This is important to mention because both the size of enterprises and the governance structure of existing schemes largely determine their degree of territorial concentration in particular areas of the Community. According to DG XII and with respect to certain sectors covered by Esprit, the relatively modest size of firms in some countries (notably Italy) is one of the main causes of non-participation of these enterprises in the schemes.

The Commission, indeed, continues to define as SME only those 'independent firms with less than 500 employees whose fixed assets (net of depreciation) are less than 75 million ECU and in whose capital structure large enterprises hold no more than a one-third participation' [*Aitken, 1988: 59*]. This practice continues to be used despite the fact that the official definition for this category of enterprises lies at a level of up to ten times below the EC definition in many member states of the South where they provide the bulk of value added and of productive capacity [*Grote, 1992b*]. The irresistible temptation for the Commission has been to identify successful industry with big firms, possibly because that is the institution's view of what makes Japanese industry successful.

Generally, however, it is not only the relatively weak participation rates of SMEs in the exclusive, club-type EC-schemes in co-operative R&D which appear to be most startling. Not less peculiar are the modes of governance of this club itself which even tends to reinforce the already existing barriers to entry resulting from official eligibility criteria. Contrary to the theory that, following 'the complexity and multiplicity of the emerging telecommunications services, only the market can efficiently link the producer with the consumer ... [and that] economics knows of no other means of fulfilling this purpose and all attempts to replace it by something else have so far failed' [*Ungerer and Costello, 1988: 100*], the practice of restoring competitiveness falls far short of these normative statements. What is warranted by Cawson [*1990: 29*] with regard to consumer electronics, actually applies to the entire Framework Programme: 'The consumer electronics industry is . . . increasingly governed by non-market means, such as state-producer networks and industry networks, and increasingly those hierarchical instruments of state influence are being refashioned at the European level.'

With respect to the decision-making structures of programmes as Esprit, Race, Brite, Eureka, etc. we are, indeed, not merely confronted with a classic phenomenon of agency capture [*Grote, 1989; 1990*] but, more precisely, with a phenomenon of 'agency creation' by a narrow distributive coalition of, in principal, not more than 12 enterprises.[41] This can be shown surveying both Esprit, the 'flagship programme' of the Framework, and the territorially more encompassing – but with respect to its corporate structure equally narrow – example of Eureka. Before completely being absorbed by DG 13 in 1987, Esprit was managed by an IT Task Force [*Stevers, 1990: 32*] which, initially, consisted of ex-officials from DG 3 and by two subgroups of this Task Force, the Senior Officials Group of Telecommunications (SOGT) and the Group d'Analyse et de Prevision (GAP). These three groupings were joined by business experts representing the leading European MNCs and by academics and were largely autonomous of government control. The fact that they were given 'broad powers to choose which individual project proposals receive funding, how EC funds are distributed between participants, and which specific technologies are supported within broad technological sectors' [*Peterson, 1990: 10*] led to 70–80 per cent of all Esprit contracts between 1981 and 1983 being awarded to the big 12 European MNCs [*Mytelka and Delapierre, 1987: 245*].

In the case of Eureka, industrial firms are entirely responsible for proposing projects for Eureka 'status' and a proposal has, so far, never been refused by Eureka's Council of Ministers [*Peterson, 1990: 13*]. Although this programme does not possess a genuine public governing body to guide the general direction of policy or perform the sort of technology assessment required to determine whether funds are spent wisely, instances of a free market are difficult to detect here as well. What emerges with respect to the overall ensemble of these programmes is a hierarchically organized European MITI of the Japanese type with enormous problems for democratic accountability. If the five billion ECU commitments by European firms and governments turn into hard cash, 'Eureka 95' 'will be the largest single investment project in Europe after the Channel Tunnel' [*Cawson, 1992*].

FIGURE 3
SHARE OF THE BIG 12 EUROPEAN MNCS AND OF SMES (%) IN FOUR R&D CO-OPERATION PROGRAMMES AND THEIR NATIONAL ORIGIN

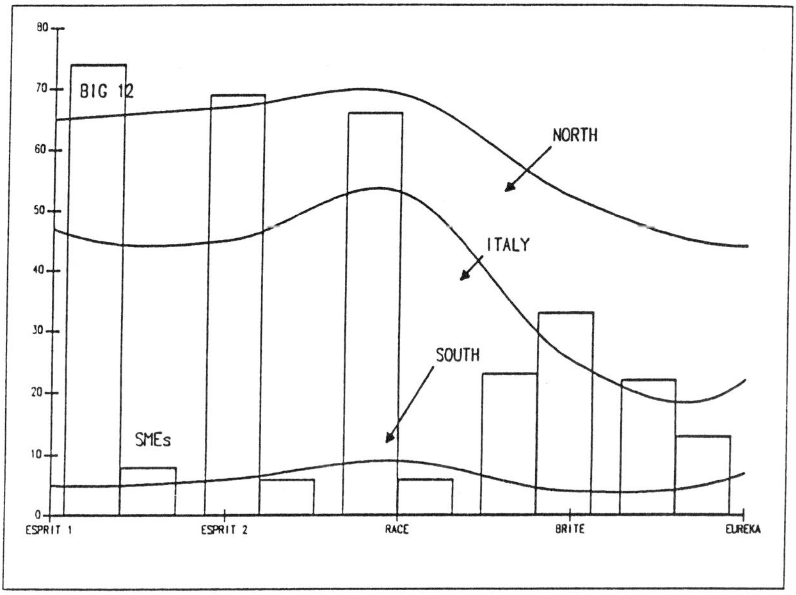

Source: van Tulder [*1990*] (author's elaboration).

Data presented in Figure 3 largely confirms what has been argued so far. Columns represent the relative participation of the big 12 and of small and medium sized enterprises while lines illustrate the territorial origin of enterprises for two geographical areas.[42] With regard to the second phase of Esprit (Esprit 2), the BIG 12 participate in 69 per cent of the projects while SMEs are involved in not more than six per cent. No wonder then that, on average, enterprises from Northern member states participate in 67 per cent of Esprit 2's projects while firms from the South participate in only six per cent of the scheme's co-operative ventures. Participation of Italian firms represents an intermediate category. It is markedly higher than that of firms from the EC–South group but lies considerably below that of firms from France, the UK and Germany (EC–North).

Differences are most pronounced in the first Esprit phase and less pronounced in Brite. In the latter programme, SMEs participate without any presence of multinationals in the single projects, in about 30 per cent of the 117 cases. This may be due to the fact that, in contrast to the other programmes, Brite's problem definition and its general framework have not been formulated by the Big 12. As a consequence, the participation rate and the extent of control exerted by the latter is much lower in this programme which is also the only one where some, albeit indirect, European trade union participation has been achieved [*van Tulder and Junne, 1988*].

With respect to Esprit, many Community documents claim that the representation of small and medium-sized enterprises would be representative. The relatively modest contribution of SMEs to R&D investments is held responsible for the fact that they participate in, on average, not more than ten per cent of the programmes. What is mentioned with less frequency is the negligible portion of Esprit's public funds which actually are paid out to SMEs. Also, as noted by Peterson [*1990: 24*], 'the total proportion of innovations which originate from SMEs is higher than their share of total R&D expenditure'. Generally, considering the innovative potential of SMEs together with their dominant share in national output in the South, and taking into account the combined effect of the official SME definition of the Commission and the hierarchical governance structures of existing R&D schemes, it becomes evident that small firms 'despite apparent European Commission provisions to the contrary, are gradually squeezed out of the market' [*Shearman, 1989: 6*]. This is further amplified by the marginal share of the territories within which populations of small firms typically prosper.

V. CONCLUSION

Both uncoordinated sectoral policies and countermeasures trying to offset the negative territorial externalities of the former by way of purely redistributive initiatives which are targeted at the creation of hard infrastructure of regional economies will not be able to generate a proper regional and social dimension to the internal market. Two demands are resulting from that in terms of a future Community policy.

First, the size of non-regulatory, direct expenditure programmes is constrained by current budgetary appropriations, and the costs of regulatory interventions are directly borne by firms, individuals, territories and the latter's representative institutions. Given these financial constraints on the one hand, and the, potentially, unlimited stock of regulatory instruments on the other, 'the only way for the Commission to increase its role is to expand the scope of its regulatory activities' [*Majone, 1989*]. Since the widely appreciated strategy of mutual recognition is patently too weak to handle problems resulting from negative externalities, we are likely to encounter a re-regulatory inflation of an unknown extent in all those domains for which the Commission has acquired competences. If this continues to follow the established patterns of sectoral policies, the likely result would be a further increase in regional disparities. Following Majone, the first demand, hence, would consist in the creation of a 'regulatory clearing house' or 'regulatory budget' at the level of the Commission whose primary function would be to control the cost-effectiveness of different regulatory programmes as well as the latters externalities.

Second, the endowment of regional economies with infrastructure determines their performance more than any other resource [*Biehl, 1990*]. The definition of infrastructure varies, of course, from author to author. We subscribe here to Joachimsen's (1966) broad definition and include both tangibles and intangibles (that is, hard and soft resources) into this category. Infrastructure is, in the normal case, characterized by high degrees of visibility and, consequently, by government provision or by private provision under public regulation. Substantial fractions of hard infrastructure (for example, the whole domain of telecommunications) are now subject to privatization, while most of the soft resources, where they exist, are anyway privately generated under a more or less strongly pronounced regime of public obligations and norms. These latter drastically diverge across the regions of the Community in terms of the extent to which regional institutions are able and willing to control, influence and stimulate the procreation and promulgation of soft infrastructure.

Among the four resources determining regional development levels – infrastructure, location, agglomeration and sectoral structure – only the former 'represents a direct instrument of government policy' [*Biehl, 1990: 30*]. There is no reason why interventions in this domain should continue to be managed by national authorities alone. As regards soft devices, the Community could, for example, make the transfer of financial appropriations of its Structural Funds contingent on the existence or creation of regional collaborative networks among firms, interest associations, chambers of commerce, research institutes, etc. This would force regional public authorities especially of Southern member states to instigate, by way of imposing certain obligations on the often short-sighted behaviour of individual entrepreneurs, those 'excess' investments in redundant capacities which Streeck has called the main characteristic of a proper European accumulation model. Contrary to the mega-networks represented by programmes as Esprit, Eureka, etc., social and political institutions at the regional level would impose constraints as well as provide opportunities for individual entrepreneurs. Both are necessary: the first to suspend competition so as to protect profit-seeking individuals from the temptations of hyper-rationality, the second for building up new kinds of meso-networks in regions which would provide support for the creation of those resources which, being left to the market, would continue to remain in short supply. The problem is that these institutions would have to be designed so as to achieve both simultaneously, in order to avoid either the emergence of narrow rent-seeking distributional coalitions or the exploitation of the public by the private sector in form of firms shopping around for subsidies. The current activities by the Community in the high-tech domain, unfortunately, not only dismiss social, territorial and political aspects of technological innovation but, moreover, provide a limited number of dominant European multinationals with considerable opportunities for skimming public funds. There is no evidence, in this case, for trade-offs between constraints and opportunities which would promote territorial cohesion across the Community regions or strengthen the autonomy and action capacity of transnational institutions.

NOTES

1. The need for RIA is consistently reiterated by the Commission [1988a: 8; 1988b: 38–50] but its effects are hard to assess since 'the access to the results of these studies has been rather difficult, as they had been published either not at all or only in widely disparate journals' [*Molle and Cappellin, 1988: ix*]. Also, RIA seems to be limited essentially to those sectors where 'the question of regional impact arises mainly: agriculture and social policies' [*CEC, 1987b: 70*]. An impact assessment procedure ('*fiche d'impact*') has recently been introduced also by DG 23 for those sectoral policies affecting small and medium-sized enterprises. As demonstrated by opinions of the associations which represent the interests of the regulatory targets, the procedure is, in practice, far from being satisfactory [*UNICE, 1990; UEAPME, 1989*].
2. An early OECD study [*1975: 98*] on industrial policy points out that 'regional policy ... is an exercise in co-ordination: it is a complex effort requiring co-ordination of many national policies and at various levels of government'. Regional policy by the European Community is essentially limited to efforts in co-ordinating the Structural Funds and even this has not always been achieved. For problems the Commission has with internal coordination of its policies. See also Grote [*1989; 1990*].
3. See Anderson [*1990*] for a critical assessment of a 'Europe of the Regions' under present institutional conditions.
4. The creation of regional government in Greece in 1987, albeit eking out a precarious existence, has precisely been a result of pressure imposed by the Community on Greek national authorities to fill the institutional vacuum between central and local government. Without the establishment of a proper regional layer of administration, Greece would have been unable to bid for IMP assistance [*Bianchi and Grote, 1990; 1991*]. There is hardly anything regions would need more than equal start-up conditions in politico-administrative terms. Experiences of the type above, hence, would lend themselves for application to all structural Community interventions. A more discriminatory use of, for example, the non-quota section of the ERDF might be a realistic option in this respect.

5. If there was at all available a solution by means of public policy, 'it could only be perceived as a permanent process of redistribution of income demanding highly centralized authority. The possibility was ignored that the measures typically employed to realize such functional solutions might, by denying sufficient territorial identity and autonomy to the regions affected, actually help to generate the problems they were intended to solve' [*Coombes, 1989: 18*].
6. Cecchini's critique of over-emphasized preoccupation with sectoral repercussions of the internal market in Italy shall be quoted extensively: 'From an economic viewpoint, the problem consists in identifying the positive and negative peculiarities of the Italian situation rather than in the easy but dangerous attempt to forecast the sectoral prospectives. This kind of forecasting is condemned to fail for at least three reasons: first, the effects of the completion of the internal market will precipitate in the entire area of the Community, with reciprocal and multiple incidents across all sectors and all countries – a fact which renders extremely uncertain and dubious any kind of purely sectoral forecast of restructuring and industrial reconversion. Second, exercises of this kind risk over-emphasizing those enterprises which, for fear of increasing competition, pronounce their preoccupations more loudly than those which find themselves in an advantageous position. Finally, the results of the research on the costs of non-Europe tend to corroborate that the impact of an abolishment of the existing (market) restrictions is likely to lead to even more positive effects to the extent that reasonable and convergent policies are applied to the national level. That all requires that the analysis of domestic prospects for development shall be undertaken primarily on a global scale' [*Cecchini, 1988: 15–16;* author's translation].
7. 'If, unlike the American economy where the social conditions of production are subordinate to economic objectives, the Commission intends to promote a process of development which offers a large measure of integration of the economic and the social, the least one can expect from this institution is that it acquires the means necessary for observing and, if possible, predicting the social changes prompted by the completion of the internal market' [*CEC, 1988a: 28*]. Or, phrased differently, as done by the authors of a FAST expert study, systematic RIA and resulting policy proposals, necessarily, 'run counter to the currently prevailing ... policy' [*CEC, 1987a*].
8. Strijker and Veer [*1988: 23–24*] mention five factors which might explain the high expenditure levels: firstly, agriculture still represents the main source of income with up to 25 per cent of output and more than 33 per cent of employment in Greece and Southern Italy; secondly, it generates income and employment in an indirect way since about 50 per cent of the EC food-processing industry directly depends on agricultural production; thirdly, agriculture is the greatest user of open space – the share of this sector in the EC's total acreage lies at around 60 per cent which has many implications for other policy domains; fourthly, the sector produces many goods for basic needs and, finally, agricultural and food products possess a high share in international trade and account for, roughly, 12 per cent of intra-Community and nine per cent of extra-Community trade.
9. Directive 72/268/EC on mountain and hill farming in certain less favoured areas.
10. The 'Samland report' (PE 144.399/B of 23.10.1990), preoccupied with the take-over of ICL by Fujitsu and the attempts by the Japanese to get hold of other European multinationals, also demands an 'industrial-political orientation' of European high-tech programmes.
11. 'Un ulteriore sviluppo logico potrebbe essere la realizzazione di una struttura nella quale inserire tutti questi programmi (Brite, Sprint, Esprit, Jessi, Race, Eureka), cioè una strategia industriale. In breve, il mercato unico è destinato a far nascere una sorta di MITI europeo o alla giapponese per la metà del prossimo decennio' [*Curzon, 1989: 257*].
12. Approved by the Council on 27 Oct. 1986. See COM (85) 838 final. Valoren relates to alternative and renewable energies, namely solar and wind energy, biomass including urban waste, small-scale hydro power and geothermal energy and also helps to make more efficient use of energy (that is, energy savings and oil substitution).

13. Many observers agree that the ERDF's bias in favour of transport infrastructure provision is also due to the fact that physical indicators (kilometres of roads accomplished) and criteria for progress of implementation (ECU per square meter) are more easily measurable than is the case for other types of investment. The monitoring capacity of the Commission is less endangered here than, for example, in the case of assistance to SMEs or the training of highly qualified personnel and its subsequent insertion into the production process.
14. 'The main effect of the Autostrada del Sole has been to encourage additional migration from the Mezzogiorno to more developed areas of Italy. The motorways had little effect on the behaviour of SMEs: it appears that the large firms and state enterprises which established themselves in the South were more attracted by state subventions than by improved land-transport links' [*Fullerton/Gillespie 1988: 89*].
15. EC regulations on drivers' hours and the use of tachographs to enforce them have been vigorously resisted in Ireland and the UK because they are seen to impose distance thresholds at particular points on the transport network [*Fullerton and Gillespie, 1988*].
16. In 1981, for example, the funds available for the Community's transport policy amounted to 10 million ECU, while expenditure on regional policy approached 2400 million ECU [*ibid.*].
17. In October 1973, the Commission submitted a first outline of a common transport policy [*CEC, 1973*] which was accepted by the EP but neither discussed nor endorsed by the Council.
18. One of the most recent ones being Sapir [*1989*].
19. The group of distinguished British economists which signs responsible for the manifesto being quoted here, argues that it is 'essential that such a policy should concentrate on eliminating the causes of regional imbalance by raising productivity levels in the poorer areas and that income transfers to alleviate the consequences of low productivity should be used as an interim measure only.' [*The Economist, ibid.*]. How DGs 16 and 22 should contribute to raise productivity levels without making use of income transfers – a certainly most interesting question – is not indicated however.
20. The Delors Report is not an official statement by the Commission, but it seems to reflect 'the same incapacity to reconcile different views of the purposes of public intervention in economic affairs as the Commission's own repeated statements over the years. "Economic and social cohesion" seems, indeed, to be the latest in a series of efforts to reconcile the irreconcilable. The truth is that problems of this order go beyond the scope of purely economic explanation' [*Coombes, 1989: 10*].
21. The combined effect of (i) business concentration, (ii) market homogenization, (iii) commissioning and, (iv) deregulation and privatization (each of these trends being mutually reinforcing) results in the geographical concentration of decision-making centres around the major urban agglomerations. This combined process of functional and social polarization, 'once initiated, becomes perpetuated, reinforced and irreversible' [*CEC, 1987a: 10–12*].
22. The service sector literature [*Illeris, 1989: 30–31*] distinguishes between type-1 services (goods-related or man-thing relationships), type-2 services (information or man–man symbol relationships) and, finally, type-3 or person-related services (man–man relationships). As demonstrated by the example of the US, type 1 and 3 services (especially hotels, catering and cleaning) are still relevant in terms of employment creation, accounting for almot 50 per cent of new jobs created between 1977 and 1987. From a strategic perspective, however, information services are of much more importance for regional development.
23. The commitment appropriations of the ESF in 1985 totalled roughly 2200 million ECU, with over a third committed to less favoured regions. Vanhoven and Klaassen [*1987: 442*] even see appropriations to less developed regions increasing from 1977 (70 per cent) to 1981 (87 per cent) and 1982 (90 per cent).
24. 'The new priority of Social Fund interventions for the training of young people, for example, has on the whole not led to more young people being trained, but rather to member states submitting more projects within existing schemes' [*Steinle, 1988*].

25. The Social Fund is 'primarily functional ..., and regional criteria become involved only in a second stage, in the allocation of aid. The Regional Fund's tasks, by contrast, are primarily geographically oriented, with functional selection criteria ... playing a role in the second stage of the policy process' [*CEC, 1987b: 72*].
26. According to Streeck [*1991: 31–45*], resources needed for combatting market and hierarchy failure are (i) a congenial organizational ecology (strategic alliances and joint ventures, trust-based co-operation between firms and their suppliers, associations of small firms and chambers under public facilitation), (ii) redundant capacities (broad and high skills, a polyvalent organizational structure, decentralized competence, social peace) and (iii) collective production inputs (co-operative labour relations, the functional interpenetration of tasks, the recognition of interdependence between competitors cum allies, knowledge and the joint production of general skills by a network of potentially competitive firms).
27. This level 'should ... be defined in a functional manner with respect to a potential development project (and) is a space where it is possible to undertake a global and coherent action and where there exist common interests sufficiently strong to provoke a dialogue between local partners, where it is possible to reach sufficient numbers of people to acquire influence and make an impact and where cultural references condusive to awareness and a common commitment already exist or are of nature to be developed' [*CEC, 1988a: 23*].
28. 'Increased consultative activity involving economic and social interests on the basis of the regional economy indicated an enhanced capacity for self-organization by productive networks, previously frustrated by an inappropriate territorial allocation of public authority' [*EPRU, 1989: 56*].
29. 'Many of the European level initiatives may be characterized as "club-type" developments. Perceiving a major threat in terms of Japanese and US technology and market penetration, core groups at both the national and European level have formed defensive groupings manifested in terms of initiatives like Esprit to protect their interests' [*Shearman, 1989: 6*].
30. The Framework Programme comprises and coordinates initiatives as Esprit, Éclair, Brite, Race, etc. A pilot phase of Esprit was agreed in 1983, and a full ten-year programme (1984–1993) was finally agreed in 1984 with a budget of 1.5 billion ECUs (Peterson 1991: 12). It has originally been defined as 'pre-competitive' to avoid falling foul of EC competition rules [*Cawson, 1992*], but recent initiatives suggest that participation will now also be possible for product-oriented research (see note 10).
31. The European Research Cooperation Agency (Eureka) is entirely intergovernmental and independent of the EC. Eureka projects have been established after 1985 when, as a result of French pressure, Europe launched its civilian equivalent of the US Star Wars defence programme. The financing of these programmes is channelled largely through DG 13 (Telecommunications, Information Industries and Innovation), 'which is now responsible for the second largest item of EC expenditure after the Common Agricultural Policy' [*Cawson, 1992*]. Eureka groups together all 12 member states, the six EFTA countries, Turkey and the EC Commission the latter participating as a nominal extra member state. It is designed to encourage 'near market, product-oriented R&D'.
32. For example, 80 per cent of growth observed in the US economy between 1909 and 1949 was attributable to technical progress rather than to increasing inputs of capital and labour [*Thwaites and Oakey, 1985: 1*].
33. The danger that these programmes actually cancel out the effects of other Community policies operated, for example, by DG 5, 16, 22 and 23, has recently been criticized by the Energy Committee of the European Parliament which insists that some modifications should be inserted into the Draft Proposal for the 3rd Framework Programme on R&D collaboration presented by the Commission. The EP's critique, however, remains rather modest and basically consists in the following: first, mention should be made of the issue of social and economic cohesion (Pergola Report; PE 141.189/Res. of 19.07.1990, p.4) and, second, there should be priority treatment for applications by small and medium-sized enterprises [*ibid.: 9–10*].

34. The positive impact of the Special Telecommunications Action for Regional Development (STAR), although representing an important step into the desired direction, cannot be more than marginal in comparison to the negative ones of the EC's 'flagship programmes' (Esprit, Race, etc.) which lack any regional dimension.
35. As argued by Fullerton and Gillespie [*1988: 99*], 'there can be little doubt that public sector monopoly provision in Europe has benefitted peripheral and/or less favoured regions ... Although the principle of universality has been extended into the supply of new services, available evidence suggests that in practice there can be marked regional variations in the availability of new services arising from the phased stages by which investments are made and networks extended geographically'. Wäldchen [*1988: 53*], as well, maintains that 'unless corrective action is taken, the development of the infrastructure for the new technologies will tend to follow established demand patterns and concentrate in the most developed regions of the Community'.
36. One should, of course, keep in mind that none of these programmes had actually been designed to further regional development objectives. The original idea was to provide support for activities exclusively in 'centres of excellence'.
37. Regions eligible for Objective 1 status of the reformed Structural Funds are: Spain-1 (Andalucia, Asturias, Castilla-Leon, Castilla-La Mancha, Communidad Valenciana, Ceuta y Melilla, Galicia, Canarias, Murcia), Italy-1 (Abruzzi, Basilicata, Calabria, Campania, Molise, Puglia, Sardegna, Sicily), Greece, Portugal and Ireland (plus N. Ireland (UK)). The total number of co-operative ventures for each scheme is given in the legend to Figure 2.
38. See Saublens [*1989*]. The data set consists of the following 15 Community-financed technology and innovation-related programmes: BAP, BC-NET, BIC, BRITE, ESPRIT, EUROTECHNET, HELIOS, IRIS, LEDA, PETRA, PAUVRETE, SPRINT, COMETT (regional), COMETT (sectoral), EURO-INFO CENTRES.
39. Note with respect to Germany that this is the only country where the province with the highest relative share in national totals (Munich) does not belong to the region with the highest share (Nordrhein Westphalen). In all other cases, what is called here 'leading department' corresponds to the national capital of the respective member state. Total national participation figures and leading regions and departments per country are: Italy 263 (Lazio/Roma), Spain 188 (Madrid/Madrid), Germany 256 (NRW/Munich), UK 314 (South East/London), France 324 (Ile de France/Paris), Greece 77 (Anatoliki Sterea Kai Nisia/Athens) and Portugal 74 (Lisboa-Val de Tejo/Lisboa).
40. Nota bene that Philips, for example, 'organizes training seminars for EC officials to acquaint them with the problems of the electronics industry and presents its own position papers on current issues' [*Cawson, 1992*].
41. Decision-making, governance and interest intermediation in the consumer electronics part of Esprit 'conform rather closely to the idea of corporatism' [*Cawson, 1992*].
42. The North (that is, France, UK, Germany) and the South (that is, Spain, Portugal, Greece). Ireland is included in the latter category, while Italy, which occupies an intermediate position between the Northern and the Southern groups, is excluded from the latter.

REFERENCES

Aberle, G., 1979, 'Transport and Regional Policy Objectives in Cost Benefit Analysis' in W.A. Blonk, (ed.), *Transport and Regional Development* (Farnborough: Saxon House).

Aitken, Peter, 1988, 'SMEs, Research and Development and Technology Policies and the European Community: Issues in Implementation', in Kenneth Dyson, (ed.), *Local Authorities and New technologies – The European Dimension* (London and New York: Croom Helm), pp. 59–84.

Anderson, Jeffrey, 1988, 'Territorial Networks of Interest in Britain and Germany: Regions and the Politics of Economic Decline' (Ph.D. dissertation, Yale University, 1988), University of Michigan, Ann Arbor.

Anderson, Jeffrey, 1990, 'Skeptical Reflections on a Europe of the Regions: Britain, Germany, and the ERDF', in *Journal of Public Policies*, Vol.10, No. 4, p.417–447.

Anderson, Jeffrey, 1991, 'Business Associations and the Decentralization of Penury: Functional Groups and Territorial Interests', in *Governance*, Vol.4, No. 1, Jan. pp. 67–94.

Bakis, H., 1985, 'Telecommunications and Organization of Company Work Space', in Centre National d'Etudes des Telecommunications (ed.), Paris.

Bartels, C.P.A., Boomstra, D. and B. Viessert, 1983, 'Prospects for the regional development of the tertiary sector', Study carried out for the EC Commission, Quedemolen.

Bianchi, Giuliano and Jürgen R. Grote, 1990, 'How to create order from noise? A Case Study of Design and Implementation of the Integrated Mediterranean Programmes', in Proceedings of the XI Conferenza Italiana de Scienze Regionali – Vol.1, Trento, 26–28 Nov. 1990, pp. 167–195; now published in Flavio Boscacci and Gianluigi Gorla (eds.) [*1991*], op. cit.

Biehl, Dieter, 1990, 'The Role of Infrastructure in Regional Development', in Proceedings of the XI Conferenza Italiana di Scienze Regionali – Vol.1, pp. 17–57, Trento, 26–28 Nov. 1990; now published in Flavio Boscacci and Gianluigi Gorla (eds.) [*1991*] op. cit.

Bonnafous, A., 1979, 'Underdeveloped Regions and Structural Impacts of Transport Infrastructure', in W.A. Blonk, (ed.), op. cit.

Boscacci, Flavio and Gianluigi Gorla (eds.), 1991, *Economie locali in ambiente competitivo* (Milan: Franco Angeli).

Bourgeois, B., 1988, 'Energy', in W. Molle and R. Cappellin (eds.), op.cit., pp. 65–88.

Brocker, J. and K. Peschel, 1988, 'Trade', in W. Molle and R. Cappellin, (eds.), op.cit., pp. 127–52.

Buda, Dirk and Jean Vogel, 1989, 'L'Europe sociale 1992 – Illusion, alibi ou réalité?' (Rapport No.2), Université Libre, Brussels, June.

Cappelin, Riccardo, 1988, 'Interdependenza tra politiche regionali e politiche economiche non-regionali nella Comunita europea', *Economia pubblica*, No. 3 (March), pp.97–112.

Cawson, Alan, 1990, 'The Politics of Consumer Electronics – The British and European Industry in the 1970s and 1980s', University of Sussex: Sussex, mimeo.

Cawson, Alan, 1992, 'Interests, Groups and Public Policy-Making: The Case of the European Consumer Electronics Industry', in Justin Greenwood et al. (eds.) [*1992*] (forthcoming), op. cit.

Cecchini, Paolo, 1988, 'La Scadenza 1992: Quali sfide per l'Italia?', in *Quaderni dell'Istituto per gli Studi di Politica Internazionale*, papers 4, ISPI Milan, June.

Commission of the EC (CEC), 1973, 'Development of the Common Transport Policy' (Mursch Report), COM (73) 850, Brussels.

CEC, 1981, Study of the Regional Impact of the Common Agricultural Policy' (RICAP Study), Brussels.

CEC, 1984a, 'Tenth Report of the Activities of the European Social Fund', *Social Europe*, Supplement, 23.3.1984, Brussels.

CEC, 1984b, 'The Regional Impact of the Community's External Policy' (Kirschen study), Brussels.

CEC, 1984c, 'The Agricultural Situation in the Community', Report 1984, Brussels.

CEC, 1984d, 'The Effects of New Information Technology on the Less Favoured Regions of the Community', NIT, Newcastle upon Tyne (Curds Report).

CEC, 1985, 'The Agricultural Situation in the Community', Report 1985, Brussels.

CEC, 1987a, 'Services, advanced technologies and the regions. Strategic Dossier No.4 of the FAST programme II (1984–87) – Forecasting and Assessment in Science and Technology', (published by DG XXII, July 1987)

CEC, 1987b, 'The Regions of the Enlarged Community – Third Periodic Report on the Social and Economic Situation and Development of the Regions of the Community, Summary and Conclusions', Brussels.

CEC, 1987c, 'Science and Technology for Regional Innovation and Development in Europe. Report to the Community's Programmes Division', DG XVI by the National Board for Science and Technology, Dublin, Nov. 1987.

CEC, 1988a, 'The Social Aspects of the Internal Market', Vol 1. *Social Europe*, Supplement 7/88.

CEC, 1988b, 'The Social Dimension of the Internal Market. Interim Report of the Interservice Working Party', *Social Europe*, Special edition, May 1988.

Coombes, David, 1989, 'The Politics of Scale: European Economic Integration, Spatial Disparity and Local Development', paper presented at the Inaugural Conference of the European Community Studies Association, George Mason University, Fairfax, Virginia, 24–25 May 1989.Cooke, Philip and Kevin Morgan, 1990, 'Learning through Networking: Regional Innovation and the Lessons of Baden Württemberg', Regional Industrial Research ReportNo. 5, University of Wales, May 1990.

Curzon, Gerard, 1989, 'Dieci motivi per temere la fortezza Europa', in Rivista di Politica Economica, anno LXXIX, serie III, Dec, 1989, pp.245–63.

Ebbinghaus, Bernhard and Jelle Visser, 1992, 'Making the Most of Diversity? European Integration and Transnational Organization of Labour', in Greenwood *et al.* (eds.) [*1992*].

European Policy Research Unit (EPRU), 1989, 'Economic Development Networks: Consultation of Economic and Social Interests for Purposes of Regional Development Strategy', Consultancy paper for Shannon Development by EPRU, University of Limerick, March 1989.

The Economist, 1975, 'The All Saint's Day Manifesto for European Monetary Union', 1–7 Nov. 1975.

Fullerton, B. and A. Gillespie, 1988, 'Transport and Communications', in W. Molle, and R Cappellin, (eds.), op. cit., pp. 88–111.

Garmise, Shari Orris and Jürgen R. Grote, 1990, 'Economic Performance and Social Embeddedness: Emilia Romagna in an Interregional Context', in Robert Leonardi and Nanetti Raffaela (ed.), *Regions and European Integration: The Case of Emilia Romagna* (London: Frances Pinter Publishers).

George, Stephen, 1983, 'Regional Policy', in Juliet Lodge (ed.), *Institutions and Policies in the European Community* (London: Frances Pinter Publishers).

Goddard, J.B., Gillespie, A.E., Robinson, J.F., and A.T. Thwates, 1985, 'The Impact of New Information Technology on Urban and Regional Structure in Europe', in A.T. Thwaites and R.P. Oakey (eds.), *The Regional Economic Impact of Technological Change* (London: Frances Pinter), pp. 215–43.

Grabher, Gernot, 1990 'The Weakness of Strong Ties: The Ambivalent Role of Inter-firm Cooperation in the Decline and Reorganization of the Ruhr', Paper presented at the conference on 'Networks – On the Socio-economics of Inter-Firm Cooperation', Social Science Center (WZB), Research Area Labour Market and Employment, Berlin, 11–13 June 1990.

Grabher, Gernot, 1991, 'Against De-Industrialization: A Strategy for Old Industrial Areas', in Egon Matzner and Wolfgang Streeck (eds.) (1991), op. cit., pp. 62–81.

Greenwood, Justin, Grote, Jürgen R. and Karsten Ronit (eds.), 1992, *Organized Interests and the European Community* (London: Sage Publications).

Grote, Jürgen R., 1987, 'Tripartism and European Integration: Mutual Transfers, Osmotic Exchanges or Frictions between the 'National' and the "Transnational"?'in Georges Spyropoulos (ed.) Trade Unions Today and Tomorrow – Vol. 2: Trade Unions in a Changing Europe (Maastricht: Presses Interuniversitaire Europeenne), pp. 356–88.

Grote, Jürgen R., 1989, 'Guidance and Control in Transnational Committee Networks: The Associational Basis of Policy Cycles at EC Level', Paper presented at conference of SOG (Structure and Organization of Government) conference of the International Political Science Association (IPSA) on 'Government and Organized Interests', Zürich, Switzerland, 27–30 Sept. 1989.

Grote, Jürgen R., 1990, 'Steuerungsprobleme in transnationalen Beratungsgremien: über soziale Kosten unkoordinierter Regulierung in der EG', *Jahrbuch zur Staats,- und*

Verwaltungs-wissenschaft 1990, TJ. Ellwein, R. Mayntz and W.F. Scharpf (Hrsg.) (Baden Baden: Nomos Verlagsgesellschaft), pp.227–54.

Grote, Jürgen R., 1992a, 'Networking: un nuovo approccio all'analisi delle interdependenze tra attori locali', *Il Nuovo Governo Locale*, No. 1 (1992), Milan, pp. 3–37.

Grote, Jürgen R., 1992b, 'Small firms in the European Community: Modes of Production, Governance and Territorial Interest Representation', in Justin Greenwood *et al.* (eds.) [*1992*] (forthcoming), op. cit.

Hebbert, M. and H. Machin, 1984, *Regionalisation in France, Italy and Spain* (London: The International Centre for Economics and Related Disciplines of the London School of Economics and Political Science).

Hepworth, M.E., 1986, 'The Geography of Technological Change in the Information Economy', *Regional Studies*.

Holland, Stuart, 1990, 'The Promotion of Networking by Regional Development Agencies and Small and Medium Enterprises within the European Community', Paper presented at conference on 'Networks – On the Socio-economics of Inter-Firm Cooperation', Social Science Center (WZB), Research Area Labour Market and Employment, Berlin, 11–13 June 1990.

Illeris, Sven, 1989, *Services and Regions in Europe* (A Report from the FAST programme of the European Communities) (Aldershot: Avebury Publishers).

Joachimsen, Reimut, 1966, *Theorie der Infrastruktur. Grundlagen der marktwirtschaftlichen Entwicklung* (Tübingen).

Majone, Giandomenico ,1989 'Regulating Europe', in T. Ellwein, R. Mayntz and R.W. Scharpf (Hrsg.) *Jahrbuch zur Staats,- und Verwaltungswissenschaft 1989* (Baden Baden: Nomos Verlagsanstalt).

Matzner, Egon and Wolfgang Streeck (eds.), 1991, *Beyond Keynesianism. The Socio-Economics of Production and Full Employment* (Aldershot and Brookfield: Edward Alger).

Molle, Willem, 1983, *Industrial Location and Regional Development in the European Community: the FLEUR Model* (Aldershot: Gower Publishing).

Molle, Willem, 1988, 'Industry and Services', in Molle and Cappellin (eds.), op. cit., pp. 45–65.

Molle, Willem and Riccardo Cappelin (eds.), 1988, *Regional Impact of Community Policies in Europe* (Aldershot: Avebury Publishers).

Mytelka, L.K. and M. Delapierre, 1987, 'The Alliance Strategies of European Firms in the Information Technology Industry and the Role of Esprit', *Journal of Common Market Studies*, Vol. 26.

OECD, 1975, *The Aims and Instruments of Industrial Policy – A Comparative Study* (Paris: OECD).

Oettle, K., 1979, 'Public Obligations and Transportation in Underdeveloped Regions', in W.A. Blonk (ed.), *Transport and Regional Development* (Farnborough: Saxon House).

Peterson, John, 1990, 'European Technology Policy – Policy Communities and the Politics of Meso-Corporatism', Paper presented at Europeanists Convention of the Council for European Studies, Washington DC, 24 March 1990 (now published in *Journal of Common Market Studies*, Jan. 1991).

Rees, Nicholas, A.G., 1989, 'The European Community, Regional Policy and the Dynamics of Organizational Policy Networks', Paper presented at the Inaugural Conference of the European Community Studies Association, George Mason University, Fairfax, Virginia, 24–25 May 1989.

Sapir, Andre, 1989, 'Does 1992 come before or after 1990? On Regional versus Multilateral Integration', Discussion Paper No.313, Centre for Economic Policy Research, London.

Saublens, G., 1988, 'Participation of less favoured regions in the Community programmes. Brussels Info. No. 61 of 02.12.1988 of the International Union of Local Authorities (IULA), in Permanent Representation of Local and Regional Authorities with the European Community (ed.).

Saublens, G., 1989, 'Listing by Intermediate Regional Authority of the Eligibility and Rate of Participation in Programmes and Actions initiated by the European Community',

Brussels Info. No. 86 of 24.11.1989 of IULA, in Permanent Representation of Local and Regional Authorities with the European Community (ed.).

Sharpe, A., 1984, 'The market, the state and regional peripherality in Western Europe', in Hebbert and Machin (eds.), op. cit.

Shearman, C., 1989, 'European Technological Collaboration: An Overview of Some of the Issues Arising', Paper presented at European Community Studies Associations's Inaugural Conference, George Mason University, Fairfax, Virginia, 24–25 May 1989.

Solow, R.M., 1957, 'Technical Change and the Aggregate Production Function', *Review of Economic Statistics*, Vol. 39, pp. 213–20.

Steinle, W., 1989, 'Labour Market and Social Policies', in Molle and Cappellin (eds.), op. cit., pp. 111–26.

Stevers, Ester, 1990, 'Telecommunications Regulation in the European Community – The Commission of the EC as Regulatory Actor', EUI Working Paper No. 89/421, Florence.

Streeck, Wolfgang, 1989, 'The Social Dimension of the European Firm', Paper presented at the Annual Meeting of the Andrew Shonfield Association, European University Institute, Florence, 14–15 Sept. 14–15, 1989.

Streeck, Wolfgang, 1991, 'On the Institutional Conditions of Diversified Quality Production', in Marzner and Streekc (eds.) [*1991*], op. cit., pp. 21–62.

Strijker, D. and J., de Veer, 1988, 'Agriculture', in Molle and Cappellin (eds.), *Regional Impact of Community Policies in Europe* (Aldershot: Avebury).

Swann, Denis, 1983, *Competition Policy in the European Community* (London and New York: Methuen's EEC Series).

Thwaites, A.J. and R.P. Oakey, 1985, 'Editorial Introduction', in A.J. Thwaites and R.P. Oakey (eds.), *The Regional Economic Impact of Technical Change*, London: Pinter Publishers, pp. 1–13.

UEAPME, 1989, 'EG – Entwicklung und Politik für Handwerk, Klein – und Mittelbetriebe – Jahresbericht 1989', Brussels: Union Européenne de l'Artisanat et des Petite et Moyennes Entreprise.

Ungerer, Herbert and Nicholas P. Costello, 1988, *Telecommunications in Europe* ((Brussels: The European Perspectives Series (Commission of the EC)).

UNICE, 1990, 'Bilan de quatre années de fonctionnement de la fiche d'impact. Proposition de l'UNICE pour l'amelioration du système' (mimeo, Brussels).

van Tulder, Rob and G. Junne, 1988, 'European Multinationals in Core Technologies' (Geneva: Wiley/IRM).

Voigt, F., 1979, 'Transport and Regional Policy –Some General Aspects', in Blonk, op. cit.,

Vanhoven, Norbert and Leo H. Klassen, 1987, *Regional Policy: A European Approach* (Aldershot: Avebury Publishers).

Wäldchen, Paul, 1988, 'Industrial Change, New Technologies and EC Regional Policy', in Kenneth Dyson (ed.), op. cit., pp. 49–59.

The IMPs: A Missed Opportunity? An Appraisal of the Design and Implementation of the Integrated Mediterranean Programmes

GIULIANO BIANCHI

I. INTRODUCTION

The seven-year lifespan of the Integrated Mediterranean Programmes (IMPs) is quickly coming to an end,[1] but an understanding of the strategic importance and potential functions represented by the IMPs as a major re-thinking of regional development in Europe is still sketchy among scholars of regional planning and economics.[2] One of the reasons for this is due to the almost insurmountable difficulties that one has in collecting coherent information concerning the implementation of the programmes in the geographic areas where they are being implemented – that is, in Greece, the main part of Italy, and substantial parts of Southern France.[3] Yet, not more than a handful of authors have thought it worthwhile to analyse possible – and multiple – impacts that the IMPs have exerted on almost 30 regional economies and societies in Southern Europe. Moreover, at the time of writing, the literature dealing explicitly with the IMPs is, for the most part, based on analyses of EEC Regulation 2088/1985 and on the information provided by the first Progress Report produced by the Commission.[4] With only one exception, there is no apparent evidence of a direct knowledge of IMP implementation activities or even of the IMPs as written documents.[5]

An early Spanish text expressed the hope that IMPs could become the comprehensive response to the development problems of Southern Europe.[6] Later, the uniqueness of the IMPs began to emerge in that they were correctly defined as 'a large-scale experiment in integrated

The author would like to thank Robert Leonardi for his help in formulating the codebook that was used to code the IMP programmes. Jürgen Grote supplied invaluable support during the entire study and made a significant contribution to the analysis of the issues discussed in section four of this contribution. Shari O. Garmise created the IMP database which served as the primary information base for the analysis. The author would also like to thank Cristina Caldonazzo for her assistance in data and word processing.

planning.[7] In 1989 a French scholar outlined an interpretation of the IMPs as a major policy innovation within the Community's regional policies, given their features which go beyond planning technicalities and become innovative contributions to political issues, such as the 'emphasis on decentralized structures, especially the regions', and the 'search for consensus in their elaboration and implementation'.[8] Even though the author is aware of the congenital shortcomings of IMPs ('the inadequacy of the goals and the slow and burdensome procedures'), his overall conclusion is that 'despite some of the faults of the IMPs, they can be evaluated as representing a generally positive experience', more or less in the same terms as stated by Shotton.[9]

Other analysts have a less optimistic attitude towards the IMPs; some even see them as some sort of threat. For instance, an organization such as the World Wildlife Fund expressed the fear that IMPs could be 'an unprecedented threat to natural resources, mainly in Greece and in some parts of Italy'.[10]

However, an objective assessment of the ecological impact of IMP provisions (see the following Table 2) does not support the WWF view. Also, a case study of the Tuscany IMP shows that 'none of the proposed actions affects environmentally sensitive or valuable areas'.[11]

IMPs have also been regarded as a threat to the interests of non-EC members of the Mediterranean area. The hypothesis is that if IMPs reduce excess agricultural production in the Mediterranean regions of France, Greece and Italy in order to substitute new productions for the EC markets at competitive prices this will be to the detriment of the market shares enjoyed by non-Community countries in the area (primarily Israel) already specializing in the new products.[12] In these articles the forecasted impact of IMPs seems to be slightly exaggerated while, at the same time, they are curiously interpreted as a mere sop thrown to the Community's Mediterranean farmers in order to satisfy their 'unease and demands' rather than as an effort to integrated development planning which, according to the logic, should go far beyond the limited boundaries of agriculture.

Yannopoulos attempts to evaluate the effectiveness of IMPs as 'adjustment policy measures' based on their original objective (that is, to help the Mediterranean regions of the Community to adjust their economies to the expected negative impact of the 1986 accession of Spain and Portugal to the Community).[13] Yannopoulos voices a lot of skepticism in his analysis. The IMPs appear to satisfy several criteria of an appropriate adjustment policy (limited duration, integration, transparency, private capital participation) but Yannopoulos claims that 'they fall short of two important competitive requirements: those of encouraging potentially viable, competitive activities and providing for market strengthening measures'.

Yet, this criticism does not really grasp the peculiar innovative potential characteristic of the IMPs which surpasses any traditional adjustment policy. It also seems to underestimate that the main cause of the relatively modest impacts of IMPs on regional economies (see the following Table 3) is their 'limited' (compared to the size of regional economies) financial endowment. In any case, resource scarcity is a general feature of EC regional policies: it also affects the reformed European Regional Development Fund. Croxford *et al.* write that no improvement in the 'allocation system of the ERDF can compensate for the inadequacy of an overall budget which has never been sufficient to make a substantial contribution to redressing EC regional imbalances'.[14]

Also, the remark that IMPs have generated a tendency to politicize the whole decision-making process is not qualified. 'Politicized decision-making' is perceived as a major threat to the integrated approach in so far as IMP funds are allocated by 'politicians, who will naturally favour projects that are electorally rather than economically productive'.[15] This risk certainly exists. But, it also existed prior to the launching of the IMPs. Politicized decision-making is a structural factor that must be taken into account not only in the IMP regions; it affects non-IMP regions too. Rather than lamenting the existence of political factors in the decision-making process, we should be alerted to the fact that the IMPs have in many ways and for the first time instilled a proper planning attitude in regions where planning had been absent; they initiated an unprecedented institutional partnership among regional, national and Community authorities; and they have stimulated some genuine participation by local officials and interest groups in the decision-making process regarding the formulation and administration of regional social and economic policies.

A more recent and accurate appraisal of the Community's regional policy highlights the role of the IMPs as the fruit of a policy evolution spanning from 'the initial period during which the issue of regional disparities had to be tackled in a secondary or mediated way, to the time when the integrated approach to regional development has been adopted'.[16] In this sense, the IMPs constitute the true 'benchmark' of the integrated approach due to the changes that they have inserted into the formulation of the Community's regional policy.[17] These views correspond to the central thesis of this article which considers the IMPs as a major break with previous trends in the Community's regional policy and the precursor to the formulation of the Community Support Frameworks. Evidence supporting the thesis will be drawn from the first major empirical study of the IMPs conducted within the 'Regions and European Community Project' directed by the editor of this volume.[18]

II. RESEARCH DESIGN AND OBJECTIVES OF THE STUDY

Within the context of the research project, a specific study was carried out on the IMPs in order to analyse the relationship between policy goals and policy instruments in what was, at the time, the Community's major initiative at integrated planning targeting the major problems of regional development. More specifically, the objectives of the study were the following:

(1) to appraise the quality of the IMP planning design in terms of coherence between 'IMP philosophy' (integrated regional development approach, as expressed in the EC Regulation 2088/1985)[19] and the structure of the specific IMPs (as expressed in the IMP written documents);[20]

(2) to assess and measure the possible discrepancies between 'expected outcomes' and 'achieved effects' in terms of the economic impact of the IMP. The economic impact has been evaluated by means of regional input–output models for three representative regions (Tuscany, Emilia-Romagna, Languedoc-Roussillon). Impact evaluation has measured the activation induced in each region by the IMP investment in terms of the increase in regional value added and net new employment which were both broken down into 17 branches of production;

(3) to identify the actors and mechanisms of the informal interaction chains put into motion by the IMPs – within and beyond the formal relationships – between the European Community, member states and region on the one hand (institutional interactions), and between the IMP programme and local society on the other (social interactions). This part of the analysis is based on field surveys of IMP operations in four regions (Languedoc-Roussillon and Corsica in France; Northern Greece and Crete in Greece). Survey work was also carried out in form of a total of 85 structured interviews conducted with national and local politicians and civil servants.

During the study, and on the basis of its preliminary findings, an additional hypothesis has been forwarded: the conception of the IMP experience as a 'societal feasibility test' for a possible new generation of EC regional planning initiatives. This hypothesis is based, firstly, on the criteria for programme design established by the IMP Regulation and, secondly, on criticism of European regional planning experiences over the last two decades.

The criteria of Regulation 2088 seem to be fundamental to a new approach to regional planning, even though they have so far received very little attention both in EC documents and in the academic literature. In fact, those criteria (which will be referred to later on as the three 'IMP principles') state that the IMPs must: (i) be elaborated as authentic programmes for integrated development; (ii) be conceived and implemented at the pertinent geographical level; and (iii) be provided with rigorous parameters for evaluation and control.

In criticizing the European experience with regional planning, many authors have recognized the theoretical weakness and limited effectiveness of the experience owing, in particular, to: (a) an extreme differentiation in terms of form and content of the various regional planning exercises;[21] (b) a widespread lack of formal planning requisites in the form of objective quantification, formal generation of strategies from policies, formal and quantified evaluation of alternative strategies, etc;[22] (c) a sort of 'divorce' between policy-making and decision-making techniques, despite the existence of appropriate, portable and 'cheap' methodology.[23]

Given the underlying assumptions, the IMPs should be considered as a fruitful opportunity to overcome these shortcomings to the extent that, from the ongoing experience, it is possible to draw really significant lessons in order to: propose a unified approach to regional planning, introduce formal requirements for plan-making; and reconcile politics and techniques.

III. THE APPRAISAL OF THE PLANNING DESIGN

In order to assess the quality of the IMP approach to planning which emerges from the existing documents, the information extracted from the coding of the contents of the IMP documents has been organized to identify, first of all, the regional 'system feature' or sector to which every single IMP operation (measure) was to be applied, and, secondly, the basic actions that make up each measure. To detect the system feature, the regional system has been broken down into system components (SC), and the basic actions were analysed on the basis of breaking the measures down to individual homogeneous operations (specific technical projects) or, as we termed them, Elementary Units of Intervention (EUI). We were able to identify and code 1,233 EUIs from our 29 IMP programmes. Each EUI was coded based on a structured questionnaire. Then, the coding of each EUI was entered into the IMP Database along with other information explicitly or implicitly provided by the IMP documents. To analyse the quality of the planning design – that is, to study Objective 1 – we have aimed at breaking down IMP interventions by system components, detecting innovative aspects of plan design, and assessing the extent to which the formulation and administration of the IMPs has satisfied the state IMP principles.

The IMP Database has also contributed to study Objective 2 by testing the IMPs' economic impact, their ability to serve the goal of integrated forms of development (that is, being able to impact on more than one sector with each measure and sub-programme), and identifying the beneficiaries and responsible actors as a rough measurement of the IMPs' potential for generating institutional partnership and social participation.

In the following sections, the general results of the analysis will be presented and will remain as close as possible to the original research objectives; however findings about Objective 2 are discussed together with the application of the three 'IMP principles' (see section III).

IMP Actions by System Component

A brief description of how the IMP actions have been distributed according to system component provides a general idea of their sectoral impact or, more precisely, how the IMPs have contributed to each sector. The analysis might also serve to illustrate some of the novel features introduced by the IMPs to Community regional and sectoral policies.

The analysis of IMP actions according to their system component (SC) demonstrates their marked multisectoral nature (see Table 1 and Figure 1: data are referred only to mainheadings of the SC list). IMP actions have been distributed over almost all possible sectors: infrastructure and transport receive 19 per cent of the resources, business services 15 per cent, agriculture and forestry 13 per cent, small and medium-sized enterprise 13 per cent, public utilities nine per cent, and tourism eight per cent; but also natural environment, livestock, fishing, and social services are given shares of two to five per cent of the total available funds. This represents a significant innovation with respect to traditional EC allocation criteria. The conclusion is confirmed by the relevance of non-agricultural sectors that cover 87 per cent of all interventions and by the substantial irrelevance of sectors such as mining, chemicals, refinery, metallurgy and shipbuilding, which had in the past largely benefited from EC policy.

As demonstrated by Figure 1, the relative importance of the single system component is not always congruent in terms of both monetary allocations and number of EUIs. The difference is particularly striking in the case of infrastructure: a 19 per cent share of the total resources allotted in all IMPs with only 11 per cent of the EUIs. This clearly means that the relative financial amount available per action in this sector lies much above that of, for example, fishing, urban and historical environ-

TABLE 1
COST AND EUI BY SYSTEM COMPONENT – TOTAL (ALL IMPs)

SYSTEM COMPONENT	COST		EUIs	
	MECU*	%	No	%
1 NATURAL ENVIRONMENT	423.695	5,81	54	4,38
2 URBAN & HISTORICAL ENVIRONMENT	170.431	2,34	49	3,97
3 INFRASTRUCTURE & TRANSPORT	1.380.309	18,92	135	10,95
4 PUBLIC UTILITIES & COMMUNICATIONS	684.463	9,38	83	6,73
5 AGRICULTURE & FORESTRY	987.186	13,53	157	12,73
6 FISHERY & AQUACULTURE	153.704	2,11	72	5,84
7 LIVESTOCK DEVELOPMENT	305.323	4,18	63	5,11
8 MANUFACTURING	92.934	1,27	15	1,22
9 TRADE	11.840	0,16	2	0,16
10 TOURISM	609.673	8,36	126	10,22
11 BANKING & INSURANCE	13.906	0,19	2	0,16
12 SMEs	928.077	12,72	174	14,11
13 BUSINESS SERVICES	1.113.570	15,26	134	10,87
14 GOVERNMENT	63.781	0,87	9	0,73
15 SOCIAL SERVICES	155.161	2,13	16	1,30
16 CULTURE & LEISURE	48.603	0,67	7	0,57
17 HUMAN CAPITAL	84.820	1,16	19	1,54
18 KNOWLEDGE	14.309	0,20	14	1,14
19 IMP MANAGEMENT	54.342	0,74	85	6,89
TOTAL	**7.296.127**	**100,00**	**1233**	**100,00**

*1,000 ECU

FIGURE 1
COST AND EUI BY SYSTEM COMPONENT – TOTAL (ALL IMPs)

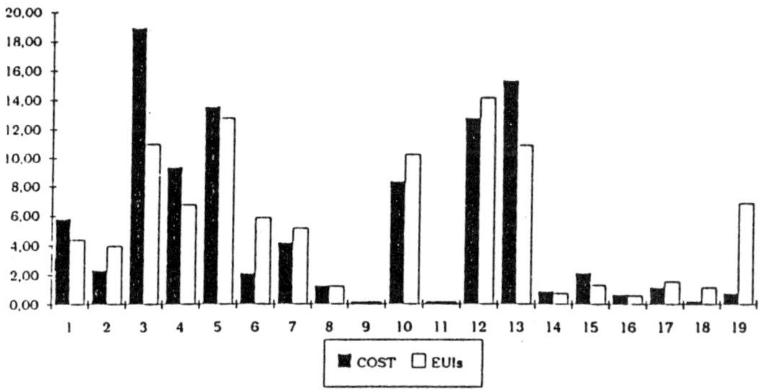

ment, or tourism. The character of intervention in the latter group – because of the high diffusion of relatively modest financial means among a relatively high number of beneficiaries – is likely to resemble the well-

TABLE 2
EUIS BY TYPE OF ENVIRONMENTAL IMPACT – TOTAL

IMPACT	TEXT		REASSESSMENT	
	No	%	No	%
1 NOT ASSESSED	517	41,93	0	0,00
2 NO IMPACT	470	38,12	566	45,90
3 POSITIVE	209	16,95	187	15,17
4 NEGATIVE	7	0,57	75	6,08
5 NEG-COUNTERMEASURE	20	1,62	0	0,00
6 UNCLEAR	0	0,00	391	31,71
NOT IDENTIFIED	10	0,81	14	1,14
TOTAL	1.233	100,00	1.233	100,00

known feature of 'interventi a pioggia' or the unregulated dispersion of funds.

Innovative Aspects of the IMPs

Besides their multisectoral nature, other innovative aspects embodied in the IMPs can be identified by looking at the emphasis they place on: ecological concerns, factors of local economic environment, small and medium-sized enterprises (SMEs), and new types of activity. With regard to the first of these issues, ecological concerns appear to be taken quite seriously at least in the IMP documents. The fact is that Regulation 2088 makes the evaluation of the environmental impact of IMP measures mandatory. Analysing the content of the documents (see Table 2), only seven EUIs, out of the total number of 1,233, are recognized to have a negative impact, whereas 470 (38 per cent) were assessed as having no identifiable impact and 209 (17 per cent) a positive one. The impact is not officially assessed in 517 cases (42 per cent).

Based on our own analysis of objective criteria, we did an independent reassessment of ecological impact of each EUI. The results do not dramatically diverge from the official information. With regards to environmentally negative impacts, however, our reassessment provides a different conclusion from the one advanced by the IMP documents. Our data shows that out of the 1,233 only six are evaluated as having a negative impact. The potential ecological impact of one third of the EUIs remained unclear because the IMP document supplied no information on the environmental impact.

The IMPs are likely to play a remarkable role in terms of changing the 'industrial atmosphere' of regional economies. Factors influencing the local economic environment are all those elements of a given regional (or local) system, which – although not directly or explicitly pertaining to the economic processes – affect firm performances by generating economies which are external to the single firm but internal to the local economic system. Such factors are – expressed in terms of structural components – infrastructure and transport, public utilities, business, public and social services, human capital, and knowledge. Interventions in these fields, on average, account for one-third of all IMP actions and nearly half of the corresponding funds. The hypothesis that IMPs are strongly oriented toward the improvement of the effectiveness of the economic environment is also supported by data on the content of action – that is, the concrete output of each IMP action. Capital stock is the target of 37 per cent of the EUIs. Only a limited number of EUIs deal with the direct production of goods. At the same time, 580 EUIs are aimed at service production. Roughly, almost half (47 with a maximum of 54 per cent in Italy) of the programmes' efforts are concentrated in service production. Moreover, a good deal of IMP actions (38 per cent) has been identified as susceptible to generate positive impacts on technological enhancement – perhaps the most powerful effectiveness factor.

The importance of SMEs in the overall strategy of the programmes has already been noted above (accounting for 13 per cent of overall financing, with seven per cent in Greece and 20 per cent in Italy). SMEs rank at the same level as agriculture and below only infrastructure and business services.[24] Such an outstanding role was never attributed to SMEs by any other EC sectoral policy. This is reinforced by the fact that looking at the content of each IMP action 38 per cent of them seem likely to produce a positive, even if indirect, impact on SMEs (with a striking 46 per cent in Italy).

In the twenty-nine IMP documents, a distinction is made between measures which continue or reinforce previous activities and those which create new activities. In contrast with traditional EC Structural Fund projects, only 18 per cent of IMP interventions are concerned with the continuation of previous activities, while 54 per cent cover completely new activities.

The Three 'IMP Principles' and Their Application in the Programme Design

Substantial innovations in content (multisectoral approach, ecological concern, emphasis on factors of local effectiveness and the role of SMEs) are coupled with important innovations in the methodology of programme design. The reference is, again, to the three 'IMP principles' according to which IMPs have to: (i) be conceived as actual programmes for local integrated development; (ii) be provided with rigorous parameters for presentation and evaluation; and (iii) be developed at the pertinent geographical level.

As to principle (i), can IMPs be considered as programmes or plans and do they really provide for integrated local development? The breakdown of each IMP into sub-programmes and measures can identify the substance of a territorial (regional or local) plan in only a handful of cases (some Greek IMPs). In the majority of cases, IMPs appear more like components of broader, yet unknown, plans (French IMPs), or like casual sets of actions, that is, mere sources of financing (most Italian IMPs). Although resembling a plan, the mutual coherence and synergistic effects of the actions are mostly declared but not demonstrated. In practice, despite the intentions underlying Regulation 2088, the programmes seem to have encountered the same experience as practically all other regional planning initiatives in Europe – that is, a lack of formal planning requisites and a limited and quite often naive use of the available and appropriate decision-making techniques. To quote from the first IMP Progress Report: 'One of the Commission's concerns during examination of the IMPs was to encourage the regional authorities to make a choice among a vast array of problems to which they had initially sought to find answers.' Now, such a 'beseecher-besought' bargaining does not exactly correspond to a decision-making process appropriate for an integrated approach to regional development.

The second question is: can IMPs promote integrated development? A comparison between the economic size of the IMPs (the potential factor of integration) and the magnitude of the regional system (the object to be developed in an integrated way) shows that in France and Italy – with the exception of the cases of Molise, Corisca, and Basilicata – the total investment of each IMP amounts to an injection of new resources equivalent to not more than a handful of ECU per capita (Table 3). These figures imply that the incidence of IMP investment on gross regional product is around one per cent (and frequently less). Weak shocks of this kind when applied to the 'economic base' of each region only allow for a minimal response in terms of appreciable economic effects. Therefore, despite their marked multisectorality, IMPs are hardly recognizable as a genuine manifestation of 'integrated development'. Ironically, the multisectoral approach operates, given the limited amount of resources and the pronounced sectoral fragmentation, to reduce the potential impact of the IMP. Moreover, the potential for local systems to react to IMP impulses is furthermore undermined by the territorial dispersion of IMP actions (see Figure 2). This argument, of course, does not apply to Greek

TABLE 3
IMP INVESTMENT & GROSS REGIONAL PRODUCT

REGIONS	ECU /1/	%GRP /2/
AQUITAINE	78	0,7
CORSE	443	5,1
LANGUEDOC-ROUSSILLON	139	1,5
MIDI PYRENEES	104	1,0
PACA	74	0,6
GREECE	322	7,6
ABRUZZI	117	1,4
BASILICATA	309	4,2
CALABRIA	96	1,6
CAMPANIA	50	0,7
EMILIA-ROMAGNA	39	0,3
LIGURIA	101	0,8
MARCHE	182	1,9
MOLISE	455	6,0
PUGLIA	56	0,8
SARDEGNA	166	2,2
SICILIA	45	0,7
TOSCANA	63	0,6
UMBRIA	251	2,6

Notes: /1/ IMP investment: inhabitants (ecu per capita)
/2/ IMP investment: Gross Regional Product (percentage)

IMPs or to those in Molise, Corsica and Basilicata. Here, IMP investments represent, on average, an impact equal to six to seven per cent of gross regional product.

Concerning the purely economic impact of the programmes, the analysis arrives at similar results. Three case studies (Tuscany, Emilia-Romagna, Languedoc-Roussillon) on IMP regional economic impact prove that IMPs in their current version cannot generate any sort of integrated development (at least in France and Italy). Economic impact analysis implies measuring the endogenous effect (internal to the spatial system; in this case: a given region) of an exogenous shock (in this case:

IMP investment and expenditure). The effects can be broken down into global effects (gross regional product increases via the Keynesian multiplier), and intersectoral effect (diffusion through Leontief's multiplier: direct, indirect, and induced effects). The impact has been spatially broken down into internal, spillover, and feedback effects. The activation is measured in terms of annual value added[25] and net new employment expressed in employees per year.

However, the point here is the global quantitative effect of the IMP investment as a possible lever for integrated development. Let us take Tuscany as an example: the economic impact of the IMP is measured by a value added increase of 131 million ECU and 7,000 new employees which is a negligible 0.25 per cent of the annual Tuscan value added and a marginal 0.5 per cent of regional employment. The suspicion, discussed in the foregoing section, that weak shocks induce minimal responses is born out in the case of Tuscany. Were this region the target area, the impulse of IMP investments would not be able to integrate anything. This is the main conclusion that can be drawn from impact analysis in studying Objective 2 mentioned above – that is, the measurement of discrepancies between IMP expected and achieved results.

To continue now with the principle ii, the analysis reveals that the 'rigorous parameters for evaluation', as requested by Regulation 2088, are substantially non-existent on the *ex-ante* evaluation side. Cost-benefit analysis is missing in 950 EUI (77 per cent of the cases), only 91 EUIs (seven per cent) give an assessed and quantified analyses. Even less satisfactory is the ex-post evaluation. Monitoring procedures are clearly dominated by a 'book-keeping approach'. While everything concerning financial transactions is scrupulously recorded, time-schedules for planning operations, although representing a rather rudimentary monitoring tool, are given for only 23 per cent of EUIs. Physical progress indicators, though explicitly required by IMP instructions, are only quantified in a very small number of EUIs (eight per cent) and in 49 per cent of the cases indicators are not even identified. Nor is there any (estimated) information on expected results – that is, investment outcome (for example: increase in tourism demand or reduction in transport cost and time). It is astonishing that IMP administrators have been asked to develop cost-benefit analysis but not to identify (and hence, not to evaluate) outcome indicators!

The most disappointing aspect of the programme design concerns principle (iii) – that is, the issue of the pertinent geographical level (or appropriate spatial unit) – perhaps the most innovative prescription put forward by Regulation 2088. EUIs turn out to have been spatially distributed in four ways (see Figure 2): 45 per cent cover the whole IMP

FIGURE 2
COST AND EUI BY SYSTEM COMPONENT – TOTAL (ALL IMPs)

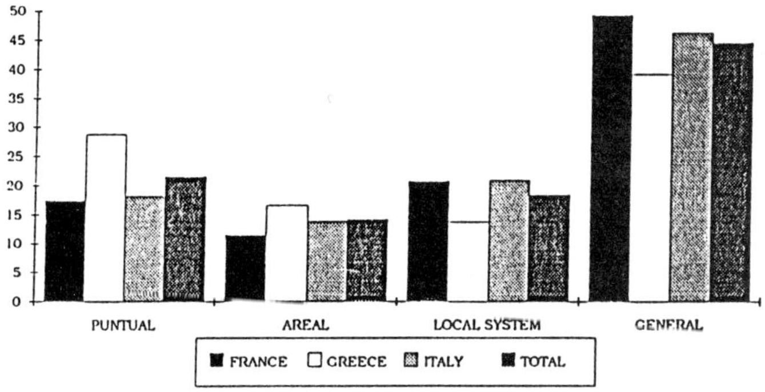

region: not a good example for 'spatial concentration' as advocated by the EC; 22 per cent are punctually located (a city, a port); 14 per cent regard geographical fractions of the region; and 18 per cent (less than one out of five) are correctly applied to specific local systems as is required by the integrated regional development approach.

Italy could have been expected to leave on its programmes at least some imprints of the relevance that economic local systems (industrial districts) have had, and still have, within contemporary Italian economic development. Yet, only a meagre 22 per cent of the IMP actions are directly addressed to proper local systems. Over half of the EUIs are attributed to the whole IMP region when their targets are structural components such as human capital, social services, government or business services, as if these interventions were 'diffused incentives' by definition. This interpretation fits perfectly with the fact that EUIs aimed at SMEs (typically agglomerated in spatial systems) are in 81 per cent of the cases assigned to the entire region.

IV. PARTNERSHIP, PARTICIPATION, AND SOCIO-ECONOMIC NETWORKS

Despite the critical appraisal sketched out here, the IMP experience has had positive results in terms of an institutional partnership that has never been achieved in the past. This applies both to the legal as well as to the financial aspects of the programmes. The major causal factor for the above has to be sought, obviously, in the set of rules established by Regulation 2088, according to which institutional partnership:

- begins with the preliminary, informal, trilateral (Community, state, region) bargaining leading to an IMP proposal;

TABLE 4
EUI BY CLASS OF FINANCIAL INTERVENTION AND FUNDING SOURCE – TOTAL

MECU	EC	NAT GOV	REG GOV	OTH PUB	PRIV	EIB NCI
1 ABSENT	7,46	46,55	53,69	90,43	69,83	94,97
2 LESS THAN 999	40,06	29,85	25,39	6,49	13,95	0,57
3 1000 TO 9999	47,53	21,98	20,19	3,08	14,27	3,00
4 10000 TO 49999	4,87	1,46	0,73	0,00	1,62	1,05
5 MORE THAN 50000	0,08	0,16	0,00	0,00	0,32	0,41
TOTAL	100,00	100,00	100,00	100,00	100,00	100,00

- progress with the formal, again trilateral, interaction resulting in IMP approval;
- is legally formalized in a programme-contract;
- involves financial contribution by the three parties (plus other possible contributors, both public and private); and
- becomes operational in form of co-managed implementation by a Monitoring Committee, in which all three parties participate in cooperation with private entities.

Institutional Partnership

This kind of partnership implies, of course, financial contributions by the actors involved. The participation rate of the Community in funding single EUIs, normally, lies at around 1,000,000–10,000,000 ECU (see Table 4). National governments' contribution rates are lower: approximately one third of EUIs are granted less than 1,000,000 ECU. The Greek government does not contribute in 18 per cent of the EUIs, whereas the non-participation rate for national authorities increases to a striking 70 per cent in the case of Italy. On average, regional governments seem to perform better than the national ones. They contribute to 313 EUIs whose costs lie below 1,000,000 ECU, and to 249 EUIs with quotas between 1,000,000 and 10,000,000 ECU. It is true that regions do not participate in 54 per cent of cases but the average percentage is affected by the complete absence of regional contributions to Greek EUIs. In Italy only 20 per cent of EUIs do not receive regional financial interventions.

Social Participation

It has already been mentioned that IMPs were expected to generate, at the local level, multiple interactions between institutions, social bodies (co-operatives, organized interests, etc.) and individuals (firms, enterprises, etc.). This may, eventually, be regarded as the most innovative and promising profile of the IMP implementation process. Some data support this point. First, local participation is expressed in terms of financial involvement. Local public authorities (provinces and municipalities) contribute to ten per cent of EUIs; private capital is involved in 28 per cent of EUIs with contributions falling into the class of above 1,000,000 ECU in 14 per cent of cases (Table 4).

Private financial participation varies markedly across the three countries. It is highest in France with private financing being present in half of the cases, decreases to below one-third in Italy, and ranks lowest in Greece at around one-tenth. Second, potential institutional-society interactions are more clearly detectable if one looks at the management and steering activities of the IMPs and at the different categories of actors being involved in these activities, which are: (i) beneficiaries (that is, final addressees of each intervention) and (ii) responsibile (that is, those in charge of carrying out the IMP operations).

Concerning the overall data set – in Figure 3, given that each EUI has normally more than one beneficiary, total percentages exceed 100 – economic entities (firms, entrepreneurs) are the most frequent beneficiaries (79 per cent of EUIs). Associations (business associations, trade unions, co-operatives) rank second (one-third) and the labourforce occupies the third position (one-fifth). Hence, elements of civil society are massively associated with IMP operations, notwithstanding the fact that, for example, in Greece, associations are beneficiaries in only 17 per cent of the cases, thus indicating a relatively weakly structured society – or limited access by society to the IMP process – in terms of social interest organizations. The relevance of local participation is also confirmed looking at the responsible side (Figure 3).

Governmental institutions are, obviously, always present, but regional government is primarily responsible in the sense that it is uniquely responsible or co-responsible for implementation in 41 out of 100 cases. National government ranks second, being responsible (alone or in association) in one-third of the cases. Moreover, merging public authorities (with the exception of the nation state) with public services (which are regional or local) gives a responsibility rate of (non-national) public administration of 73 per cent of EUIs. IMPs seem to provide, indeed, some room for decentralization.

The brand new feature, however, is that economic entities, associations, and public interest groups are involved as responsible actors for IMP implementation in 14 per cent of cases respectively. From a purely quantitative perspective, this phenomenon is not overwhelming. Seen

FIGURE 3

EUIS BY TYPE OF BENEFICIARY AND RESPONSIBLE

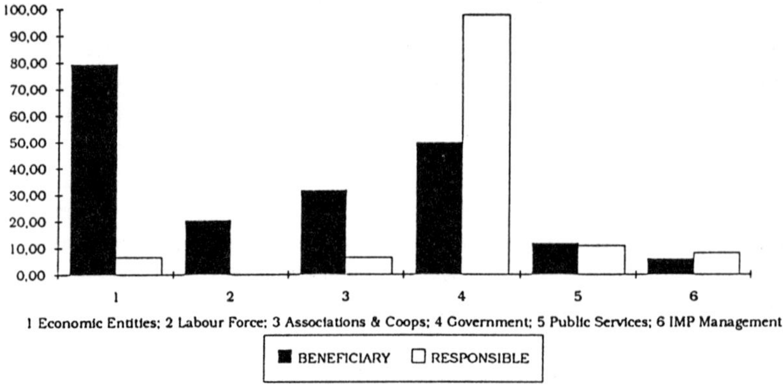

from the qualitative angle, though, it represents a relevant break within the Community regional planning experience.

Socio-economic Networks

Going beyond the formal aspects covered with the content analysis of the IMPs, we will now move on to look at the information from 85 structured interviews carried out with national and regional politicians, civil servants, and interest group leaders on the issue of the IMPs and how they have been implemented.[26] In assessing these interviews, we will attempt to: (a) appraise if, how, and to what extent an institutional partnership and social participation have progressed as a result of the IMPs; (b) understand the consistency and nature of the informal interaction chains among various institutions and between the institutions and groups in civil society that the IMPs have activated within formal (legal) relationships; (c) ascertain whether the IMPs have fostered regionalization in terms of regional identities, regional institutions, and regional bargaining powers *vis-à-vis* the central authorities.

The field survey covered four 'sample' regions: Languedoc-Roussillon (a region with a remarkable experience in planning and a strong commitment to bridging the critical gap between the growth pole of Montpellier and the less developed department of Lozère); Corsica (a classical example of a region with a low development rate intertwined with the presence of a 'national minority'); Northern Greece (a relatively sound example of IMP management within the Greek context); and Crete (an IMP test-case since its programme-contract was the first to be signed, 1985, and, hence, it has the longest experience in IMP implementation).

As was to be expected, the most critical situation is found in Greece. From the outset, the IMP administrative activities revealed many interconnected difficulties. In France the IMPs have been incorporated into the current planning system, thus constituting indistinguishable (but often minor) elements of ordinary regional management. However, this common feature is expressed in two opposite manifestations. In Languedoc-Roussillon, for instance, one councillor expressed the most often encountered attitude in the following form: 'the IMPs allow us to do more of the same things, but not different or new things'. In Corsica, on the contrary, the IMP was expected to have a real impact on the island's historic problems, but expectations have been deluded by the sectoral fragmentation of the IMP projects. No clear priority has been given to even strategically important sectors for the Corsican economy such as handicraft/artisanry and tourism.

Given the extremely heterogeneous situation which exists across the three countries in terms of administrative complexity, capacity to co-ordinate policies, autonomy in implementation of the Funds on the one hand and, on the other, in terms of the willingness on the part of private entities to co-operate and to assume responsibility – the overall experience with the IMPs must be judged positively despite the endless list of complaints and shortcomings during the first phase of the operation. Generally, what is lacking both in the design of the IMPs and in the perceptions of many officials of sub-national administrative units is the notion of a system to which the new Community measures could have been applied. However, this system defined as either functional, social, industrial, or geographical does not exist. In most cases no proper *ex ante* analysis has been undertaken which would have helped to detect the existence of those systems, their internal structure or their interdependencies with civil society and the public sector.

Hence, in order to achieve a better boundary specification of those areas where synergies are to be created, it seems necessary to adopt a network perspective in future Community regional planning. The adoption of such a perspective would help to guarantee more effectiveness and, at the same time, more transparency in providing financial allocations. First of all, the regional and local systems could be analysed in terms of their internal structure. That would imply a measure of the relative position of enterprises in particular 'resource exchange networks' of a purely private (information, raw material, financial, customer contacts, pre-competitive co-operation, etc.) and of a more public nature (relationship of firms to regional and local administration, interdependencies of these relationships, existence, strength, and relevance of regional or sub-regional interest associations, etc.). Having undertaken this kind of analysis, one could proceed with building and creating these networks or the missing links in the existing networks (for example, middlemen, 'technology brokers', etc.) in cases where co-operation is still underdeveloped.

Both the theoretical analysis of regional networks and the practical construction of these networks would assure (to a much higher extent than has been the case so far) that future Community policies would impact on the relationships linking two or more actors to each other rather than on single, partly isolated and territorially or functionally dispersed units which are not able to generate the desired transaction chains. One of the objectives of the Community in designing IMPs has been (although not explicitly stated in these terms) to establish a semi-institutional network between various kinds of actors (EC Commission, EIB, national and regional governments, private and public development agencies and organized interests at the most appropriate, that is, the regional level) and at different layers of complexity (EC, national, regional, sub-regional).[27] The existence of such networks would help the Commission to partly solve its problems with administrative overload as a result of severe shortage of staff and, at the same time, would lead to the emergence of mechanisms which can facilitate implementation and monitoring. Closer links between fund-allocating institutions and the recipients of funds would help solve the common problem of accountability and transparency in Community policies.

The general conclusion of the field surveys on the issue of partnership and participation can be summed up as follows. The integrated approach, as such, cannot be made responsible for the failure of the programmes, the shortcomings and the contradictions which have appeared in some specific instances. It is quite obvious that despite the attempts to experiment with pilot projects and other preparatory measures the IMPs were designed and put into practice without any serious consideration of the local institutional and societal context. Secondly, the outcomes of the IMPs have proved to be massively dependent on the surrounding institutional environment (autonomy and efficiency of regional and local authorities) and on local social networks (co-operative attitudes and cultures of individuals, firms, administrations and sub-nationally organized interests) rather than the juridical structure of the programme or the institutional home of the programme in Brussels. Finally, institutional partnership and social participation do not stem automatically from the fact that the first is formalized in a programme-contract and the second is made potentially possible through transactions between the IMP public management and private recipients of IMP funds. The survey demonstrates how intensively they are both correlated with the existence of networks which ease public-private transactions and, thereafter, reduce the administrative overload of public bodies while promoting co-operation among private actors.

In other words, there appears to be three determining factors which explain how target groups behave within the process instigated by the IMPs: (i) enterprise rationale (size, degree of mutual integration, agglomerated/isolated location, family/staff management, attitude to innovation, etc.); (ii) tiered structure of government and the way this affects the behaviour of governmental machines and officials, especially with respect to decentralization; (ii) the organization of business interests and public interest groups.

In the case of the IMPs, at least in the four regional cases examined here, it appears that the determinants for success or failure are more likely to be found in institutional performance and network functioning of the local society rather than in its economic structure. Should this prove to be the case, then future Community regional policies must build rather than take these two issues into explicit consideration and where they are weak make provisions for their strengthening through reforms, financial assistance, and training.

V. OVERALL EVALUATION OF THE IMPS

The IMP programme represents a major discontinuity within Community regional policy. In the regions where they have been implemented the IMPs have triggered off a chain of events and transactions. The announcement of an IMP intervention has, typically, generated expectations in local communities which can be met only in cases where non-formalized types of programme participation (co-decision-making, co-management, networks) are provided by the key actors present at the local level. Unsatisfied expectations may increase pressure on regional, national, and Community authorities for more coherent forms of regional planning and decentralization but, as our field survey has demonstrated, there is also the risk that they might degenerate into frustration and lack of co-operation.

Effective IMP implementation proves the viability of planning as an approach to policy making and creates an institutional and social participation within and beyond the range of the immediate IMP operation. In this sense, the IMPs have actively contributed to launching (Greece), or relaunching (France, Italy) the idea of regional planning as a broadly acceptable and desirable tool for dealing with regional problems and opening up opportunities for regional and locally targeted spatial development. Simultaneously, the IMPs represent a new impulse in the wave of regionalism by advancing and advocating the urgency and obligation to refresh (Italy), to reinforce (France) or merely to introduce (Greece) the role of regional authorities as effective administrators of development policies. Moreover, as has been outlined here, the IMPs possess a number of other innovative features with respect to the traditional approach to Community regional policy.

It is not excessive to consider the IMPs as a major innovation in the history of EC regional policies. In fact, not only are they the point of arrival after a long and non-linear process of evolution which started off with the Treaty of Paris (1951) and Treaties of Rome (1957), but they also represent the testing ground for the multitude of new principles, methods and procedures which are embodied in the 1988 reform of the Structural Funds. It is by way of the integrated approach that Regulation 1787/84 outspokenly broke with both traditional Community regional policy and the history of legislative ambiguity and compromise that had long clouded the course of an effective regional policy at the European level.

The integrated development approach has, for the first time, clearly become manifest in EC legislation in the form of the IMPs. One can legitimately say that the present phase of EC regional planning characterized by the IMPs constitutes the end of the prehistory of European regional planning and opens up a new phase of Community policy-making in this domain. It appears to be quite obvious that the reform of the Community's Structural Funds has its roots in the integrated approach and, more specifically, in the experiences gained with the IMPs. The Single European Act, in its awareness that the complexity of the creation of an internal market carries with it the potential risk of increasing inter-regional disparities, made it mandatory for the EC and member states to reinforce Community economic and social cohesion. This was to be done by co-ordinating national economic policies, 'cohesion oriented' Community policies, coherent Structural Fund interventions and the use of other financial instruments.

All Structural Funds have been reorganized to make them more effective in the achievement of social and economic cohesion. As is well known, Regulation 2052/88 provides for a general frame of reference in this respect. Regulation 4253/88 deals, not without contradictions, with horizontal coordination and Regulations 4254, 4255, 4256/88 with the reform of the ERDF, the ESF, and the EAGGF-Guidance Section respectively. The key issues of the reform clearly stem from the IMP version of the integrated development approach and from lessons gained with their design and initial implementation. These key issues can be summarized in the following two points: increase and concentration of available resources and the generalization of the integrated approach. These reform perspectives also carry with them the possibility of serious institutional implications given that a future Community regional policy, once it is really spatial and multisectoral in nature, could put forward claims on the member states for a consistent reallocation of decision-making, shifting powers upwards from the state to the Community level and downwards from the state to the regional level.

The integrated approach, typical of the third phase of Community regional policy (1984–88) takes into consideration interdependencies among the Community's regional and other sectoral policies.[28] Spatial, social, and economic environments (that is, relations rather than single and isolated units) are, by definition, the specific targets of intervention with reference both to material (infrastructures, economic activities) and non-material (human capital) components of local systems. The outcome, however, continues to be not remarkably different from that of previous approaches. Ambitious objectives have clashed with considerable resource limitations and, above all, with the diffusion of micro forms of interventions. Integrated development is a long way off from becoming a reality. Admittedly, the analysis rests on an estimation of the potentially achievable results given the programme design and economic impact assessment. However, the convergence between results from content analysis and findings from field survey support the following interpretative hypothesis: limited amounts of resources, diffused and fragmented over a multiplicity of actions, are not able to reach the 'critical mass' which is necessary and capable of inducing qualitative changes in those local and regional systems to which the interventions have been applied.

At this point, the consequences of the fundamental contradiction between the three fundamental assumptions of the IMPs (integrated development plan, pertinent spatial unit, rigorous evaluation parameters) on the one hand and their factual implementation on the other emerge dramatically. The inadequacy of appropriate spatial units for regional planning has prevented the application of interventions to those structural components possessing a higher reaction and diffusion capacity. Moreover, the lack of *ex-ante* (expected impacts) and *ex-post* (induced impacts) evaluation has prevented at the beginning the fine tuning of the programmes and after their implementation their review and adequate re-design before proceeding on to the second phase. In other words, the IMPs conceived of as the completion of a long evolution of the Community's regional policy and the starting point for a new generation of programmes seem to remain jammed precisely in the cracks between those innovative and promising potentials.

Indeed, the Commission has stated clearly that it had not encouraged research and consultancy for the IMPs in order to avoid theoretical studies and to concentrate on already available expertise. The result has been a confused form of empiricism which, as we have seen, has left many imprints on the implementation of the three 'IMP principles'. The Commission is fully aware of the shortcomings which have made impossible more satisfactory results and states the need in the future to tighten up the conceptual framework with specific reference to 'key-concepts' such as the concentration of interventions, institutional and social partnership, and pertinent geographical level of planning. The second IMP Progress Report stated that the experience gained so far from IMP operations 'will doubtless be immensely valuable when operational programmes stemming from the reform of the Structural Funds are drawn out and implemented'.[29]

This optimism can be shared: indeed the IMP experience could prove to be immensely valuable provided IMP design and implementation can be critically evaluated in order to derive lessons to be embodied in a new generation of integrated development programmes in which the ideas underlying Regulation 2088 can be fully realized.

NOTES

1. According to EEC Regulation No.2088/1985 (OJ No.L197, 27.07.1985), the IMPs are designed as multiannual programmes that are supposed to last for a maximum of seven years. The financial contribution of the Community amounts to 6.6 billion ECU (4.1 billion from the EC budget, of which 1.6 are from the Structural Funds and another 2.5 billion are provided in the form of loans from the European Investment Bank). Given that the EC participation rate cannot exceed 70 per cent of the total cost of any planned investment, member states, regional authorities and other public and private bodies must cover the remaining 30 per cent. The rights and duties of the parties involved in an IMP are defined in a 'programme-contract' which makes the IMP provisions compulsory and legally binding, therefore formalizing the concept of institutional partnership. Implementation of the IMPs is managed by a Monitoring Committee whose members are representatives of the three contracting parties, plus the representatives of local interest groups and institutions. The Monitoring Committee is supported by an administrative staff that is composed of regional administrators. Responsibility for monitoring the administration and impact of the IMPs has been allocated to an independent technical unit which is selected on an independent basis by the Community through an open bid process, and the activities of the technical unit are paid for by a specific line in the IMP budget. Given that the IMPs became operational in 1986 and 1987, they are expected to be completed by the end of 1993.
2. See N. Konsolas, 'EEC Regional Policy and the Integrated Mediterranean Programs', in M. Tykkylainnen (ed.), *Development Issues and Strategies in the New Europe* (Aldershot: Avebury, 1992), pp. 41–52.
3. The 29 IMPs are distributed as follows: fourteen regions (Abruzzi, Basilicata, Calabria, Campania, Emilia-Romagna, Lazio, Liguria, Marche, Molise, Puglia, Sardinia, Sicily, Tuscany, Umbria) plus one interregional programme (Northern Adriatic for aqua-

culture) in Italy; five regions (Aquitaine, Corse, Languedoc-Roussillon, Midi-Pyrénées, Provence-Alpes-Cote d'Azur) and two departments (Ardèche, Drome) in France; the whole of Greece (six regions: Aegean Sea Islands, Attica, Central and Eastern Greece, Crete, Northern Greece, Western Greece and Peloponnese, plus one programme for information technology that covers the entire country).

4. 'Integrated Mediterranean Programmes: 1986–1987 Progress Report', Doc XXII/1/57/88–EN 24.03.1988.
5. G.N. Yannopoulos, 'The Management of Trade Induced Structural Adjustment: An Evaluation of the EC's Integrated Mediterranean Programmes', *Journal of Common Market Studies*, Vol. 27, No. 4 (1989).
6. J.B. Jaureguis, 'Los Programas Mediterraneos Integrados: una respuesta a la Europa del Sur', *Revista de Instituciones Europeas*, Vol. 1 (1985).
7. R. Shotton, 'The Integrated Mediterranean Programmes', Paper presented at the Centre for European Studies Conference on 'The Mediterranean Regions: Problems and Perspectives', City University of New York, New York, 1988.
8. P. Py, 'Les Programmes Intégrées Méditerranéens'. Presentation to the Conference on 'La politique régionale communautaire a l'égard de l'Europe du Sud', Montpellier, France 9–10 May 1989.
9. R. Shotton, 'IMPs: Programme Definition and Implementation – A Comparison of Experiences', Introductory report at the first session of the sixth IMP Regions' Conference, Viterbo, 18–20 May 1988.
10. WWF (World Wildlife Fund) International, 'EEC, CAP and IMPs', Report No.1. Gland, 1988. See also D. Baldock and T. Long, 'Bad News for the Environment: The EC' IMPs', *European Environment Review*, Vol. 1, No. 5 (1987).
11. S. Angelini, 'A Case Study on Integrated Rural Development: The Integrated Mediterranean Programme of Tuscany', MSc thesis, Wye, University of London, 1989.
12. See G.N. Yannopoulos, 'The Integrated Mediterranean Programs: Their Effects on the EC's Relations with Mediterranean Non-Member Countries', *Jerusalem Journal of International Relations*, Vol. 3 (1988) and A. Tovias, 'Les effets extérieurs des politiques internes des Communautés Européennes sur les pays tiers: le cas des pays méditerranées', *Revue d'intégration européenne*, Vol. 12, No. 1 (1988).
13. G.N. Yannopoulos, op. cit., 1989.
14. G.J. Croxford, M. Wise, and B.S. Chalkley, 'The Reform of the European Development Fund: A Preliminary Assessement', *Journal of Common Market Studies*, Vol. 26, No. 1 (1987).
15. W. Kingston, 'The Failure of Regional Aids', *European Affairs*, Vol. 1 (Spring 1990).
16. See C.M. Geurts, 'The Reform of the EC's Structural Funds', Paper presented at the workshop on 'The European Community, Regions and European Integration: Results of the Comparative Study of Policy Sectors in Preparing for 1992', European University Institute, Florence, 30–31 March 1990.
17. R.Y. Nanetti, 'The Community's Structural Funds and the Search for a European Regional Policy', American Political Science Association Conference, San Francisco, 30 Aug.–2 Sept. 1990.
18. For an illustration of the scope and methods of the project, see the 'Introduction' to this volume.
19. See also the general introductions to the two Progress Reports of the EC Commission: Doc XXII/1/57/88–EN 24.03.1988 (CEC 1988), and SEC (89) 1665 (CEC 1989).
20. The 'written documents' are the 29 volumes containing the IMP programme contracts and the actions to be implemented in each region concerned. As a written document, an IMP typically breaks down into five chapters: (a) General aspects (geographical location, socio-economic situation, priorities, objectives and financing); (b) Content by Sub-Programmes; (c) Context: relationship of IMP Measures to other EC, State and regional intervention on the same area; (d) Financing plan; (e) Implementing organization and procedures. IMP Sub-Programmes refer to the development priorities. A specific Sub-Programme deals with actions, equipment, studies, etc., to back up implementation and monitoring activities. Each Sub-Programme consists of a set of

Measures which carry a Technical Sheet, containing the information that have been entered in the IMP Database.

21. See R. Barras and A. Broadbent, 'The Analysis in English Structure Planning', *Urban Studies*, Vol. 16 (1979); G. Bianchi, 'L'esperienza di programmazione regionale in Italia: una breve rassegna critica', in Bielli, M., La Bella A. (eds.) *Problematiche dei livelli sub-regionali di programmazione*, Milano: F. Angeli, 1982; G. Bianchi, 'Local Integrated Development: Appropriate Analytical Tools, Planning Models, Spatial Units', Lecture delivered at the EEC-IASM-ISPES Workshop on 'IMP Experience: Analysis and Perspectives', Rome, 10–11 Dec. 1987. Also in IASM-ISPES 1990 (Italian version); R.H. (ed.) Williams, 1984. *Planning in Europe. Urban and Regional Planning in the EEC* (London: Allen & Unwin, 1984).
22. G. Bianchi, B. Johansson, and F. Snickars, 'Models as Integral Parts of Regional Information Systems', in P. Nijkamp and P. Rietvold (eds.), *Information Systems for Integrated Regional Planning* (Amsterdam: North Holland, 1984).
23. See B. Issaev, P. Nijkamp, P. Rietvold and F. Snickars, *Multiregional Economic Modelling: Practice and Prospect* (Amsterdam: North Holland, 1982); C.S. Bertuglia, G.A. Rabino and R. Tadei, 'I modelli matematici e la valutazione dei piani'. Relazione presentata al Colloquio internazionale su 'La valutazione nella pianificazione urbana e territoriale: teoria e casi di studio', Capri-Napoli, 5–9 April 1988; and D.E. Boyce, 'Renaissance of Large-Scale Models', *Papers of the Regional Science Association*, Vol. 65 (1988).
24. In this context, it should be remembered that at the beginning the main motivating factor in creating the IMPs was the potential competition that would come from the two Iberian countries in the field of agricultural products.
25. Here transformed into ECU at 1989 rates. The impact analysis has been calculated at 1986 prices taking the signing of the IMPs as the reference year.
26. The structured interviews were carried out by Jürgen Grote and Charles Michele Geurts in Languedoc Roussillon, Jürgen Grote and John Loughlin in Corsica, and Robert Leonardi, Fouli Papageorgiou and Susannah Verney in Northern Greece and Crete.
27. This type of networking has become explicit in new programmes initiated by the Community as a means of implementing Structural Fund programmes in the 1990s, for example, LEADER and EUROFORM.
28. The first period (1957–75) was characterized by numerous and diffused micro-interventions which did not have measurable effects and the second period (1975–84) by the formal introduction of a proper regional policy which continued, however, to remain fragmented and underfunded as was the case during the first phase.
29. CEC, 'Integrated Mediterranean Programmes. 1988 Progress Report', SEC(89)1665, Brussels, 1989.

Regional Elites, Regional 'Powerlessness' and European Regional Policy in Ireland

CARMEL COYLE and RICHARD SINNOTT

I. INTRODUCTION

The decision of the EC Commission to mount a comparative study of regional issues and processes in Objective 1 regions was both problematic and pertinent in the Irish context. It was problematic in so far as Ireland has a highly centralized system of government with rather limited devolution of powers to the sub-national level. Moreover, this sub-national tier of government operates at the level of the county rather than the region. It was pertinent since the need for a major overhaul of the system of local government in Ireland has been on the political agenda for some time. Moreover it had gained new momentum in the light of the revised Structural Funds which emphasized geographically based programmes drawn up in consultation with local and regional authorities. Since the study was completed there have been some important reforms introduced to the local government system, including the proposed introduction of a comprehensive tier of indirectly elected regional authorities.

The study begins with an overview of the system of local government in Ireland – its historical development, structure and functions and recent reforms. The methodological problems encountered in adapting the study to a Irish setting and the solutions adopted are outlined. The analysis of the data then provides a comprehensive overview of the attitudes of regional elites to regional problems in the context of the internal market in 1992. Finally, the results of the analysis are evaluated in the wider context of the current trends in regional policy in both the national and the EC arenas.

II. LOCAL GOVERNMENT IN IRELAND

Historical Background

The present system of local government in Ireland has its origins in the

Local Government (Ireland) Act, 1898. This Act transferred to elected county councils the administrative functions which were hitherto carried out by Grand Juries. The latter consisted of wealthy landowners who assisted the Crown judges on their twice-yearly assizes. The Grand Juries were authorized to propose public works, to oversee the maintenance of public buildings and to pay the salaries of county officers.

The 1989 Act thus ended the dominant role of the ascendency class in local politics in Ireland and put local government on a representative basis. After Independence in 1922, the new Irish administration left the structure of local government largely as inherited from Britain. It did, however, abolish the independent Local Authority Board, which had been responsible for overseeing the various local authorities, and transferred its functions to a newly established central government department, the Department of Local Government (now the Department of the Environment). This was the first step in what has to-day become a highly centralised system of control over the local authorities.

Structure and Legal Basis

The administrative division of Ireland remains to-day more or less as established in the 1898 Act with the county being the basic unit of local administration. There are 27 directly elected county councils – one for each county but two for County Tipperary which had two Grand Juries, one for each riding. In addition, four of the major cities – Dublin, Cork, Limerick and Waterford – were designated county boroughs independent of, and with the same powers as, the county councils. The Local Government (Reorganisation) Act, 1985 revised the boundary between Dublin city and county and established three new electoral counties for Dublin county to reflect the huge growth there over the past number of years. However, these new county councils never became operational and are now about to be superceded by more recent reforms (see below). Under the same Act, Galway City was upgraded to county borough status.

A second tier of local administration was created in the form of urban and rural district councils with their own directly elected members. These councils operated independently of the county councils but their functions were rather limited – essentially taking over the public health functions of the Urban Sanitary Authorities and the Poor Law Guardians. In 1925 the rural district councils were abolished and their functions were assumed by the county councils. To-day there are 49 urban district councils and six borough corporations.

The lowest level of local administration is the Town Commissioners which have been in existence since the beginning of the nineteenth century. The Towns Improvement (Ireland) Act, 1854, which is still in operation, provides for the election of a Board of Town Commissioners by the inhabitants of towns with a population of 1,500 people or more. Twenty-five towns in Ireland still have their own directly elected Boards of Town Commissioners. However, they are no longer rating authorities and are funded directly by the county councils. Many of their original functions are now the concern of the larger local authorities and some of the smaller towns are, in fact, administered by their county councils.

The subsidiary role of local government in the Irish political system may be seen in the absence of any constitutional basis for local authorities. Rather, local authorities have their origins in, and derive their powers from, Acts of the Oireachtas (Parliament). Moreover, they may only exercise those powers which are specifically enumerated in legislation. They have no general competence in matters of local interest and may be held to be acting ultra vires – outside their powers – if they perform functions which are not laid down by law. Enabling legislation tends to be in specific rather than in general terms and many functions may be performed only with the sanction, approval or concurrence of the Minister for the Environment or another appropriate Minister.[1]

Functions of Local Government

By contrast with other European countries, the range of functions performed by local authorities in Ireland is very limited and mainly concerned with the physical environment. For accounting purposes the functions of local authorities are classified under eight programmes. Figure 1 summarizes the competence of the local authorities in these areas.

Figure 1 highlights the rather limited role of local authorities in Ireland. They have effectively no involvement in the major policy areas like education, agriculture, social welfare, police, public transport and public utilities such as electricity and gas. This fact indeed epitomizes the fundamental inadequacy of local government in Ireland – it is seen as the sole preserve of one Minister and one Department, namely the Department of the Environment. The absence of any direct links to the key economic Departments, and especially the Department of Finance, has deprived the local authorities of a role in the submission of projects and programmes for EC funding. As will be seen later, this has become especially problematic in the context of the recent reforms of the Structural Funds.

It is also quite clear from Figure 1 that the trend in recent times has been to remove functions from the competence of the local authorities and transfer them to newly created single-function executive agencies

FIGURE 1
FUNCTIONS OF LOCAL AUTHORITIES

Programme	Responsibility	Recent Changes
Housing and Building	Provision and up-keep of low-cost housing: provision of mortgages for people on low incomes.	1960: National Building Agency established to supplement the local authorities' housing programmes. 1970: Housing Finance Agency set up to provide low cost housing loans. Operates mainly through local authorities.
Road Transportation and Safety	Road maintenance and improvement; public lighting; traffic management; licensing, registration and taxation of vehicles; road safety.	1970: Dept. Environment assumed all financial responsibility for national road system. 1988: National Roads Authority established under aegis of Dept. of Environment. Effectively transferred responsibility for national road system from local to central Government.
Water Supply and Sewerage	Provision of public water supply and sewage schemes.	
Development Incentives and Control	Preparation of development plans with respect to land use and zoning, traffic, urban renewal and the preservation and improvement of amenities.	1965: County Development Teams established in less developed Western counties to foster economic development and coordinate public services. Local authorities represented on Teams. 1976: An Bord Pleanala (Planning Appeals Board) appointed to hear and determine appeals against decisions of planning authorities.
Environmental Protection	Waste collection and disposal; pollution control; fire brigade service; etc.	1992: Environmental Protection Agency set up under aegis of Dept. of the Environment with licencing, monitoring and enforcement functions for developments with potential for serious pollution.
Recreation and Amenity	Provision and maintenance of parks, leisure centres, museums, art galleries, etc. and grant-aiding cultural and sporting events.	

FIGURE 1 (cont.)
FUNCTIONS OF LOCAL AUTHORITIES

Programme	Responsibility	Recent Changes
Agriculture, Education, Health and Welfare	Primary responsibility in these functional areas rests with agencies other than the local authorities. The main involvement of the local authorities is to provide financial support for some services. They may have some residual functions e.g. administration of higher education grants, and there is usually local authority representation on the boards of the agencies.	1971: Eight Regional Health Boards were established to take over the administration of the health service from the local authorities. 1988: The County Committees of Agriculture appointed by the local authorities to provide advisory service to the farming community, were replaced by a national agency, TEAGASC (Agriculture and Food Development Authority).
Miscellaneous Services	Includes the preparation of lists of voters and jurors, the provision of courthouses and pounds, etc.	

operating at regional or national level, rather than devolve functions from central to local government.

The Management System

The local authority management system in operation in Ireland is sometimes hailed as Ireland's contribution to the development of politics and public administration in Western Europe.[2] Altogether there are 30 county/city managers – one for each of the county councils and county boroughs, except for Dublin City/County and Galway City/County which each have a joint city/county manager. By law the county manager is deemed to be manager of all elected authorities in the county, thereby strengthening the position of the county as the pre-eminent unit of local government. His appointment and dismissal are the responsibility of the Local Appointments Commission – a national recruitment agency for local authority personnel – and the elected representatives are only empowered, with a two-thirds majority, to suspend him for alleged incompetence or misconduct and to request the Minister for the Environment to remove him from office.

The management system was designed to give practical expression to the classical politics/administration dichotomy in public administration theory. Under this system the functions of local authorities are classified as 'reserved' and 'executive'. Reserved functions cover major policy issues, finance, legislation and the nomination of elected representatives to public bodies. These are the sole domain of elected representatives. Anything that is not specified as a 'reserved' function is deemed to be an 'executive' function and falls within the competence of an appointed county manager.

The system has generally worked well in terms of administrative efficiency but has come in for criticism as undemocratic because it vests authority in the hands of non-elected officials. In theory the county manager acts within the general policy framework laid down by the council. In practice, however, as permanent, professional, salaried officials, the manager and his staff are in a strong position *vis-à-vis* the unpaid, part-time, perhaps transient elected councillors and play a key role in initiating policy and in advising the council. The pre-eminent position of the county manager is very clearly shown in the survey data below. When politicians were asked to rank various groups by the amount of power which they wielded in the region, 73 per cent of the respondents placed the county manager in second place, only one percentage point behind government ministers (see Table 7).

Financing Local Government

The narrow range of functions performed by local authorities in Ireland is reflected in their level of spending. In 1990 expenditure by the local authorities represented about 4.7 per cent of GDP and 12 per cent of total public spending.[3]

Local authorities have three main sources of revenue to finance current expenditure, namely:

(a) Central Government grants and subsidies. There are two types of grants:

- Grants for road works: Spending on road works is classified as current expenditure for local authority accounting purposes but the State grant to finance this service comes from the Government's Public Capital Programme. Local authorities' receive 100% grants in respect of works carried out on national roads and additional general (bloc) grants to supplement the local authorities' own funds for the maintenance and improvement of regional, county and urban roads.
- Rate Support grants to compensate local authorities for the loss

TABLE 1
LOCAL AUTHORITY FINANCE

	Total 1990 IR£m	Provisional Outturn 1989 IR£m
EXPENDITURE	1,062.15	1,030.84
RECEIPTS:		
Government Grants and Subsidies	466.08	440.8
Commercial rates	240.03	229.76
Supply of Goods and Services	350.22	368.28
TOTAL RECEIPTS	1,056.33	1,038.84

of revenue arising from the abolition of rates on domestic dwellings and land referred to below.

(b) Rates on commercial property. Rates on domestic dwellings and certain community and farm buildings were abolished in 1978 while rates on land were declared to be unconstitutional in 1982.

(c) Charges for supply of goods and services: rental on local authorities houses; home-loan repayments; service charges for water; refuse collection; planning applications; etc.

Table 1 gives a summary of the estimated expenditure and receipts of local authorities for 1990, with comparative outturn figures for 1989.[4]

Local Government Reform

Ireland is almost unique among her European neighbours in not having implemented any major reorganization of the local government system in the post-war period. As we saw earlier, the few administrative reorganizations which have taken place have been mainly negative from the perspective of the local authorities. The abolition of rates on domestic dwellings and on land deprived local authorities of a substantial part of their independent source of finance and also broke the intimate link between taxation and representation at the local level.

Over the years a number of reports have been published by government, social/interest groups and academic institutions on the reform of local government, none of which have been implemented to date.[5]

In 1990 the scheduled local authority elections were postponed pending the outcome of yet another enquiry into local government reorganization and reform.[6] The Report of this latest Advisory Committee advocates a comprehensive reform of local government, including the granting of a constitutional basis to local government and a significant devolution of powers from central to local authorities in accordance with the principle of subsidiarity.

The key recommendations of the Report relate to the structure of local government and propose a three tier system – at regional, county and sub-county or district level as follows:

(a) The retention and the strengthening of the position of the county as the basic unit of local government. The only significant change recommended is the reorganization of Dublin County Council into two new councils (Dublin North and Dublin South) and the upgrading of the Borough of Dunlaoghaire to city status.
(b) The introduction of a comprehensive second tier of local authorities at the sub-county or district level to replace the current system of Urban Councils and Town Commissioners. However, the Advisory Committee was not unanimous on the exact nature of this second tier and put forward two divergent models for consideration: directly elected district councils or district committees of county councils.
(c) The establishment of eight standard regions in the country for all public sector groups and the setting up of indirectly elected statutory regional authorities in each of the regions to promote public sector co-ordination.

To date, the government's response has mainly focused on the proposed structural reforms. It has indicated its intention to proceed with the proposals to retain and enhance the county as the basic unit of local government and to establish a system of indirectly elected regional authorities. However, as with the Advisory Committee, there is disagreement among the government coalition partners on the structure and nature of the second tier of sub-county/district authorities and so a decision on this matter has been postponed.

The key issue of local taxation did not come within the terms of reference of the Advisory Committee. Their remit extended only to a consideration of the basis on which contributions from central government to the local authorities should be made. Two earlier reports on the financing of local authorities, both published in 1985,[7] reached broadly similar conclusions. The option of introducing a system of local income tax was rejected on the grounds that it would only further complicate an already complicated tax system. A local sales tax was also dismissed in the context of the small size of the country. Instead, both reports advocated the introduction of a new local property tax, with a revised valuation system to overcome the defects of the earlier domestic rates system.

III. REGIONAL GOVERNMENT IN IRELAND: LIMITATIONS AND PROSPECTS

Regional Structure

Ireland does not have a system of regional government. The division of Ireland into four Provinces – Ulster, Munster, Leinster and Connacht – dates back to Ireland's ancient Celtic past and has no modern significance in terms of administrative or political structures, although some people do retain a strong provincial identity and loyalty. There are no directly elected provincial or regional authorities with executive, administrative and planning functions between central government and the local authorities. The traditional arguments put forward in defence of this arrangement are that a population base of just over three million is too small to sustain a viable system of regional government and regional administration and that such a system could only be developed at the expense of undermining the existing – and very entrenched – position of county government.

The absence of an adequate regional dimension in the Irish local government system has been highlighted in recent years not only in the national arena but also in international fora such as the OECD[8] and the European Parliament.[9]

Regionalization: Uncoordinated and Administrative

The failure of successive Irish governments to devise an adequate regional structure has resulted in the continued growth of the East region – and especially the greater Dublin area – at the expense of other parts of the country. Moreover, the vacuum has resulted in the ad-hoc growth of single function regional agencies and offices arising mainly from the decentralization of government departments and state agencies and operating, for the most part, independently of each other. Today, we are left with a proliferation of regional bodies operating in differently constituted sets of regions. There are formal statutory regional bodies with responsibility for the health service, for tourism promotion and for the development and protection of inland fisheries. In addition, many national state agencies are organised on a regional basis, for example, the Industrial Development Authority. Just recently, the country was divided into seven regions for the purpose of preparing the National

Development Plan for EC Structural Funds, thereby introducing a further disparity into the regional divisions in Ireland (see below).

Shannon Free Airport Development Company

Only one body operating on a regional level in Ireland could be broadly described as a regional authority in the sense of having a devolved function for a wide variety of services in the region. This body, Shannon Free Airport Development Company (SFADCO), was originally set up in 1959 to ensure the growth of Shannon airport in respect of passengers, trade and services. Over the years both its remit and its geographical basis have been extended so that today it is responsible for industrial development, tourism and regional development in the Mid-West Region (covering counties Clare, Limerick and parts of Tipperary, Offaly and Kerry).

SFADCO is not an elected body or part of the local government system. It is a government agency with an appointed Board of Directors. The chairmen of the local authorities in the region are members of a consultative forum within SFADCO but this forum is purely advisory and has no formal powers or functions. None the less SFADCO is acclaimed for its success in promoting development of the Mid-Western region and cited as a role model for other regions. The data analysis below will show a generally higher level of satisfaction with the operation of government by both politicians and socio-economic interest groups in the Mid-West region compared to other regions.

Udaras na Gaeltachta

Another body, Udaras na Gaeltachta (Irish-speaking districts Authority), is something of a hybrid between a local and a regional authority. The Udaras was established in 1979 to encourage the preservation and extension of the Irish language and to foster industrial development in the Gaeltacht (Irish speaking districts). There are Gaeltacht areas in parts of seven counties mainly along the western seaboard, so the jurisdiction of the Udaras extends into a number of different regions. Also, while the Udaras is not an integral part of the local government system, the majority of its Board members are directly elected in a manner similar to local government elections.

The Impact of the EC on Regionalisation

Given the generally low level of economic development in Ireland, priority access to financial aid from the EC was a powerful factor behind the decision to seek membership of the Communities. With Ireland's accession to the European Communities, the focus shifted from internal regional disparities to disparities between Ireland and other member states as the government sought to have the whole country classified as a single underdeveloped region. Since then, the Irish government has been pressing for a comprehensive Community regional policy from its own increasingly centralized position within Ireland.

There was an inherent bias towards national administrative arrangements in the European Regional Development Fund (ERDF) as established in 1975. The Funds were primarily an instrument to provide financial support for the regional policies of the member states and consequently it was left to Member States to administer them as they saw fit.[10]

From the outset, responsibility for the operation of the ERDF lay with the Department of Finance. Given the small size of the funds and the national quota arrangements, the priority of the Irish government was to get the maximum amount of funds with the minimum delay. To this end, the Irish bureaucracy appears to have been particularly successful.[11] No new administrative arrangements were established in Ireland to deal specifically with the ERDF. Instead the Department of Finance simply extended the existing procedures and criteria for determining capital investment to encompass ERDF projects. ERDF receipts were thus effectively used to augment the Public Capital Programme for which the Department is also responsible.

This arrangement left Ireland ill-prepared for the new approach to regional policy which lay behind the reform of the Structural Funds, i.e., a move away from funding individual projects in favour of multi-annual integrated programmes for clearly defined geographical areas, drawn up in consultation with local and regional authorities.

Preparation of the National Development Plan

The effect of having the whole country designated as a single underdeveloped region means that the Irish government *is* the regional authority for the purposes of EC funding and so only a single national programme is required. This fact has enabled the government to present its decision to establish a sub-national structure for the purpose of preparing the National Development Plan as something of a benevolent gesture on its part. This sub-national structure involved the establishment of two types of groups in seven sub-regions:

- Working Groups composed of representatives of the main government departments and state agencies plus the managers of the local authorities. Their functions were to prepare a development plan for their sub-regions which could then be integrated into the National Development Plan.

- Advisory Groups composed of the chairmen of the local authorities and representatives of the main social and economic interest groups in the sub-regions, who received submissions from interested parties for transmission to the Working Groups.

To the great disappointment of many of the interests which had been involved in the working and advisory groups, the National Development Plan which the Irish government submitted to Brussels in March 1989 was based on national sectoral programmes rather than sub-regional ones. There was a good deal of criticism at what was seen by many as a snub to the regional groups, and it was argued that the 'consultation' mechanism was simply a cosmetic exercise to pander to the aspiration of Brussels. The Commissioner for Regional Policy, Bruce Millan, expressed 'regret' at the lack of adequate community and regional participation in the preparation of the National Development Plan.[12] The government, for its part, upheld its right and duty to determine the final shape of the National Plan and to mediate the conflicting demands of the different regions and of the various groups within the regions. The decision to impose national control was defended on the grounds 'that the requirements of efficiency, effectiveness and expediency all demand that the National Development Plan and its operational programmes be implemented through the already existing structures with which everyone is familiar and that have evolved to meet the particular circumstances and population structures of this country'.[13]

The government has recently announced its intention to retain and merge the Working and Advisory Groups to form Regional Review Committees. However, the new Committees will still only have a consultative role. The final decision about the operation of the Structural Funds will be the responsibility of the Monitoring Committee which will be composed of the representatives of central government, the Commission and the European Investment Bank. It is not yet clear how these Review Committees will be integrated into the proposed new statutory Regional Authorities which the Government is committed to establishing under its forthcoming local government reform programme discussed above.

IV. ATTITUDES OF REGIONAL POLITICIANS TO REGIONAL ISSUES

Methodological Considerations

Given the institutional background described above, it was inevitable that a comparative study of attitudes of regional politicians to regional political structures and regional issues would encounter comparability problems when extended to the Irish case. There are no regional councillors, regional structures are more administrative or consultative than political, and even the geographical definitions of the regions are variable. In the face of these problems, one might have been tempted to conclude that to proceed further would be akin to attempting to study the deep sea fishing industry in a land-locked country and abandon the effort. However, in Ireland there are certainly regional issues, there is some experience with regional structures and a group of politicians with a reasonable approximation to regional experience can be identified. In other words, there seemed to be enough to go on to make the effort at cross-national comparison worthwhile. This is particularly so in the light of the ongoing debate in Ireland about regional political structures and in the context of the recently accepted proposals for an indirectly elected tier of regional authorities.

In adapting the questionnaire to Irish circumstances every effort was made to retain the concept of 'region' where possible and to replace it with an appropriate functional equivalent where necessary. Thus, politicians were asked to respond to the questions regarding, for example, regional development in terms of the region in which their local constituency was located. In other cases, however, the term region had to be replaced altogether, for example, all references to 'regional council' or 'regional councillor' were replaced by 'local authority/local councillor'. On occasion, even substituting local for regional was not sufficient. For example, while it would certainly be meaningful to ask an Italian or Spanish respondent to assess the degree of influence of his or her regional government on national government, asking an Irish respondent to assess the degree of influence of his or her local government on the central government seemed to be rather superfluous! In such cases the question was simply dropped. Finally, other minor amendments were made to the terminology in the common questionnaire in order to incorporate local usage, for example, 'artisanry' was replaced by 'craft and small industry'.

Finding a functional equivalent of 'regional councillor' for the Irish case also represented something of a methodological challenge. Local councillors are too local and, with the exception of Udaras na Gaeltachta, there is no elected body between that level and national government. The solution to the problem was to focus on local politicians who also have a role beyond the county council or corporation. This 'supra-local' involvement was defined to include membership of the various regional bodies described in the earlier part of this article, membership of the Dail or Seanad (the two houses of the legislature) or membership of the executive of the General Council of County Councils. (A detail breakdown of the sample is given in Appendix I.)

Five of the seven regions into which Ireland was recently divided for the purpose of preparing the National Development Plan were included in the study (see Appendix I) and the response rate was, after considerable follow-up, 34 per cent. A number of factors affected the rate of response:

(i) The originally planned timing of the survey coincided with the general election of June 1989. The issuing of the questionnaires was held over until mid-July. However, even at this stage many politicians would have been in the throes of the Seanad (Upper House) election campaign. The postponement also meant that the field work coincided with the holiday period.

(ii) In the light of the absence of a system of regional government or regional administration in Ireland, the centrality of the concept of 'region' in the survey undoubtedly made some of the questions difficult and remote for many respondents.

(iii) Given the very heavy demands on their time, many politicians would probably have been discouraged by the length of the questionnaire which in the Irish case ran to nineteen pages.

The net result was a response rate somewhat less than the normal for postal questionnaires. The self-selection process involved may have introduced an element of bias which must be borne in mind when interpreting the responses. Further qualifications must be borne in mind in light of the composition of the population samples, especially in attempting to compare the Irish findings with those from countries with established representative institutions at regional level. Taking everything into account however, we can conclude that the sample provides a reasonably representative view of political opinion at regional level in Ireland.

The study was not limited to political opinion. A second population to be sampled was defined as those involved in administration, policy-making, and interest representation at regional level or at national level with specific regional responsibilities. The details of the organizations sampled are given in Appendix II. The response rate was a satisfactory 54 per cent. However, given the smaller target sample size (n=55) and the rather general terms in which the target population is defined, the representativeness of this sample is subject to greater qualification than is required in the case of the politicians. The sample is treated essentially as a control group *vis-à-vis* the politicians. This sample group shall be referred to from here on as the interest/administrative elites sample.

A key question in research of this sort is what significance should be attached to the views articulated by the respondents? This problem arises with all attitude research but is particularly acute in policy-oriented research. It is further exacerbated in this case by the fact that one is not dealing with a sample from the totality of those with an interest in the issues, but from a group that is likely to be predisposed to certain views. Asking a sample of politicians who are active at the regional level for their opinion on increased regional powers is somewhat akin to tackling the question of attitudes to a motorway proposal by taking a sample of road-haulage contractors. The opinions gathered will not be invalid, but they may only be one side of the picture. The problem is further complicated in this case by the fact that responses may be influenced by the partisan struggle between government and opposition, with the government party politicians being more defensive about the regional status quo and members of opposition parties delighting in the opportunity to implicitly criticise the government. This problem is more likely to occur in Ireland, where the question of regional involvement in the Structural Funds' process has been a matter of overt political controversy.

We have taken a number of steps to minimise these problems. In the first place, we pay particular attention to relative support given to the items in the questionnaire. Thus, in all the tables that follow, the statements or items relating to a particular theme are arranged in ascending or descending order of agreement or disagreement. Secondly, we use the interest/administrative elites sample as a check on the politicians' responses. We do not argue that the interest/administrative elites are right and the politicians wrong, but where there is agreement between politicians and interest/administrative elites on a particular perception or policy preference, then greater weight should be attached to that view. Thirdly, we tackle the possibility that responses by politicians might simply reflect a government versus opposition partisan divide by controlling for the effect of party affiliation. Fourthly, we attempt to control for in-built localist bias in the responses by controlling for the extent to which both government and opposition politicians are linked into the national policy-making network. Finally, in our concluding section, we attempt to place the results of the analysis in the context of the current debate about regional structures in Ireland, taking into account viewpoints that are important in the debate, though not necessarily expressed in the data.

Perceptions of Regional Performance

The majority of politicians interviewed were dissatisfied with the overall policy direction of the government in their region and even more dissatisfied with the rate of economic development. This dissatisfaction varied very considerably between the regions, or rather, between the Mid-West on the one hand and all of the other regions sampled (Dublin, South-East, North-West and Midlands-East) (see Table 2). Seventy per cent of

TABLE 2
GENERAL EVALUATION OF DEVELOPMENT OF THE REGION

	All %	Mid-West %	Dublin %	South-East %	North West %	Midlands East %
Satisfaction with overall policy direction of government						
-Politicians	43	70	33	33	41	43
-Interest/Admin.Elites	63	73	69	67	36	70
Satisfaction with rate of economic development						
-Politicians*	32	50	18	30	30	29
Satisfaction with operation of government						
-Interest/Admin.Elites**	54	21	25	18	4	32

* This question only put to politicians
** This question only put to Interest/Administrative Elites

politicians in the Mid-West were satisfied with the overall policy direction of government and 50 per cent of them were satisfied with the rate of economic development. This compares with satisfaction rates of between 33 and 43 per cent on the policy question in the other regions and between 18 and 32 per cent on the rate of economic development. The positive evaluation of the policy direction of government in the Mid-West is particularly significant. As we saw earlier, the Mid-West has long had distinctive regional institutions and is the only region within Ireland that comes close to having a stable regional identity and institutions to match. The contrast between the perception of the rate of economic development in the Mid-West (50 per cent satisfactory) and the other regions (satisfaction ranging from 18–32 per cent) also requires explanation. The existence, within the region, of a major international airport (sustained in part by a compulsory stopover policy in relation to all transatlantic flights coming into Ireland) and the Shannon Industrial Estate undoubtedly have something to do with this differential perception. It may also be that there is a carryover effect from the existence of an identifiable and reasonably stable set of regional institutions into a general feeling of optimism about economic development.

TABLE 3
POLARIZATION BETWEEN GOVERNMENT AND OPPOSITION PARTIES

	Government	Opposition	All
Satisfaction with overall policy direction of government in region	53%	25%	43%
Agree rate of economic development in region is satisfactory	48%	19%	31%

Regional politicians' assessment of regional performance must also be judged in the context that the interest/administrative elites take a considerably more sanguine view of government policy in the region. Thus 63 per cent of the interest/administrative elites sample judged the overall policy direction of government in their region to be satisfactory. We do not have data on their perception of the rate of economic development in their region but when asked about the operation of government in their region 54 per cent expressed satisfaction. There is some tentative evidence that indicates much less inter-regional variation in satisfaction with the operation and the overall policy direction of government among this group. The evidence is only tentative because the number of respondents in this sample is small and is therefore not very reliable when broken down over five regions. However, it is notable that only in the North-West region do the interest/administrative elites differ significantly from the national figure for satisfaction with government performance – in the North-west only 36 per cent were satisfied with government policy and only four per cent with the operation of government. The contrasting interregional patterns among politicians and interest/administrative elite respondents in satisfaction with government policy in the regions lends some weight to the view expressed above that the existence of regional political institutions influences the attitude of politicians.

The 20 per cent gap in the evaluation of regional performance as between politicians and interest/administrative elites suggests the need to probe further into the determinants of the politicians' response. Is it the case that politicians' responses are determined by their particular political concerns and political position? An obvious hypothesis is that the polarization between government and opposition parties, which extends from the national down to the local level, is a significant determinant of politicians attitudes. Table 3 confirms this hypothesis with a 30–35 per cent contrast in the degree of satisfaction with policy and with rate of

TABLE 4
EFFECT OF CONTACT WITH GOVERNMENT MINISTERS AND MINISTERS OF STATE

	Regular Contact	Little/No Contact	All
Satisfied with overall policy direction of government in region	67%	25%	43%

economic development as between government and opposition politicians. Regional politicians also seem to be influenced by the extent to which they are linked in to the national policy making network, at least in so far as their assessment of the overall policy direction of government in their region in concerned (Table 4).

Two-thirds of those who have regular contact with government ministers and ministers of state expressed satisfaction compared to only one quarter of those with little or no contact. There is of course a risk here that, since members of the government party are more likely to be in more regular contact with government ministers, this relationship simply reflects the government/opposition polarization noted in Table 4. In Table 5 we look at the relationship between regularity of contact and assessment of policy in the region controlling for the effects of membership of the government party. The results suggest that the degree of

TABLE 5
EFFECT OF CONTACT WITH GOVERNMENT MINISTERS AND MINISTERS OF STATE

	Government		Opposition	
	Regular Contact	Little/No Contact	Regular Contact	Little/No Contact
Satisfied with overall policy direction of government in the region	85%	33%	42%	16%

contact with government ministers has an affect on the assessment of regional policy independent of membership of the government or opposition parties. Those in more regular contact with members of the government were less critical of policy in their region, irrespective of whether they belong to the government or opposition party. It should be noted that in the case of opposition politicians the significance level (.07 derived from a chi-square test) is slightly above the conventional cut off point. The evidence of the persistence of the relationship among opposition politicians should therefore be regarded as somewhat tentative. However, even bearing this in mind, we can conclude that the effect of exposure to the national policy making apparatus is not reducible to the adversarial relationship between government and opposition.

Perceptions of Regional Preparedness for 1992

Dissatisfaction with government policy in the regions and with the rate of economic development spills over into specific doubts about the adequacy of various aspects of regional preparedness for 1992. Table 6 divides a series of items relating to the theme of the adequacy of preparation of the regions for 1992 in respect of various sectors and social and economic conditions into those which a majority judges to be inadequate and those in which this judgement represents a minority view. Three of the six areas deemed by a majority to be inadequate are core elements of the economic and physical infrastructure of the regions i.e. the road network, the port system and the railway network. Interestingly the other infrastructure element (air service to and from the regions) was exonerated.

A negative judgement was also passed by a majority of the politicians on two aspects of the structure of industry, that is, the structure of small and medium-sized industry and the general question of the restructuring of industry in preparation for 1992. Finally, politicians also judged the 'utilization of historical/environmental resources' to be inadequate. The latter perhaps reflects the commonly held view that historical artifacts and an attractive environment are a particular plus operating in Ireland's favour in relation to tourism post 1992, if only they were properly developed. It is notable that there was very little dissent on the part of the interest/administrative elites in regard to these judgements by the politicians. In fact, the interest/administrative elites would add 'level of technological innovation in industry' to the list of problem areas, otherwise they tended to concur with the politicians. Those areas where a clear majority of politicians were happy with preparedness for 1992 tend to be those that are less essential to the internal market. Thus, farm structure, the health service and social service network were seen as much less problematic. The educational sector and the level of training of the labour force were also favourably evaluated.

TABLE 6
SECTORS PERCEIVED TO BE INADEQUATELY PREPARED FOR 1992

	Politicians	Int./Admin. Elites
Majority deem Inadequate		
-Road Network	81%	84%
-Functions of urban areas	64%	42%
-Utilisation of historical/ environmental resource	64%	60%
-Structure of small/ medium sized industry	63%	61%
-Port System	61%	49%
-Railroad Network	60%	63%
-Restructuring of industry	58%	70%
Minority deem Inadequate		
-Commercial Network	47%	30%
-Level of technological innovation in industry	44%	58%
-Farm Structure	42%	43%
-Air Service	36%	40%
-Health Service	36%	22%
-Social Service Network	34%	29%
-Third Level Education	27%	26%
-Skill level of labour force	22%	22%

Just as there tends to be, in general, a considerable level of agreement between politicians and interest/administrative elites in regard to these judgements, there is relatively little evidence of a polarization between government and opposition politicians. The only exception in this regard is in the adequacy of the railroad network which was judged by 58 per cent of government politicians to be inadequate whereas this assessment is made by 71 per cent opposition politicians.

The Problem of Centralization

When we examined the sources of these negative perceptions of regional performance, the problems were overwhelmingly perceived to be related to ones of political structure and the allocation of power (see Table 7). Very large majorities of the politicians identified time taken to implement decisions (90 per cent), allocation of financial resources (89 per cent), level of consultation between the region and the central government (85 per cent) and co-ordination with local authorities (75 per cent)

TABLE 7
SOURCES OF DISSATISFACTION WITH THE OPERATION OF GOVERNMENT IN THE REGION

	Politicians	Int./Admin. Elites
-Time taken to implement decisions	90%	80%
-Allocation of financial resources	89%	69%
-Level of consultation between the region and central government	85%	77%
-Coordination with local authorities	75%	43%
-Use of University/research facilities	71%	37%
-Planning capacity	65%	67%
-Feasibility of projects	56%	44%
-Quality of politicians in the region	42%	43%
-Preparation and committment of public servants	36%	22%
-Availability of local authorities for consultation with socio-economic organisations	35%	8%

as the main problems with the operation of government at a regional level. With the exception of the last of these items (co-ordination with local authorities) interest/administrative elites tended to concur, though they were less unanimous than the politicians about the problematic nature of the allocation of financial resources (69 per cent for the interest/administrative elites as opposed to 89 per cent for the politicians). Majorities of the politicians also agreed that use of the university/research facilities, planning capacity and feasibility of projects were also problem areas. Perhaps not surprisingly, majorities denied that the quality of politicians was a problem. However, they also denied that the preparation and commitment of public servants was a problem or that the availability of local authorities for consultation with socio-economic organizations in the region was a problem. This points to the conclusion that the problem is seen as one of structure rather than personnel.

Interest/administrative elites appear to regard local authorities as not being particularly important. At least this is a plausible interpretation of the fact that only 43 per cent of them see co-ordination with local authorities as being a problem and only eight per cent see the availability of local authorities for consultations with socio-economic organizations in the region as being problematic. The latter figure in particular is more likely to be due to the perception that the local authorities are not

TABLE 8
GROUPS WHO WIELD MOST POWER IN THE REGION

Government Ministers	74%
Local Authority Managers	73%
National Party leaders	69%
Press	58%
Catholic Clergy	46%
Other senior local authority officials	38%
Agricultural organisations	36%
Private economic and financial groups	32%
Semi-State Bodies	31%
Local Party leaders	31%
TD's (Members of Lower House of Parliament)	30%
County Councillors	26%
Trade Unions	20%
Clergy of other denominations	15%
Senators	15%

sufficiently influential to warrant additional points of contact rather than to satisfaction with the performance of local authorities in this area.

Centralization of power is even more evident when we turn to the politicians' perceptions of the distribution of power in their region. Approximately 70 per cent identified government ministers, local authority managers (who are centrally appointed) and national party leaders as the groups who wield most power in the region. In contrast, local politicians, whether they be local elected representatives (county councillors), local TDs, or local party leaders were perceived to be influential by only 25–30 per cent. In fact both the press (58 per cent) and the Catholic clergy (46 per cent) were perceived to be more influential than any local elected representatives or local interest organizations (see Table 8).

Antidote to Centralization

When it comes to redesigning, or perhaps one should say designing regional government institutions, the politicians show a mixture of conservatism and radicalism. As Table 9 shows, they are quite conservative when it comes to allocating particular areas of competence to the regions as against the national government. Those policy areas for which there is in excess of 60 per cent support in favour of the region are areas that are organized on a local or regional basis at present, or in which there has been a tradition of regional involvement. These areas are craft and small industry 96 per cent, industrial development 87 per cent, urban areas 84 per cent, health 78 per cent, environmental conservation 78 per cent, public works 76 per cent, cultural affairs 72 per cent and agriculture 63 per cent. Somewhat slimmer majorities would also advocate more power for the regions in the areas of transportation, employment policies, and primary and secondary education. However, majorities opposed giving more power to the regions in regard to taxes, banking and

TABLE 9

PREFERENCE FOR MORE POWER IN THE REGION

	Politicians	Int./Admin. Elites
Craft and Small Industry	96%	98%
Industrial Development	87%	81%
Urban Areas	84%	89%
Health	78%	71%
Environmental Conservation	78%	61%
Public Works	76%	85%
Cultural Affairs	72%	83%
Agriculture	63%	62%
Transportation	57%	59%
Employment Policies	54%	52%
Primary and Secondary Education	54%	46%
Taxes	46%	35%
Banking and Credit Facilities	37%	45%
Third Level Education	35%	36%
Scientific Research	31%	38%
Police	30%	40%
Foreign Trade	19%	11%

credit facilities, third level education, scientific research, police and, not unexpectedly, foreign trade.

When it comes to choosing a role for hypothetical elected regional councils, the responses were more radical. Faced with a series of potential roles for such a council respondents could accord the role first priority, second priority or third priority, or designate it as having fairly high

TABLE 10

ROLE OF HYPOTHETICAL REGIONAL COUNCIL

	1st Pr'ty	2nd Pr'ty	3rd Pr'ty	Fairly High Pr'ty	Imp.	Not Imp.
Investigate the social and economic problems of the region and propose solutions to them	31%	11%	18%	35%	3%	2%
Defend the interests of the region in the national arena	25%	18%	16%	30%	11%	1%
Help the individual citizens in their dealing with the public administration	7%	9%	7%	38%	28%	11%
Defend the interests of the less privileged sectors of society	7%	20%	12%	42%	17%	2%
Defend the interests of individual localities of the region	6%	7%	11%	31%	37%	8%
Control the activity of the regional government and of the regional and local officials	5%	12%	5%	32%	38%	8%
Protect the national interests in the context of regional deliberations	1%	3%	7%	40%	31%	18%
Mediate the conflicting demands of the various groups in the region	1%	5%	9%	24%	53%	7%

priority, being important or not being important. Two items that suggest a developmental role likely to bring the region into conflict with national government emerged clearly as the priority items. Thus, 31 per cent of respondents indicated that 'investigating the social and economic problems of the region and proposing solutions to them' should have first priority, while a further 25 per cent ticked 'defend the interests of the region in the national arena'. These two items were given either first, second or third priority by 68 per cent of respondents. In contrast to this ambitious comprehensive role for elected councils, politicians seemed to deliberately eschew a particularistic and traditional role, for example 'helping citizens in their dealings with public administration' (22 per cent, first, second or third priority) and 'defend the interests of the individual localities in the region' (23 per cent first, second or third priority). It is notable also that the role assigned to councils was developmental rather than redistributional – contrast the 68 per cent conceiving of the role in terms of regional development or the interests of the region as against 38 per cent defining it in terms of 'defending the interests of the less privileged sector of society'. One could also look at the data in Table 10 in terms of a contrast between a preferred emphasis on a council role in relation to the external environment of the region rather than on roles that involve processes internal to the region. Now that regional authorities are about to be established in Ireland, these views take on added significance.

The Role of the European Community

We have already touched briefly on the role of the European Community in relation to the regions by examining the perceived preparedness of the regions for 1992. As we have seen the politicians' views in this regard tended to be negative. Despite this assessment there is considerable optimism about the prospects for each region in the post 1992 period. Table 11 divides the series of possible outcomes into positive outcomes, neutral outcomes and negative outcomes. Obviously, the neutral category of outcomes is of less interest to us in this regard because it tells us nothing about the optimism or pessimism of respondents. Thus 96 per cent of politicians (and of interest/administrative elites) see 'more competition' as a result of 1992 and three-quarters of each group see a greater 'concentration of industry'. Setting these aside, majorities expect ten favourable outcomes in the post 1992 period, ranging in substance and degree of support from stimulating the adoption of new environmental standards (93 per cent) to 'improvement in the standard of social services' (53 per cent). In between these two are a series of outcomes that one immediately associated with 1992, for example, 'access to new markets',

TABLE 11
PROSPECTS FOR THE REGION IN THE POST 1992 PERIOD

	Politicians	Int./Admin Elites
Positive		
– Stimulate the adoption of new environmental standards	93%	95%
– Access to new markets	91%	95%
– Provide access to new financial resources	84%	87%
– Stimulate the modernisation of agricultural production	81%	76%
– Restructure the commercial distribution network	78%	85%
– Stimulate technological innovation	77%	86%
– Stimulate institutional reform	72%	75%
– Development of regional administration	67%	55%
– Allocation of functions between national and sub-national levels of government	54%	57%
– Improvement in the standard of social service	53%	51%
Neutral		
– More competition	96%	96%
– Concentration of industry	73%	76%
Negative		
– Worsen situation in underdeveloped areas	53%	73%
– Slow down the decision-making process	48%	53%
– Increase unemployment	40%	42%
– Loss of regional identity	38%	38%
– Increase the cost of production	32%	20%

'access to new financial resources', 'modernization of agricultural production', 'restructuring commercial distribution network', etc.

In the light of our interest in the institutional structures and processes at regional level, it is also interesting to note two-thirds of politicians expect the 1992 programme to stimulate institutional reform in the regions and assist in the development of regional administration. A slimmer majority expects 1992 to effect the 'allocation of functions between national and sub-national levels of government', presumably in favour of the latter.

TABLE 12
ROLE OF THE EUROPEAN COMMUNITY

	Politicians	Int./Admin.Elites
Financing of projects for underdeveloped areas	93%	91%
Promotion of technological innovation	91%	94%
Providing a European Perspective for scientific research	79%	85%
Monitoring of labour market	77%	53%
Coordination of foreign trade	76%	60%
Evaluation of regional investment projects	73%	57%
Monitoring of financial markets	71%	65%
Formulate guidelines for vocational education	70%	52%
Control over the enforcement of environmental and urban planning standards	68%	57%
Control of immigration from non-Community countries	45%	42%
Promotion of integration of non-Community immigrants	42%	33%
Financing of European Defence Policies	27%	23%

Among the negative outcomes of 1992, only one – 'worsen situation in under-developed areas' – is expected by a majority, and the majority (53 per cent) is a slender one. This particular prediction is in fact the only in which the interest/administrative elites differ (in a more pessimistic direction) from the politicians. All of this is not to say that the other matters are perceived as unproblematic, for example, 48 per cent of the politicians, and 53 per cent of the interest/administrative elites foresee a 'slow down in the decision-making process'; approximately 40 per cent of each sees an 'increase of unemployment'.

Politicians do not just have expectations in regard to the role of the European Community, they also have preferences (see Table 12). Not surprisingly, the overwhelming preference was for roles with funding implications – financing projects for underdeveloped areas (93 per cent), and promotion of technological innovation (91 per cent). The interest/administrative elites concurred. To these one might add the function of 'providing a European perspective for scientific research' – it does not require too much imagination to envisage this also involving the provision of funds. It is notable however that roles that do not involve funding and employ some transfer of power to the EC were also endorsed by majorities in excess of two-thirds – co-ordination of foreign trade, the evaluation of regional investment projects, formulating guidelines for vocational education, and control over the enforcement of environmental and urban planning standards. Two neutral functions-monitoring the labour market and monitoring the financial markets – received similar levels of endorsement.

Table 12 also indicates, however, that interest/administrative elites have some reservations about assigning these kind of interventionist roles to the Community. Intervention by the Community was rejected outright by both politicians and interest/administrative elites in regard to one sensitive area – immigration, whether this takes the form of control of immigration from non-Community countries or promotion of integration of non-Community immigrants. This is quite clearly an area that is to be kept out the Community's hands and reserved for a lower level of government, presumably the national level. Finally, only a relatively small minority of respondents of either category are prepared to envisage the financing of European defence policies as an appropriate role for the Community. In regard to this latter item, what is perhaps noteworthy is that even as many as one in four are prepared to countenance such a role.

As we have seen in Table 11, regional politicians expect a lot of the European Community and their optimism in regard to the outcome of 1992 is presumably predicated on the capacity of the Community institutions to deliver. Some, at least, of the expectations in Table 12 will require new organizational structures. In Table 13, we examine support among politicians and interest/administrative elites for a range of new Community structures.

Table 13 indicates overwhelming support for a whole array of new organizational structures in the post 1992 period. There is virtual unanimity that all of the proposed structures are indispensable, or at least necessary. One detects here a tendency to treat the Community as a *deus ex machina*. Once a problem is identified there is assumed to be a Euro agency or a Euro consortium that will solve it. However, there are significant variations in the degree of enthusiasm for such structures and also in the endorsement of the structures as between politicians and the interest/administrative elites.

TABLE 13
PREFERRED NEW ORGANISATIONAL STRUCTURES

	Politicians		Int./Admin.Elites	
	Indispens.	Necessary	Indispens.	Necessary
European Environment Agency	37%	60%	29%	60%
European level representation for local/regional elected politicians	37%	54%	23%	44%
Central European Bank	32%	62%	33%	58%
Postgraduate Eurodiplomas in scientific fields	31%	61%	17%	70%
Offices representing the regions in Brussels	30%	56%	27%	40%
Community Programmes for trans-regional sectoral policies	27%	64%	29%	67%
European Telecommunications Agency	26%	69%	21%	70%
European Agency to monitor labour market	26%	68%	19%	65%
European Securities and Exchange Commission	26%	67%	13%	78%
Inter-regional consortia for planning of services and public infrastructures	26%	66%	9%	80%
Agencies for inter-regional cooperation for management of services and infrastructures	23%	67%	13%	69%
European Administrative Court	23%	48%	14%	60%

Between a quarter and a third of the politicians deemed the new structures to be 'indispensable' while a further two thirds considered them to be 'necessary'. The exception is a 'European Administrative Court'. A majority did support that proposal but over a quarter actually oppose it and these figures are similar for politicians and interest/administrative elites. A possible explanation for this might be the fact that, unlike other European countries (except Britain), Ireland does not have a separate body of administrative law or an administrative court, nor has there been any great demand for either.

The interest/administrative elites were somewhat more discriminating

TABLE 14
COMMON INITIATIVES FOR THE POST 1992 PERIOD

	Politicians		Int./Admin.Elites	
	Indispens.	Necessary	Indispens.	Necessary
Policies to protect the environment	61%	38%	50%	48%
Integrated programmes for contiguous border regions	45%	50%	43%	57%
Formulate development programmes	44%	56%	42%	58%
Stregthen regional airline service	38%	59%	42%	56%
Lobby the EC Commission	37%	62%	33%	54%
Cultural/tourist exchange programmes	34%	62%	26%	74%
Plans for applied research	27%	65%	18%	80%
Promotion of joint ventures between industry	27%	64%	21%	79%
Action to promote product/services	25%	71%	17%	73%
Training of administrative personnel	20%	72%	23%	69%

in their evaluation. Four of the proposals deal directly with structuring the relations between regions in different countries and between the regions and central institutions of the Community. One in five of the interest/administrative elites was opposed to new structures for inter-regional co-operation and almost one in three opposed greater regional representation at European level.

Interestingly the doubts of the interest/administrative elites on the proposals for new structures for region-to-Brussels links did not extend to opposition to 'common initiatives among the regions located in different countries' (see Table 14). One partial exception is that one in eight of the interest/administrative elites sample was opposed to common trans-national regional lobbying directed at the Commission. Otherwise, there was virtual unanimity that all of the proposed trans-national regional initiatives were a 'good thing'. Except on the question of environmental protection policies, the pattern which emerged is one of no very marked differences between the views of politicians and the interest/administrative elites. However, as in Table 13 the interest/administrative elites were less convinced than the politicians about the indispensability of the suggested initiatives. One is again faced with the 'motherhood and apple pie' problem. When everyone is so much in agreement, the conclusions to be drawn from data are likely to be banal.

One way to bring some perspective to bear on the responses in Tables 13 and 14 is to ignore those initiatives which respondents considered to be 'necessary' and focus instead on those deemed to be 'indispensable' and then interpret this as an indication of what should receive priority. Analysing the data in this manner there is only one area which a majority of either group deemed to be indispensable, that is, 'policies to protect the environment' (Table 14).

V. SUMMARY AND CONCLUSION – THE PROGNOSIS FOR REGIONALIZATION IN IRELAND

Our survey revealed widespread discontent among regional politicians with both the economic and the political state of the regions in Ireland. On the economic front, the findings clearly demonstrate widespread dissatisfaction among the politicians with the overall policy direction of government in the regions and with the rate of economic development (Table 2). There was also a high degree of pessimism expressed by both the politicians and the interest/administrative elites on the state of readiness of the regions for the advent of the single market in 1992. Over 50 per cent of both groups deemed the structure of industry and the key infrastructural areas (roads, ports and the railroad network) to be inadequate (Table 6).

While the survey data indicated sharp differences between government and opposition parties on the overall operation of government in the regions, there was broad agreement on the nature of specific regional issues and problems. On these, our analysis did not find a significant degree of polarization between the politicians and the interest/administrative elites, between the five regions, between government and opposition, or between national and local politicians.

Underlying this was widespread discontent regarding the allocation of power between central government and the regions. In most European countries the role of local government has expanded in the period since the Second World War. In some cases this was the outcome of a genuine desire to enhance local democracy. In others, it was simply a necessary concomitant to the growth of the welfare state – devolving powers to sub-national tiers of government was seen to be the most efficient way of delivering services. Over this period, however, Ireland has seen the gradual erosion of its local government system.

As the role of the State expanded, the tendency has been to create new single function agencies at national or regional level rather than to devolve powers and functions to the local authorities. Moreover, central government has not traditionally engaged in dialogue with the local authorities on matters affecting their interests, or provided them with a forum for having an input into the policy process of central administration. Local authorities in Ireland have not been able to gain the right to regular formal consultation with central government.

Over 85 per cent of the politicians in the survey were dissatisfied with the decision-making process, with the level of consultation between the region and central government and with the allocation of financial resources (Table 7). Large majorities of the interest/administrative elites sample (70–80 per cent) were also dissatisfied with these areas. County councillors were ranked in the bottom third of those groups which were perceived as having most power in the region – well behind the non-elected senior local authority officials and the main interest groups (Table 8).

Despite the general discontent with aspects of the present system, demands for change were quite conservative. When asked to indicate the preferred distribution of power between the region and central government, respondents in both the politicians' and the interest/administrative elites' sample came down very strongly in favour of the region in those areas which have traditionally had a regional input, although not necessarily coming under the umbrella of the local authorities. There was somewhat less demand for devolution of functions which, in other countries, are normally part of the local government system but which in Ireland have remained under the control of central government (Table 9).

On the other hand, when asked to indicate the importance which they would attach to a range of roles for a hypothetical regional council, politicians gave as their top priorities those roles which are most likely to involve them in confrontation with central government, for example, 'investigate the social and economic problems and propose solutions to them' (Table 10). They attached less importance to functions which were essentially internal regional concerns.

What these two sets of demands seem to be saying is that the priority demand is for a greater degree of influence and consultation in these areas which are fundamental to regional development, rather than for the devolution of a wide range of additional functions to the local level. The importance attached to access to the national policy-making process was also highlighted in Tables 4 and 5 which showed a definite positive relationship between satisfaction with the direction of government policy and degree of contact with members of the government, even among opposition politicians.

A lot of hope and expectation is being put on new Community institutions which are likely to emerge in the post 1992 period. Large majorities of both politicians and the interest/administrative elites support the setting up of new institutional structures at EC level, including many aimed at inter-regional co-operation (Table 13). Over 90 per cent of politicians were in favour of establishing European level representation for local/regional elected politicians (Table 13). A combination of frustration at lack of involvement in the policy process at the national level and the positive attitude towards sub-national involvement emerging from the EC Commission and the European Parliament has encouraged local authorities in Ireland and elsewhere to look to Europe to champion their cause. To a large extent, however, the interest in Europe has been rather narrowly confined to a single policy areas, namely, the Regional Policy. Undoubtedly, a key factor in the preoccupation with this area is the prospects of financial aid for cash-starved local authorities. It is important, however, to keep the likely impact of Community funding in a realistic perspective. The total budget of the European Communities represents only about one per cent of the GDP of the member states, or roughly two per cent of their total public spending. With over 50 per cent of the budget earmarked for agricultural price support, this leaves only a small amount for spending on regional, social and other programmes.

Another reason why local authorities have focused on the Community's Regional Policy is that it is one of the few areas where the involvement of sub-national units of government is an integral part of the policy and of the implementating regulations. This is an important development for local and regional authorities since the Treaty of Rome does not recognize them as having a formal role in the Community policy process. Local authorities in Ireland, however, have not benefitted as much as their European counterparts in this regard for all the reasons discussed earlier – excessive centralism, the designation of Ireland as a single region, the decision to operate the ERDF through the Department of Finance and the fact that the local authorities are represented in central government by the Department of the Environment which is not a key economic department. Ireland has not signed the European Charter of Local Self-Government which was adopted by the Council of Europe in 1985 and, indeed, was one of the countries who opposed giving the Charter the status of a Convention.

The very high level of enthusiasm among politicians for a new representative organization at the trans-national level must be evaluated against the background that county councillors in Ireland have never managed to mobilize a concerted campaign to influence policy at the national level. The general practice has been for individual authorities to adopt their own strategies on how best they could influence central government, despite the existence of a number of national organizations representing the interests of elected public representatives. This lack of horizontal coordination is undoubtedly an important factor in their failure to make an impact on national government. This may have been partly due to lack of resources but it must also be explained by a certain amount of inertia on the part of the councillors themselves.

Moreover, enthusiasm for Euro consortia has to face the fact that policy-making remains primarily the responsibility of the Member States. For the foreseeable future, the national arena will remain the locus of power and influence. It will be the national governments acting jointly in the Council of Ministers who will ultimately determine the direction of EC policies. It will not, therefore, be sufficient for local government representatives to concentrate their effort on Europe. Initially they may find themselves knocking on an open door and getting a warmer reception in Brussels than they might receive at home, but at the end of the day they will find that the national authority cannot simply be bypassed or ignored. Moreover, given the diversity of sub-national structures and the very marked differences in terms of powers and functions, it may well prove difficult for any supra-national organization of local and regional authorities to come up with a coherent and comprehensive strategy, at least in the short to medium term.

None the less, involvement at the European level and the contacts with colleagues in other Member States may prove helpful for regional politicians in Ireland in devising a more effective strategy on the home front. Moreover, as the debate on European unity progresses, there is increasing concern being expressed for the implications for national sovereignty and the proper balance and distribution of power between national governments and Brussels. It is in this context that the concept of 'Europe of the Regions' and the principle of subsidiarity are gaining momentum. This principle, which calls for the decentralization of decision-making to the lowest effective and efficient levels of administration, has become more than just a Euro buzz-word. It is invoked in the Single European Act and in the Social Charter on the Fundamental Right of Workers.

In the Draft Treaty on Political Union subsidiarity is invoked as one of the basic principles of the new Union. A demand for decentralization in Ireland certainly exists. Since this research was undertaken, significant reforms of local and regional government have been announced. It remains to be seen to what extent the demand for the decentralization will be met by a combination of the proposed reforms and new developments in the implementation of European Regional Policy.

NOTES

1. For a fuller account of the system of local government in Ireland see D. Roche, *Local government in Ireland* (Dublin: Institute of Public Administration, 1982).
2. For a more detailed account of the city and county management system see N. Collins, *Local Government Managers at Work* (Dublin: Institute of Public Administration, 1987).
3. Source: Department of Finance, Dublin.
4. Department of the Environment *Returns of Local Taxation 1990* (Dublin: Stationery Office).
5. The following were the main reports on the reform of local government in Ireland:
   - Ireland. Government White Paper, 1971, *Local Government Reorganisation* (Dublin: Stationery Office).
   - Ireland, 1973, *Local Government Discussion Document* (Dublin: Stationery Office).
   - Ireland, 1985, *Local Government Reform* (Dublin: Stationery Office).
   - Institute of Public Administration, 1971, *More Local government* (Dublin: Institute of Public Administration).
   - Muintir na Tire, 1985, *Towards a New Democracy: Implications of Local Government Reform* (Dublin: Institute of Public Administration).
6. Ireland, 1991, *Local Government Reorganisation and Reform* (Dublin: Stationery Office).
7. (a) Commission on Taxation, *Fourth Report of the Commission on Taxation* (Dublin: Stationery Office, 1985).
   (b) National Economic and Social Council, Report No. 80, *The Financing of Local Authorities* (Dublin: NESC, 1985).
8. OECD, *Innovation Policy: Ireland* (Paris: OECE, 1987).
9. European Communities: European Parliament, Hume Report on the Regional Problems of Ireland, Document B 910/85, 6 April, 1987.
10. J. Hart, 'The European Regional Development Fund and the Republic of Ireland', in M. Keating and B. Jones (eds.), *Regions in the European Community* (Oxford: Clarendon Press, 1986), p. 210.
11. B. Laffan, 'While you're over there in Brussels, get us a grant': the management of the structural funds in Ireland', *Irish Political Studies*, Vol. 4 (1989), pp. 49–50.
12. *Irish Times*, 11 Sept. 1989.
13. An Taoiseach (Prime Minister), Mr Charles J. Haughey, T.D. speaking at the Irish Council for the European Movement Conference on the NESC Report, University College Dublin, 2 Oct. 1989.

APPENDIX I

POLITICIANS' SAMPLE

DEFINITIONS OF TERMS EMPLOYED IN THE SURVEY

'REGIONAL COUNCILLOR'

The survey was originally designed to be administered to 'regional' politicians and so the first task was to find a functional equivalent of 'regional councillor' which would be meaningful in an Irish context. Local councillors alone were considered to be too local but given the focus of the study on sub–national government, local councillors had to be at the core of the Irish research. It was therefore decided to opt for 'supra-local councillors' i.e. those members of local authorities who also had experience beyond the local level. The survey thus comprised all those local councillors who hold, or have recently held, one or more of the following public offices:

- Member of Dail or Seanad Eireann (Irish Parliament)
- Member of the executive of the general Council of County Councils
- Public representative on the boards of one or more of the following regional bodies:

  Health Boards
  Regional Development Organisations (now disbanded)
  Regional Tourism Organisations
  Regional Advisory Bodies for Structural Funds
  Udaras na Gaeltachta
  Other public regional bodies.

'GOVERNMENT'

Given that the survey was carried out immediately after the June 1989 general election, questions relating to the operation of the 'Government' would in all likelihood have been understood to refer the Fianna Fail Government of March 1987 to June 1989. The new Government which was formed following the June 1989 election is a coalition between Fianna Fail (the majority partner) and the Progressive Democrats (PDs). There were no members of the PDs in our survey. The basic criteria for inclusion in the survey was membership of a local authority and as the PDs were only formed after the local elections of May, 1985 their local authority membership is very low, consisting only of those councillors who defected from other politicians parties. These few PD councillors did not meet the other criteria for inclusion in the survey outlined above. The terms 'Government' and 'Government Party' therefore only refer to Fianna fail.

'REGIONS'

As explained in the main text, Ireland does not have a comprehensive system of regional administration. Rather, a multiplicity of regional bodies operate in differently constituted sets of regions. Given the context of the study, the particular regional sub-division of the country chosen is the one most recently constituted by the Government for the purpose of preparing the National Development Plan. Note the use of the term 'sub-region' rather than 'region' since Ireland has been designated as a single region for the purposes of Structural Funding. The sub-regions are as follows:

Sub-Region 1: Dublin	–	Dublin City and County
Sub-Region 2: South-East	–	Carlow, Kilkenny, Tipperary South Riding, Wexford, Waterford
Sub-Region 3: South-West	–	Cork, South Kerry
Sub-Region 4: Mid-West	–	Clare, Limerick, Tipperary North Riding, South West Offaly, North Kerry
Sub-Region 5: West	–	Galway, Mayo, Roscommon
Sub-Region 6: North-West	–	Donegal, Sligo, Leitrim, Cavan, Monaghan
Sub-Region 7: Midlands-East	–	Louth, Meath, Kildare, Wicklow, Laois, Longford, Westmeath, Remainder of Offaly

BREAKDOWN OF SAMPLE

A total of 311 questionnaires were sent to politicians in 5 (sub-) regions, of which 106 responded, giving a response rate of 34 per cent. The distribution of the questionnaires across the regions was as follows:

Region	N°of Questionnaires Sent out	Returned	Response Rate
Dublin	50	18	36%
South-East	64	27	42%
Mid-West	55	21	38%
North-West	73	26	36%
Midlands-East	69	14	20%
Total	311	106	34%

APPENDIX 2

INTEREST/ADMINISTRATIVE ELITES SAMPLE

This sample comprised representatives from the following organisations/groups:

- Regional Development Agencies
- Employer's Organisations
- Trade Unions
- Local Tourism
- Farming Organisations
- Administrative Elites

The response rate, at 54% was quite satisfactory and was broken down as follows:

Organisation	N° of Questionnaires		Response Rate
	Sent out	Returned	
Regional development Agencies	29	15	52%
Employers' Organisations	18	9	50%
Trade Unions	10	7	70%
Local Tourism	5	3	60%
Farming Organisations	10	3	30%
National Administrative Elites with specific regional responsibilities	29	18	62%
Total	102	55	54%

Prefecture Councils in Greece: Decentralization in the European Community Context

SUSANNAH VERNEY and
FOULI PAPAGEORGIOU

I. DECENTRALIZED ADMINISTRATION AND LOCAL GOVERNMENT: EXISTING STRUCTURES

Greece must rank as the most centralized state within the European Community. Politically, there is no alternative power source capable of challenging central government. Other directly elected institutions exist only at the local level and are weak, fragmented and constitutionally subject to government tutelage.[1] Within the public administration system, the over-concentration of decision-making in Athens has been notorious, with even the most trivial details frequently referred from the bureaucracy to the political hierarchy for a ministerial decision.

The new needs of European Community membership have thrown the deficiencies of the system into sharp relief. In particular, the difficulties encountered by the over-centralized bureaucracy in planning and implementing regional development programmes were eloquently expressed by the former Director of KEPE, the state Centre for Planning and Economic Research, when she declared that, even though there have been plans in Greece, there has been no planning'.[2]

Greece's administrative division into prefectures (*nomoi*) divided into sub-prefectures dates back to the foundation of the nation-state in 1833. As the territory of the Greek state expanded, the number of prefectures increased from the original ten to the current 55.[3] At two points during the post-war period, a number of administrative functions were transferred to the prefectures. The first step towards turning the prefectures into a level of planning and implementation was taken in the 1950s when each prefecture for the first time was allocated a separate public works budget and set up a Prefecture Fund to handle it.[4] In the 1980s, following Greece's accession to the EC, a wide range of additional responsibilities in sectors such as town planning, health and education were also transferred to the prefectures.[5] However, these attempts to decentralize administrative functions in the interests of bureaucratic rationalization should not be confused with an effective decentralization of political decision-making power.

The prefecture is a branch of the administration. It is headed by a prefect who embodies the central government in the prefecture and who is in charge of the decentralized services of the central Ministries which are located there. The prefect's traditional status as a dependent political appointee was reinforced by Law 1235 of 1982, allowing the government to appoint and dismiss prefects at will.[6]

The lack of any popular mandate clearly leaves the prefect few margins for independent political initiatives. At the same time local government, which does enjoy a popular mandate, is also considerably circumscribed. In 1833 the largely autonomous local communities of the Ottoman period were regrouped into new units and brought under a stifling central control which has only relaxed to some extent during the past decade. Until 1982 all local authority decisions had to be approved for expediency by the prefect, a restriction which still applies in a number of important cases including the sale of municipal land. The prefect's obligation to scrutinize all municipal decisions for compatibility with the law continues to provide central government with a means of delaying the implementation of decisions not to its liking.

In contrast to those other West European countries which have redefined their local government units during the last two decades, local government in Greece continues to be based on the municipalities and communities (*demoi* and *koinotites* in Greek) established in 1912. The communities, initially with a minimum of 300 inhabitants, now officially represent 1,000–10,000 people, while the municipalities are supposed to have at least 10,000 inhabitants. However, there is no obligation on units whose population falls below the specified levels to merge with others.[7] Consequently, Greece with a population of less than 10 million currently has 5,999 local government units, of which an astounding 5,695 are communities with less than 1,000 inhabitants.

Even more striking, 3,284 of these communities represent less than 500 inhabitants.[8] It is obviously impossible for such dwarf units either to develop into a serious level of planning and implementation or to do anything but raise a shrill voice of protest in the face of central government dictates. Clearly there is a need for intermediate layers of government between the two levels – central government and first-tier local government (the municipalities and communities) – specified in the 1975 Constitution.

II. PREFECTURE COUNCILS

During the history of the Greek nation-state, there have been several experiments with intermediate tiers of local government, mostly focused on the prefecture.[9] It is perhaps an obvious choice, as the prefecture is already established in the popular consciousness as a political entity. Long accepted as an administrative unit, it also serves as the electoral constituency for national elections. However, a disadvantage of creating intermediate local government institutions at this level is that with 55 prefectures, the units are still too small either to stand up to central government or to provide an efficient unit for the regional planning process.

In the post-Second World War period, Law 3200 of 1955 established prefecture councils with a remit to discuss the prefecture public works programme and to make proposals concerning the development of the prefecture, the functioning of the public services and issues of labour, health, social welfare, etc. Given this purely advisory role and the fact that they were to meet only twice a year, these councils were particularly unlikely to disrupt existing decision-making structures. While their members included one local government representative from each sub-prefecture, the councils were basically composed of high-level state functionaries in the prefecture, such as the chief of police and the head of the financial service. They should thus be seen essentially as part of the administrative system.

Although the 1950s were marked by some attempts at bureaucratic modernization, like Law 3200 of 1955, the prevailing political climate was hardly conducive to experiments with new forms of political participation including local government institutions. Following the Civil War of 1946–49, the Greek government aimed at the political demobilization of those sectors of the population who had been politically awakened and radicalized through the Communist-dominated Resistance of the Second World War. One method was the excessive expansion of the state bureaucracy, offering social security benefits only to those deemed politically fit for civil service jobs. Thus it has been suggested that the clientelist system, benefiting only a section of the population regarded as holding politically acceptable views, substituted for the development of a Welfare State covering the population as a whole.[10] In consequence, social welfare provision, one of the main areas of local government responsibilities elsewhere in Western Europe, remained backward in Greece.

The climate for local government became even bleaker when new demands for political participation, expressed by the 'Unyielding

Struggle' movements of the 1960s, led to the imposition of military dictatorship in 1967. Under the Junta, elected local councils were replaced by government appointees. With the Colonels' fall in 1974, the establishment of a true parliamentary democracy in contrast to the repressive parliamentarism of the pre-dictatorship period, opened up new opportunities for political participation. However, the government of New Democracy (ND), in power throughout the 1970s, had a fundamentally centralist approach and did not take advantage of the provision in the 1975 Constitution allowing new tiers of local government to be created by Acts of Parliament.[11]

Then in 1981, PASOK (the Panhellenic Socialist Movement) came to power with an ideological commitment to decentralization[12] and the following year relaunched the prefecture councils. By common consent, the councils of 1955 had been a failure and in some areas had not functioned at all during previous years.[13] Under Law 1235 of 1982 the councils' functions continue to be mainly advisory. For example, they are allowed to propose the inclusion of particular projects in their prefecture in public sector programmes and to give opinions on prefecture cultural, social and developmental affairs. However, they have also been explicitly allocated a role in the development planning process, with decision-making powers concerning the drawing up and amendment of the prefecture public works programme. The councils also have to approve the Prefecture Fund budget, previously the responsibility of the Ministries of Finance and the Interior.

Two other factors significantly upgraded the role of the prefecture councils. First, under Law 1235/1982, they have to meet once a month or whenever two-thirds of their members demand it, thus considerably increasing their possibilities of effective intervention. Second, a major change in their composition has led to a fundamental shift in their nature. From civil service committees adorned by a local government component, they have been transformed into advisory councils representing the various organized interests of the prefecture.

The prefect has continued to act as president of the council. But other state functionaries, although allowed to attend council meetings, no longer have the right to vote. Local government representatives now make up half the council. In addition to the sub-prefecture representatives specified in Law 3200/1955, the council now also includes the mayor of the leading municipality in the prefecture and two representatives of the Local Association of Local Authorities (TEDK). The remaining members are elected by the prefecture-level governing committees of professional organizations, agricultural co-operatives, labour movement organizations and chambers of commerce.[14] Thus the council has ceased to be an integral part of the central administration system. But although Article 1 of Law 1235/1982 described them as 'organs of popular representation', they should not be confused with directly elected local government institutions. Rather they appear to have been designed as a local interest group input into the prefecture-level policy-making process.

However, Law 1235 explicitly stated that these prefecture councils were a transitional institution, which would help to prepare the way for new tiers of local government. With the introduction of the EC's Integrated Mediterranean Programmes (IMPs), the creation of new subnational levels which could be used as basic units in the planning process, became a necessity. For the purposes of the IMPs, the country was divided into six areas (Aegean Islands, Crete, Northern Greece, Western Greece and the Peloponnese, Central and Eastern Greece, and Attica), but subsequently Law 1622 of 1986 defined 13 administrative Regions (*Perifereies*) and legislated for a major upgrading of the prefecture councils.

Law 1622 provided for prefecture councils ranging in size from 27 to 51 members according to the population of the prefecture. Seventy-five per cent of the members would be directly elected, while 15–20 per cent would continue to be chosen by interest groups.[15] There was also a reversion to the concept of a civil service component, with the inclusion of between two and five administrative representatives to be selected by the prefect. Law 1622 still denied the councils legislative powers, but gave them considerable new responsibilities, including drawing up the prefecture's medium-term development programme. Together with the abolition of the Prefecture Fund and the transfer of all its responsibilities to the councils, this meant the latter would essentially have gained control over the prefecture public works budget.[16] Other new responsibilities were to include a variety of social welfare tasks, such as the provision of nurseries and care for the elderly.

The PASOK government, in power until June 1989, did not implement Law 1622. Then in March 1990, the 'ecumenical' government supported by Greece's three major parties, PASOK, the right-wing New Democracy (ND), and the communist dominated Coalition of the Forces of the Left and Progress (Synaspismos or Syn), legislated for elections to the new local government institutions to take place in October 1990, with the new councils scheduled to come into existence in January 1991. But after its electoral victory in April 1990, the new ND government cancelled the elections and the decentralization process in Greece took a major step backwards.

III. THE SURVEY

Our survey, conducted in May and early June 1989, was conceived as a 'snapshot' of an infant institution on the eve of its evolution into a more substantial organ of decentralized government. In turn, proponents of decentralization saw the elected prefecture councils as only the preliminary to the creation of more effective units at the new regional level. However, in the end Law 1622/1986 has remained an exercise in wishful thinking. Hence, in practice our report concerns an institution which seems likely to continue functioning in its present form for the immediately foreseeable future.

Our research was conducted through a series of face-to-face interviews,[17] using a modified version of the 'master' questionnaire developed in Florence and first used to complete the Italian survey of political and interest group leaders. The overlap between prefecture council and interest group membership meant that in the Greek case, in contrast to the other countries included in the survey, it would have been a dubious exercise to conduct separate studies of council members and observers. Instead, the interviews focused exclusively on prefecture councillors (including both elected public officials representing municipal governments and those representing locally important interest groups). The Greek study was thus a survey of a political/interest group elite operating at a level above local government.

In order to obtain a geographically representative sample, we initially chose one prefecture from each of the 13 administrative Regions, with the aim of interviewing 12 councillors in each case. The sample was subsequently increased to include three other prefectures in Attica to take account of the fact that more than one-third of Greece's population lives there. Our total sample was 155 prefecture councillors. The number of interviews completed by area is shown in Table 1.

IV. PROFILE OF THE PREFECTURE COUNCILLORS

The representation of organizations in our sample reflected the provisions of Law 1235/1982 defining the membership of the council, with local government clearly predominant. Fifty-five per cent came from local government, 16.8 per cent from chambers of commerce, 8.7 per cent from labour centres, 7.4 per cent from agricultural co-operatives, 4.7 per cent from professional organizations and 3.4 per cent from agricultural associations. A further four per cent came from other organizations. Less than five per cent had served on the old councils before 1982, while the majority (57.5 per cent) had joined since the beginning of 1987. This was

TABLE 1
INTERVIEWS CONDUCTED BY PREFECTURE

Prefecture	Region	Number of interviews	Percentage of sample
Achaia	Western Greece	12	7.7
Arkadia	Peloponnese	10	6.5
Athens	Attica	6	3.9
West & East Attica	Attica	14	9.0
Corfu	Ionian Islands	7	4.5
Dodecanese	Aegean Islands	11	7.1
Evia	Central Greece	11	7.1
Evros	Eastern Macedonia	9	5.8
Grevena	Western Macedonia	9	5.8
Herakleion	Crete	12	7.7
Magnissia	Thessaly	10	6.5
Mytilini	Northern Aegean	9	5.8
Pella	Central Macedonia	8	5.2
Piraeus	Attica	15	9.7
Thesprotia	Epirus	12	7.7
		155	100.0

due both to the change in local government representation at the beginning of that year as a result of the municipal elections and to the fact that representatives from organizations serve only a two-year term.

Our survey suggests that the prefecture councils are largely staffed[18] by well-educated, upwardly mobile professionals who are already established in provincial political life.

Agewise, the members of our sample ranged from 24 to 73 years old. More than half fell into the 30–45 age group while a further third were aged from 46 to 60. Only a small minority (6.9 per cent) were over 60 and even fewer (2.4 per cent) under 30. A striking 53.5 per cent of the respondents claimed to be graduates of universities or other institutes of higher education, compared to the four per cent among the population aged 10+ shown in the 1981 census.[19] In addition, a further 13.6 per cent of our councillors had completed some kind of further education. In marked contrast, only 9.7 per cent of the respondents' fathers were university graduates, while almost two-thirds had gone no further than primary school.

A comparison of the professional backgrounds of our sample with those of their fathers confirms the extensive social mobility which has taken place, reflecting a more general trend in Greece as a result of rapid socio-economic change since the Second World War. Among the fathers, the most numerous occupational category were farmers (39 per cent), followed by self-employed craftsmen, small-scale traders and entrepreneurs, and shopkeepers (24 per cent), and workers (7.8 per cent skilled and 3.9 per cent unskilled). Liberal professionals accounted for only 5.7 per cent, and civil servants and teachers (all levels, including university) for 6.1 per cent.

Meanwhile, the majority of the councillors came from white-collar strata, with professionals (42.5 per cent) clearly dominant. However, the inclusion of delegates from agricultural organizations, labour centres and professional chambers, has prevented the councils' complete bourgeoisification. Thus our sample also included farmers (14.9 per cent), skilled workers (5.8 per cent) and self-employed craftsmen, small-scale traders and entrepreneurs, and shopkeepers (nine per cent). Given the usual trend in elected bodies, it could be expected that direct elections would change the social composition of the councils, increasing the representation of the professional classes at the expense of farmers and workers.

The political background of our councillors was also indicative of historical differences between their generation and that of their fathers. While two councillors claimed to have had a relative in Parliament, the majority could not be regarded as the offspring of traditional political families even at the local level. Although 84.6 per cent of the councillors declared that their fathers had shown some degree of interest in politics, this is not surprising in the Greek context, where the traditional predominance of clientelism has meant that party political concerns penetrate even minor bread-and-butter issues of daily life. In the main, this interest was not translated into activism. Only just over a third of our sample had relatives who had participated actively in politics, while the main areas of activity cited – the wartime National Resistance (32.4 per cent), the local community council (28.4 per cent) and party member/cadre (16.2 per cent) – reflected the lack of opportunities for active political involvement in post-Civil War Greece.

The political careers of our councillors themselves appear to be an

TABLE 2
PARTY POLITICAL COMPOSITION OF OUR SAMPLE, COMPARED TO THE ELECTORATE AS A WHOLE AS INDICATED BY THE PARLIAMENTARY ELECTIONS OF JUNE 1985 AND JUNE 1989

Party	Members of sample who declared party membership Number	Percent	Election results June 1985	June 1989	Difference between sample and electorate 1985	1989
PASOK	81	65.9%	45.8%	39.2%	+20.1%	+26.7%
ND	22	17.9%	40.8%	44.3%	-22.9%	-26.4%
Syn	16	13.0%	11.7%	13.1%	+1.3%	-0.1%
Small parties	4	3.3%	1.7%	3.4%	+1.6%	-0.1%
Total	123	100.0%				

Note: As the Syn was only formed in December 1988, the 1985 figure consists of the combined vote of its two major component parties, KKE and the former Eurocommunist KKE-Eseterikou. Of our 16 Syn councillors, 15 belonged to KKE and one to EAR.

almost exclusively post-dictatorship phenomenon. Asked to list up to four political party positions and four public offices which they had held, the councillors cited a total of 538 posts. Only 1.3 per cent pre-dated the Colonels' fall in 1974 while 82.5 per cent began in the 1980s. The existence of this more politically active generation, product of the freer political conditions of the post-1974 era, suggests a societal and not purely an administrative need for new instititutions, including local government, as channels of political expression.

Table 2 compares the political affiliation of those respondents who declared party membership, with the preferences of the electorate at large as indicated by the results of both the previous general election of June 1985 and that of June 1989 which took place immediately after our survey. The councils' striking over-representation of the then governing party, PASOK, mainly at the expense of the official opposition, ND, is due to the fact that their membership is based on interest groups and local government. Professional organizations in Greece are highly party politicized, traditionally being dominated by the governing party.[20] Meanwhile, for much of the post-war period, local government has been a bastion of non-right political forces, which in the post-dictatorship era meant particularly PASOK and the Greek Communist Party (KKE). Thus the imbalance in party representation would have been even more pronounced before PASOK's losses in the 1986 municipal elections reduced its local government representatives on the councils.[21]

However, this imbalance may be less significant than it seems. That our sample was by no means made up of professional party cadres was indicated by the fact that those devoting more than one-tenth of their time to their party at the national, prefecture and local levels accounted respectively for only 5.0, 26.4 and 18.3 per cent of our respondents. Only one-fifth of our respondents were current holders of at least one party post, while 29.0 per cent did not list any party posts (in addition to the 19.4 per cent who did not belong to a party). Overall, our sample had held far fewer party political (148) than public posts (390). This reflects the way the councillors are chosen, on the basis of public service posts and not through selection by political parties. It would seem reasonable to assume that this would affect the way in which the councillors see their role, less as party politicians rather than as representatives of local interests. This supposition seems to be borne out by evidence from our survey (to be discussed later).

That 42.7 per cent of our councillors claimed to spend more than half of their time on non-political (personal and professional) activities suggests that they are very much part-time politicians. Asked how much of their time they currently devote to the councils, 63.3 per cent of our sample claimed the proportion was ten per cent or less; in only 1.9 per cent of cases was the figure over 30 per cent and in no case did it exceed 50 per cent. This is hardly surprising given that service on the council is unpaid, making it hard for the councillors to develop into professionals.

Here it is worth noting that the implementation of Law 1622/1986 would have included the creation of a salaried president of the council, to have been elected by the councillors from among their number. The role of the Prefect would have been correspondingly downgraded. Although the Prefect would have retained voting rights, he would no longer have presided over council meetings or set the agenda. Hence, this government appointee who can be recalled at any moment would have faced an alternative power source in a new full-time cadre of a council legitimated by direct elections. Supporters of decentralization expected this development to inaugurate a long-term, if limited, shift in the centre-periphery power balance.

V. ASSESSMENT OF THE PREFECTURE COUNCILS

At present, the councils seem to suffer from a generally low public profile. A team from the Hellenic Agency for Local Government and Local Development (EETAA) who conducted a pilot study in Larissa,[22] found that local society seemed unaware of the existence and functioning of the councils. Our survey suggests that the role played by the councillors in the political life of their prefectures is chiefly determined by their other political posts.

That members of the public mainly addressed the councillors in their other capacities, for example, as mayor or president of the local labour centre, was indicated by our finding concerning the statistically significant variations in contact levels with individual citizens between councillors representing different organizations. Asked to indicate contact levels on a five-point scale from 'at least once a week' to 'never', the overwhelming majority of councillors from associations, local government and agricultural co-ops claimed they saw individual citizens at least once a week, compared to only 32 per cent of councillors from chambers and 14.3 per cent of those from professional unions. Statistically significant differences according to organization were also noted in frequency of contacts with the prefect and with civil servants and representatives of interest groups at the prefecture level, factors in prefecture political life with whom our respondents could have been expected to have had frequent dealings in connection with council business.

The councillors did not evaluate their political influence on the life of the prefecture very highly. The majority rated it as 'medium' (40.3 per cent) or 'little' (33.1 per cent). As Table 3 shows, this indicates that the councillors see themselves as one of the least influential groups in the political life of the prefecture. The table also illustrates the extensive centralization of political life. The groups seen as most influential have national political posts: national party leaders and government ministers, with the press also seen as playing a significant role. Of the 'local' political factors, the most significant is perceived to be the government-appointed prefect, followed by private economic interests, prefecture-level party leaders, local personalities, Members of Parliament (MPs) and state economic agencies.

The higher rating of the local party boss in relation to the MP is indicative of the post-dictatorship shift away from traditional clientelism, in which the MP is the key figure in the distribution of civil service jobs and public sector investments, towards a new bureaucratic clientelism mediated through the party machine.[23] The prefecture councils seem already to have played some role in further undermining the patronage role of the MP. The EETAA team reported that local community council

TABLE 3

EVALUATION OF THE INFLUENCE OF VARIOUS FACTORS ON THE POLITICAL LIFE OF THE PREFECTURE

Factors Group	Great or Very Great	Medium	Little	None
National party leaders	85.1%	11.0%	3.9%	-
Government ministers	69.4%	25.3%	4.5%	0.6%
Press	65.6%	26.6%	7.1%	0.6%
Prefect	61.1%	30.5%	7.1%	1.3%
Members of Parliament	55.2%	33.8%	9.7%	1.3%
Private economic interests	52.6%	27.3%	17.5%	2.6%
Prefecture party leaders	49.3%	40.9%	9.1%	0.6%
Trade unions	47.7%	39.9%	11.1%	1.3%
Local personalities	44.5%	35.3%	17.6%	2.6%
State economic agencies	41.6%	39.0%	18.2%	1.3%
Agricultural associations & co-ops	35.9%	37.9%	22.9%	3.3%
Church	34.7%	35.9%	19.6%	9.8%
Local party leaders	34.4%	50.6%	11.0%	3.9%
Prefecture councillors	18.8%	40.3%	33.1%	7.8%
Senior civil servants at Regional, prefecture & local levels	14.2%	44.8%	33.8%	7.1%

leaders in Larissa had started lobbying the prefecture councils for allocations from the public investment budget rather than appealing to local MPs to apply pressure on the centre to obtain public works funding as in the past.[24] It is interesting that even with the current comparatively weak councils, some shift away from traditional channels of influence towards local government institutions seems to have begun. This trend would undoubtedly be accelerated if the prefecture councils were to be directly elected.

Despite the councils' current comparative lack of influence and prestige, our sample regarded them in a very positive light. The overwhelming majority (94.8 per cent) disagreed that the creation of the prefecture councils had been an error. When the questions moved on from the prefecture councils as an institution to their own councils in particular, levels of support remained high but less enthusiastic. Asked for an overall evaluation of their own council, only 7.9 per cent described them as 'very satisfactory'. However, only 14.6 per cent described them as 'not at all satisfactory'. These assessments of their own councils were strongly influenced by the respondents' party affiliation. Thus 95.1 per cent of PASOK members agreed that their own council had functioned satisfactorily, compared to 45.4 per cent of ND and 12.5 per cent of Syn councillors. Meanwhile the statement that 'realistically speaking, in this prefecture it is difficult to foresee major accomplishments of the councils' found 100 per cent of Syn and 90.9 per cent of ND members but only 34.6 per cent of PASOK members in agreement.

Moving on from what the councils could be expected to do in the future to what they had achieved already, the general assessment was overwhelmingly positive. Eighty-six per cent believed that the creation of the councils had more positive than negative results while 5.2 per cent believed there had been as many positive as negative results. Only a small minority claimed the councils had more negative than positive results or neither negative nor positive results. Even half of those who had rated their own council's performance as 'not at all satisfactory' believed the creation of the councils had more positive than negative results.

Our respondents were then asked an open-ended question, requiring them to cite two successes and two failures of their own councils. Analysis of the successes and failures in Table 4 shows that the largest categories concerned specific public works projects (35.1 per cent of successes and 23 per cent of failures) and planning (22.5 per cent of successes and 33.0 per cent of failures). Seven per cent of successes concerned the functioning of the prefecture councils themselves, for example, 'decision-making through democratic procedures' and 'a consensus on local issues regardless of party political positions'. Functioning of the councils also accounted for 10.8 per cent of failures, two examples given being 'the negative involvement of a local MP in council affairs' and 'decisions being taken by a minority controlled by the prefect'. Issues concerning the relationship between the prefecture and the central government accounted for only 1.5 per cent of successes and 6.0 per cent of failures.

The respondents' own selection of successes and failures indicates that the major focus of the councils' work is on planning and decisions concerning public works, whether this involves cutting up the allocations of the Prefecture Fund budget at local level or pressing for the inclusion of particular projects in other public sector programmes. However, as Table 5 shows, when asked to indicate the priorities of the prefecture council

TABLE 4

RESPONDENTS' EVALUATION OF THE MAJOR SUCCESSES AND FAILURES OF THEIR OWN PREFECTURE COUNCILS

Sector	Successes	Failures
Planning, studies, distribution of funds	15.8%	26.9%
Institutional questions of local government	11.2%	6.9%
Agricultural infrastructure	10.2%	5.4%
Regional and other conferences	9.7%	1.5%
Issues related to functioning of council	7.1%	10.8%
Ecology-environment	6.1%	6.9%
Water, sewage, electrification	5.1%	5.4%
Roads, transport	5.1%	3.8%
Education	4.6%	-
Sports and tourism	4.5%	1.6%
Physical planning	3.6%	4.6%
Industry	3.6%	3.0%
Integrated Mediterranean Programmes	3.1%	1.5%
Issues of popular participation & information	2.0%	3.0%
Prefecture-central government relations	1.5%	6.0%
Issues of functioning of prefecture	1.5%	3.8%
Management of state property	1.5%	3.0%
Cultural affairs	1.0%	3.0%
Hospitals, social services	1.0%	0.8%
Co-operatives	1.0%	-
Firefighting	-	1.5%
Charity	0.5%	-
Total	100.0%	100.0%

TABLE 5
RESPONDENTS' EVALUATION OF THE PRIORITIES OF THE PREFECTURE COUNCIL

	1st priority	2nd priority	3rd priority
Defend the interests of the prefecture at the national level	36.2%	19.2%	11.3%
Investigate the prefecture's social and economic problems and propose solutions	25.7%	19.2%	21.3%
Defend local government interests at the prefecture level	15.1%	19.9%	25.5%
Protect national interests in prefecture-level discussions	13.2%	16.6%	7.8%
Promote national party political struggle in the prefecture context	3.3%	4.0%	5.0%
Mediate the conflicting interests of the various groups in the prefecture	2.6%	2.6%	1.9%
Defend the interests of the less protected sector of society	2.0%	9.9%	9.2%
Control the activities of the Regional and prefecture administrations and of local government	1.3%	7.9%	14.9%
Aid individual citizens in dealings with the public administration	0.7%	0.7%	2.8%

from a list of nine options, 'defending the interests of the prefecture at national level' was the most popular choice, selected as first priority by 35.9 per cent and second or third priority by another 43.1 per cent. Second choice was 'investigating the social and economic problems of the prefecture and finding solutions for them', followed by 'defending the interests of local government at the prefecture level'. These results suggest that the councillors see the councils as primarily a prefecture pressure group operating at the national level, and only secondarily as an organization dealing at a practical level with local problems.

Given the endemic party politicization in Greece, it is interesting that 'promoting the national party political struggle in the prefecture context' was a comparatively low priority. This may be due to the composition of the councils, as members selected to represent organizations may be less interested in promoting party struggle than those elected as political party candidates. In turn, this would reinforce the tendency to see the councils more as a regional pressure group than as a miniature parliament operating at the prefecture level. The low priority given to 'defending the interests of the less protected sector of society' reflects the councils' general lack of social welfare functions, something which differentiates local government in Greece from its West European equivalents. Interestingly enough, given the traditional prevalence of clientelism based on face-to-face relations between politicians and their supporters, 'aiding individual citizens in their dealings with the public administration' came out as lowest priority of all. Second lowest priority was 'mediating the conflicting interests of the various groups of the prefecture'.

Initially this seems surprising. Given that more than half of the councillors are currently selected by local interest groups, they might have been expected to be particularly concerned with promoting sectoral interests. But because these councillors are not directly elected by the base of their organizations and receive no specific mandate for the prefecture council, in practice they represent little more than their own personal view. The broader political culture of Greece should also be borne in mind. The concept of politics as mediation between different interest groups has not taken root to the same extent as in other West European countries as indicated by the very small proportion of our sample who saw this as the principal role of the politician.

When analysing the frequency of contact with interest group representatives, shown in Table 6, the dual role of those councillors who are also themselves interest group leaders should be borne in mind. It should be noted that there were significant variations in frequency of meetings according to organization, once more suggesting that most of our councillors' contacts were made in their other capacities (for example, as president of the local labour centre or mayor of the largest municipality in the prefecture). Meanwhile, the comparative infrequency of contacts with national level interest group representatives indicates that the latter have yet to see the prefecture as a legitimate level for the promotion of their objectives.

Despite this, the majority of respondents felt that the councils had some impact on the interests of their organizations (described by 40.4 per cent as 'relatively decisive' and 23.2 per cent as 'very decisive'), while only 13.7 per cent felt it had been 'not at all decisive'. Moreover, 73.8 per cent summed up this impact as positive as opposed to the 26.2 per cent who felt it had been negative. It will be interesting in the future to see to

TABLE 6
FREQUENCY OF CONTACT BETWEEN PREFECTURE COUNCILLORS AND INTEREST GROUP REPRESENTATIVES

	Interest group representatives		
Frequency of contact	National level	Prefecture level	Local level
Once or more per week	1.3%	14.1%	32.9%
Fairly regularly	20.1%	44.3%	44.3%
Only occasionally	34.9%	32.9%	15.4%
Rarely	32.9%	6.0%	5.4%
Never	10.7%	2.7%	2.0%
Total	100.0%	100.0%	100.0%

what extent the prefecture councils succeed in evolving into a forum for the mediation of differing interests at prefecture level.

Given the intense party politicization of most public fora in Greece, the question naturally arises whether the councils have become, like the majority of interest groups, 'an apple of discord' between the major political parties.[25] Certainly, 90.2 per cent of our sample believed that politics at the prefecture level should be seen primarily as part of the national political struggle. Yet as mentioned above, the suggestion that the councils' role is to promote the national party political struggle in the context of the prefecture did not score particularly highly in our sample's assessment of the councils' priorities.

Indeed, our survey suggested that in practice, our councillors inclined towards the opposite view. It was notable that a clear majority disagreed that it is hard for ideologically opposed parties to find themselves in agreement on regional problems: 60.8 per cent 'more or less' or 'completely' disagreed, an assessment which was not influenced by political party affiliation. One of our more striking results was that 86.4 per cent of our sample claimed that in their own councils, co-operation in solving a particular problem was more common than marked differences of opinion. This would seem to confirm the EETAA team finding in Larissa concerning cases where councillors overcame political party antagonisms in order to confront specific issues.[26] Here it is worth remembering the perception of the largest group of our respondents, who saw the councils primarily as a regional pressure group operating at the national level.

VI. ATTITUDES TOWARDS DECENTRALIZATION

As an interim verdict, it appears that the prefecture councils created by Law 1235/1982, despite their limited powers, constitute an important step forward in the decentralization process. As we have seen, even in the short time in which they have functioned, the councils have already begun to have an impact on Greece's traditional political structures. They have also contributed to raising awareness of the need for further decentralization, particularly among the prefecture-level political elites who actually participate in the councils.

In the past, decentralization was predominantly a left/centre demand in the face of the right-wing state. However, in the 1980s with PASOK occupying the state machine, New Democracy, like the left and centre before it, began to use local government as a forum for opposition. Indeed, even before losing power to PASOK in 1981, there had already been some relaxation in ND's centralist practice. The need to adapt to Greece's imminent EC membership has been regarded as the reason behind the new Municipal Code and law on local government financing which the party introduced in 1980.[27] Subsequently, ND's ideological relaunch under Constantine Mitsotakis, party leader since 1984, included the adoption of a neoliberal programme based on 'rolling back the frontiers of the state'. In many sectors, this could be interpreted as favouring decentralization, in the sense of allowing the untrammelled operation of private enterprise at the local level.[28]

Thus among our sample, support for decentralization could be described as overwhelming. As Table 7 shows, when our sample was asked whether the central state or the prefecture should have more powers in specific sectors, the pro-decentralization majority was high in 13 of the 16 cases. The exceptions were the university system, scientific research and exports. Moreover, in 15 cases there were no statistically significant variations in attitudes by party. Only in the case of the police were the ND councillors notably less decentralist than the others: 52.4 per cent favoured the prefecture having more powers than central government, in contrast to 81.3 per cent of PASOK and 85.7 per cent of KKE members. However, given the traditional links between the police and the right, perhaps more striking is the fact that even in this case a small ND majority favoured decentralization.

It should of course be borne in mind that as prefecture councillors, the members of our sample have a particular interest in decentralization. This was indicated by the fact that all our ND respondents supported direct elections to the prefecture councils, despite their party's centralist tradition. This suggests that, at the prefecture level, there is a cross-party consensus around the need for decentralization, regardless of national party preferences.

TABLE 7
WHETHER THE PREFECTURE OR THE CENTRAL STATE SHOULD HAVE MORE POWER OVER SPECIFIC SECTORS

Sector	Central state	Prefecture
Cultural affairs	4.6%	95.4%
Taxes for local projects	6.8%	93.2%
Small and medium enterprises/artisanry	9.9%	90.1%
Conservation of the environment	11.2%	88.8%
Agriculture	14.4%	85.6%
Health	17.6%	82.4%
Public works	17.9%	82.1%
Employment	20.5%	79.5%
Police	22.0%	78.0%
Transportation	26.3%	73.7%
School education	27.6%	72.4%
Subsidies	31.1%	68.9%
Industrial development	40.0%	60.0%
Scientific research	58.1%	41.9%
Exports	59.3%	40.7%
University education	67.1%	32.9%

VII. LOCAL GOVERNMENT AND THE EUROPEAN COMMUNITY

Entry to the European Community has intensified the already long overdue need for radical change in the public sector planning process.

Our parallel study on the Integrated Mediterranean Programmes revealed that Greece's over-centralized structures are a major obstacle to the absorption of Community funding. As European Community membership seems likely to play an important role in promoting decentralization, the question naturally arises how our regional elite sample, in the front line of decentralization, viewed their EC environment.

Greece's EC membership was a highly controversial domestic issue. Accession in January 1981 was preceded by an intensely polemical debate, characterized by 'the politics of exaggeration',[29] in which the cleavage closely followed party lines. ND built its 'European' image around its pro-accession policy, to which PASOK was strongly opposed. While the Synaspismos had yet to be formed, its dominant member-party, the KKE, was also a vehement opponent of EC membership, while other forces, including the then Eurocommunist party, were conditionally in favour. However, PASOK's government practice following its 1981 electoral victory, ten months after accession, indicated a tacit acceptance of what was already a *fait accompli*. PASOK's stance became more openly pro-European after its second election victory in 1985. Later in the decade, the pressure of *perestroika* pushed the KKE in the same direction. In the spring of 1988 the publication of its 'Theses on 1992' marked a distinct break with the party's tradition of opposition to Greece's EC orientation which dated back to the first discussions about the Association Agreement in the late 1950s. A basic minimum consensus around the EC had also been a *sine qua non* for the formation of the Synaspismos later the same year. Although within the KKE the issue of the Community continued to be a cause of friction between conservatives and 'renewalists' which contributed to the 1991 party split and the KKE hardliners' subsequent withdrawal from the Synaspismos and return to an anti-EC stance. However, at the time of our survey, the Left's official policy was acceptance of EC membership.

The growing consensus around the EC in national party politics was reflected in our regional politicians' overwhelming support for the broadening of the Community's scope. Thus, asked whether the EC should acquire more functions after 1992, over 70 per cent of our sample agreed in ten out of 12 specific sectors with over 85 per cent agreeing in nine sectors, as shown in Table 8. Not surprisingly, given Greece's economic backwardness relative to the rest of the EC, our sample was almost unanimously in favour of the Community acquiring more responsibilities related to 'financing projects in disadvantaged areas'.

TABLE 8
WHETHER THE EC SHOULD ACQUIRE A GREATER ROLE IN SPECIFIC SECTORS AFTER 1992

Sector	More than before	Same as before	Less than before
Financing of projects in disadvantaged areas	98.7%	1.3%	-
Promotion of technological innovation	90.7%	1.3%	-
Control over the application of standards in environmental and urban planning	95.5%	2.6%	1.9%
Ensuring a European perspective for scientific research	94.7%	4.6%	0.7%
Monitoring financial markets	90.1%	7.9%	2.0%
Evaluation of regional investment projects	89.6%	8.4%	1.9%
Coordinating foreign trade	87.3%	8.0%	4.7%
Formulating basic guidelines for vocational training	86.5%	7.7%	5.8%
Monitoring the labour market	86.4%	11.0%	2.6%
Controlling immigration from non-Community countries	70.4%	20.4%	9.2%
Promoting the integration of non-Community immigrants	47.0%	33.1%	19.9%
Financing a European defence policy	35.1%	31.8%	33.1%

Of the two sectors where only a minority favoured the expansion of the EC's powers, one was 'the promotion of integration of non-Community emigrants'. In Greece during the 1980s this had become associated with allowing freedom of movement to workers from neighbouring Turkey, a country which is perceived as posing a direct threat to Greece's national integrity. Presumably, the influx of refugees from Albania at the beginning of the 1990s will now have made this an even more unpopular issue. The other area where a majority disagreed with the EC acquiring more powers – and indeed where one-third of the sample wanted a decrease in the EC's role – was the financing of European defence policy. This was also the only sector where our sample's attitudes varied significantly by party: 63.6 per cent of ND members favoured the expansion of the EC's defence role as opposed to 29.6 per cent of PASOK and 18.8 per cent of

Syn members. Interestingly enough, it may have been their party's traditional Atlanticism which made the ND councillors more reluctant to see the EC's expansion into defence than into other sectors; while on the contrary, the opposition of the PASOK and Syn members was probably due to fears that the EC would develop into a West European NATO.

The response of the PASOK councillors indicates a divergence of opinion from their party leadership, given that Prime Minister Papandreou had accepted the search for a common identity on security matters within the framework of European Political Cooperation as long ago as the Milan summit in June 1984 and had announced his intention of taking Greece into the West European Union in 1987. However, our sample's attitudes are now outdated: their parties' positions had been strongly influenced by the cold war division of Europe into blocs. Since we conducted our field work, the collapse of the East European regimes has led to the question of European defence being reformulated in a completely new framework. The Eurobarometer survey conducted in October 1990 indicated that there had been a major change in Greek public opinion on this point. At this time, two-thirds of Greek respondents apparently now regarded a common defence organization as a necessity,[30] which meant that of the 12 EC members, Greece had the third highest majority in favour of the Community acquiring a security dimension. It would be particularly interesting to measure responses to this question among regional elites after the Gulf War and the Yugoslav crisis.

Support for the creation of new EC institutions to meet the challenges of the post-1992 period was again almost unanimous. In 12 out of 13 sectors, over four-fifths of the sample were in favour. A slightly less enthusiastic response was elicited by the proposal for the creation of a European administrative court to settle disputes between regional and central governments, although a clear majority still agreed with the idea.

However, a comparison of attitudes by political party, shown in Table 9, indicated that the Syn councillors in every case were less enthusiastic than their colleagues about the proposed institutions and sometimes significantly so. But given that until a few years ago, the Syn's main component, the KKE, was still denouncing European Community funding as damaging because it tied Greece more firmly into an allegedly dependent relationship with the EC, what is more striking is that in only one case (that of the European administrative court, which was also less popular with the other parties) was a majority of Syn councillors against the creation of new Community institutions.

Certainly, even in the very recent past, co-operation between regions within the EC would almost undoubtedly have been anathema to the

TABLE 9

SUPPORT FOR THE CREATION OF NEW EUROPEAN COMMUNITY INSTITUTIONS – BREAKDOWN BY POLITICAL PARTY

Institution	Total sample	PASOK	ND	Syn
European environmental agency	99.4%	100.0%	100.0%	87.5%
European conference of regional administrators	94.1%	97.5%	100.0%	75.0%
European level representation for regional councils	92.9%	98.8%	86.4%	68.8%
University postgraduate diplomas in scientific fields	92.7%	96.3%	100.0%	43.8%
European agency to monitor labour market	90.8%	96.3%	90.9%	62.5%
European telecommunications agency	89.9%	95.1%	95.5%	43.8%
Community Europrogrammes for transregional sectoral policies	89.5%	91.4%	90.9%	68.8%
Central European Bank	89.3%	92.6%	90.9%	50.0%
European stock market	88.4%	90.1%	95.5%	43.8%
Services representing the regions in Brussels	86.8%	88.9%	86.4%	68.8%
Interregional Euroconsortia for the planning of services and public infrastructures	84.3%	88.9%	90.9%	50.0%
Euroagencies for interregional cooperation for the management of services and infrastructure	82.8%	82.7%	95.5%	50.0%
European administrative court to settle disputes between regional and central governments	62.3%	58.0%	77.3%	43.8%

TABLE 10
ATTITUDES TO DIFFERENT FORMS OF INTERREGIONAL COOPERATION AFTER 1992

Sector	Opportune	Not necessary
Policies to protect the environment	96.7%	3.3%
Cultural and tourist exchange programmes	95.5%	4.5%
Plans for applied research	95.4%	4.6%
Training of civil service personnel	94.1%	5.9%
Formulation of development programmes	93.5%	6.5%
Improvement in regional airline services	92.8%	7.2%
Activities to promote products and services	90.8%	9.2%
Promotion of joint ventures between industries	90.7%	9.3%
Creation of a pressure group to lobby the EC Commission	78.4%	21.6%

KKE, on the grounds that it would bind Greece more firmly into a capitalist Western Europe. Now our Syn councillors were as overwhelmingly enthusiastic about this idea as the rest of our sample. The only marginal difference concerned the promotion of joint ventures between industries. But again, given the prominent position occupied by foreign capital in the KKE's demonology, what is more important is that 56.3 per cent of the Syn members in our sample were in favour. The responses to this question, shown in Table 10, suggest that proposals for inter-regional co-operation would fall on fertile soil in Greece.

So far, however, Greek participation in intra-European local government meetings has been minimal. Only with the Integrated Mediterranean Programmes did Greece begin to take part in meetings of the European regions. One obstacle, the uncertainty concerning political attitudes towards the EC, has now clearly been removed: there seems no doubt that any future Greek government will support the integration process. However, the lack of suitable decentralized bodies remains a major problem. While the creation of directly elected prefecture councils could help to rectify this situation, the latter's restricted powers will probably limit their scope for participation in inter-regional co-operation. This may become a serious problem if integration acquires a new

TABLE 11
RESPONDENT'S ASSESSMENTS OF OWN PREFECTURE'S LEVEL OF PREPARATION FOR 1992

Sector	Satisfactory	Unsatisfactory
Level of technological innovation in industry	5.3%	94.7%
Restructuring of industries	6.0%	94.0%
Structure of small and medium industry	8.4%	91.6%
Rail network	9.3%	90.7%
Skill level of labour force	12.9%	87.1%
Farm structure	17.9%	82.1%
Functionality of urban areas	20.6%	79.4%
Utilisation of historical/ environmental resources	22.7%	77.3%
University system	22.8%	77.2%
Air network	27.2%	72.8%
Road network	27.3%	72.7%
Ports	32.8%	67.2%
Social service network	32.9%	67.1%
Commercial network	34.0%	66.0%
Level of associational presence and membership	38.1%	61.9%
Health service	43.9%	56.1%

momentum at sub-national level, as seems likely. The creation of representative institutions with greater autonomy at the new Regional level would clearly provide a solution, but seems politically unlikely for the foreseeable future.

Our survey also revealed anxiety about the effects of accelerated economic integration on Greece. As Table 11 shows, a high majority of the sample considered their prefecture unprepared to meet the challenge of 1992 in all specified sectors. The state of industry, whether this concerned the structure of small and medium enterprises, industrial restructuring or the level of technological innovation, provoked particularly gloomy assessments.

However, this bleak picture was relieved by a certain amount of

TABLE 12

ANTICIPATED IMPACT OF 1992 ON THE RESPONDENT'S PREFECTURE

Sector	Will have an impact	Will not have an impact
Greater competition	94.8%	5.2%
Stimulate the adoption of new environmental standards	94.1%	5.9%
Stimulate the restructuring of agricultural production	92.2%	7.8%
Stimulate institutional renewal	91.5%	8.5%
Provide access to new financial resources	90.8%	9.2%
Modernise regional administration	90.3%	9.7%
Stimulate the restructuring of the commercial distribution network	90.1%	9.9%
Stimulate technological innovation	88.4%	11.6%
Access to new markets	88.2%	11.8%
Improve social services	79.9%	20.1%
Concentration of industry	59.5%	40.5%
Increase unemployment	56.6%	43.4%
Confusion of administrative functions	53.6%	46.4%
Worsen situation in disadvantaged areas	47.1%	52.9%
Slow down decision-making	38.1%	61.9%
Increase production costs	36.2%	63.8%
Loss of regional identity	35.5%	64.5%

optimism, as a further question revealed. Our respondents were asked whether they expected the single market to have an impact on their prefecture in 18 specified sectors. As Table 12 shows, there was a clear pattern to the answers. In almost all cases, only a minority or small majority expected potentially negative consequences of 1992 to affect their prefecture. Meanwhile beneficial results were anticipated by high majorities of councillors.

Combining these answers with those from the previous questions suggests that at least in some sectors currently regarded as unsatisfactory, for example, technological innovation, our councillors seemed to be expecting the shock of 1992 to stimulate desirable changes. Sometimes these expectations appear a little inconsistent, for example, when 88.2 per cent of the sample expected 1992 to open up new markets when, at the same time, the majority also regarded the ports, air, road and rail networks as unsatisfactory. This suggests there may be a somewhat unrealistic perception of what EC membership can be expected to do for Greece.

While our survey indicated an apparently serious lack of self-confidence about Greece's ability to function in the unified market, it also suggests that West European integration, mythologized before accession as potential salvation or catastrophe for Greece, is now viewed in a very positive light. Our results here are reinforced by Eurobarometer data, which show a considerable change in public attitudes during the decade that Greece has been a full Community member. From the 38 per cent of Greek respondents who regarded EC membership as 'a good thing' in December 1980, on the eve of the country's accession,[31] the proportion had risen to 66 per cent in October–November 1988, the last report published prior to our survey.[32] Perhaps this is not surprising, given the inflow of EC funds, which by 1989 were equivalent to 4.9 per cent of Greece's gross domestic product.[33] That the trend of Greek public opinion in relation to the EC continues to be positive was indicated by the latest Eurobarometer survey, conducted in October 1990, which showed 75 per cent of Greek respondents now saw the EC as 'a good thing', while 78 per cent believed the country had benefitted from accession.[34] Our survey results, in which nearly all proposals for the expansion of the EC were greeted with the same virtually unanimous support, suggests that the initial hostility and suspicion expressed towards the EC from many quarters in Greece has been replaced by a rather all-embracing pro-Europeanism.

In conclusion, we should emphasize two points: (1) the timid steps towards decentralization taken after the Second World War – despite an acceleration of the process in the 1980s – have left Greece with a weak system of regional government. It is doubtful whether this system can meet the challenge of European integration and the developing 'Europe of the Regions'. The prefecture councils investigated in our study differ from regional authorities in other European countries with respect to political power and executive authority. As our study showed, the councillors perceive their role mainly as a pressure group defending local interests at the central government level. The councils' relative lack of autonomy and essentially clientelistic status, coupled with a low level of confidence about regional ability to compete in the unified market as mentioned above, has restricted them to a parochial outlook not compatible with the notion of Europeanism.

(2) Our study shows that there is scope for optimism. The process of building a regional 'image' is already under way and there is also an awareness of the need to develop a regional identity within the EC. Although the pro-European attitude of many councillors is non-discriminating, the climate is favourable towards EC programmes and interventions at both national and regional levels. The concept of partnership with the EC seems to be viewed positively in the Greek regions.

In addition, since the early 1980s the prestige of local government in Greece has increased substantially. However, there is an urgent need for more political power, more autonomy and more executive authority, both at the prefecture and regional levels. The cancellation of the directly elected prefecture councils was consistent with a tradition which has seen successive Greek governments reluctant to decentralize, but whose continuation in the context of a unifying Europe is becoming increasingly hazardous. If Greece does not act soon to create effective sub-national levels of government, it may have difficulty integrating in a future Europe of the Regions. As our parallel paper on the IMPs shows, substantial decentralization seems to be a necessity for the development of a more rational planning process. In turn, this is essential for the Greek regions to escape from their parochialism and for Greece to participate fully in the European integration process.

NOTES

1. Article 102 Paragraph 5 of the 1975 Constitution declares that 'the State exercises supervision over local government organizations'. See Pontiki [*1987: p. 143*].
2. Katseli [*1987, p. 66*].
3. On the increase in the number of prefectures, see Andronopoulos and Mathioudakis [*1987, p. 53*]. Technically there are only 51 prefectures in the sense of geographical departments; however, because of the administrative sub-division of the prefecture of Attica, there are currently 55 prefecture administrations.

4. See Law 3200/1955 and Presidential Decree 3620/1956.
5. See Laws 1235/1982 and 1416/84, and Presidential Decrees 443/1983, 470/1983 and 472/1983.
6. On the prefects' position in relation to central government, see Bakogiannis [*1985*].
7. 1980s legislation trying to encourage voluntary mergers has had minimal effects in the face of deeply entrenched localism.
8. Figures from Christofilopoulou [*1990*].
9. The chief examples are the attempted reforms of Prime Minister Trikoupis at the end of the nineteenth century and the 1923 law establishing prefecture councils. A notable exception was the 'Local Government Code' of the Second World War 'Government of the Mountains' established by the National Resistance, which focused on the sub-prefecture. The code is reprinted in full in Papagiannis [*1990*]; for a brief introduction to the abortive history of prefecture councils, see Sagias and Spourdalakis [*1990*].
10. Tsoucalas [*1987*].
11. Article 102 Paragraph 1: see Pontiki [*1987: 143*].
12. See PASOK [*1981*], especially pp. 101–5.
13. See the parliamentary debate on 10 February 1982 cited by Katsoulis [*1984*].
14. As the number of sub-prefectures ranges from one to eight per prefecture (for details, see Velonias [*1987: 91–5*]) and the number of interest group representatives is not to exceed those coming from local government, the size of the councils varies considerably. The choice of organizations to be invited to select a member for the council is left up to the prefect, the only restriction being that each council should include one representative each from 'the classes of the farmers, the workers/employees, the employers and the professionals'.
15. The organizations to be represented were now specified as 'the chambers of the productive classes', unions of agricultural co-ops, labour centres, the technical chamber, the lawyers' association, the geotechnical chamber, the economic chamber and the artists' chamber.
16. Ibid., Article 57.
17. The interviews were co-ordinated by Maria Stratigaki and conducted by Beatriki Evangelinidou, Maria Liapi, Naoum Papazoglou and Georgios Pavlakis.
18. Although not measured in the survey, women councillors were a rarity.
19. *National Statistical Service* [*1987: 115*].
20. For a study on interest groups in Greece and their relationship with the state and the political parties, see Mavrogordatos [*1988*].
21. See EETAA [*1989*].
22. Ibid.
23. This development is particularly associated with the rise of PASOK. See Lyrintzis [*1984*].
24. EETAA [*1989*].
25. Mavrogordatos [*1988: 195–6*].
26. Informal interview with EETAA team member Michalis Spourdalakis, 5/3/90.
27. See Kaler-Christofilopoulou [*1989: 220*].
28. For the party's current attitudes towards decentralization, see New Democracy [*1987*].
29. Tsoukalis [*1981: 106*].
30. Eurobarometer [*1990: A39*].
31. Eurobarometer [*1980: 32–3*].
32. Eurobarometer [*1988: B56*].
33. See OECD [*1989: 68*].
34. Eurobarometer [*1990: A22*].

REFERENCES

In English

Christofilopoulou, Paraskevy, 1990, 'Local Government in Greece' in J. Hesse (ed.), *Local Government and Urban Affairs – An International Perspective* (Baden-Baden: Nomos Publications), forthcoming.

Eurobarometer, 1980, *Public Opinion in the European Community*, No. 14 (Dec.); (1988) *Public Opinion in the European Community*, No. 30 (Dec.); (1990) *Public Opinion in the European Community*, No. 34 (Dec.).

Kaler-Christofilopoulou, Paraskevy, 1989, 'Decentralisation in Post-dictatorial Greece', unpublished Ph.D. thesis for the London School of Economics and Political Science.

Katseli, Louka, 1987, 'Building a Process of Democratic Planning' in Z. Tzannatos (ed.), *Socialism in Greece* (Aldershot: Gower Press), pp. 64–73.

Lyrintzis, Christos, 1984, 'Between Socialism and Populism: The Rise of the Panhellenic Socialist Movement', unpublished Ph.D. thesis for the London School of Economics.

National Statistical Service of Greece, 1987, *Statistical Yearbook of Greece 1986* (Athens: National Statistical Service).

Tsoukalis, Loukas, 1981, *The European Community and its Mediterranean Enlargement* (London: George Allen & Unwin).

In Greek

Andronopoulos, V. and Mathioudakis, M., 1987, 'Regional Administration/Local Government: Historical Development', *Dioikitiki Metarrythmisi* 31–32 (July–Dec.) pp. 35–61.

Bakogiannis, Kostas G., 1985, 'The Legal Status of the Prefect', *Dioikitiki Metarrythmisi*, 24 (Oct–Dec.), pp. 9–17.

EETAA research team [Panos Kazakos, Ion Sagias, Michalis Spourdalakis, Michalis Christakis], 1989, unpublished pilot study on the prefecture council of Larissa.

Getimis, P., 1988, 'The Establishment of the Local State in Greece', in T. Maloutas, D. Oikonomou (eds.), *Problems of the Development of the Welfare State in Greece* (Athens: Exantas).

Katsoulis, Dimitris, 1984, 'The assembly of prefecture councils ... a new institution?', *Topiki Aftodioikisi* 40 (July–Aug.) pp. 33–48.

Mavrogordatos, George Th., 1988, *Between Pityokambtes and Prokrustes: Professional Organizations in Contemporary Greece* (Athens: Odysseas).

New Democracy, 1987, *Programme for Public Administration and Local Government* (Athens: New Democracy).

OECD, 1989, *Report on Greece 1989/1990* (Paris: Organization for Economic Cooperation and Development).

Papagiannis, P., 1990, *Local Government in Free Greece: From the Greek Enlightenment to the Codes of the Resistance* (Athens: Nea Skepsi).

PASOK, 1981, *The Contract with the People: Declaration on Government Policy* (Athens: PASOK).

Pontiki, 1987, *The Greek Constitution in Demotic Greek and Katharevousa with Comments and Observations* (Athens: Pontiki Publications).

Sagias, Ion and Michalis Spourdalakis, 1990, *Prefecture Councils: History, Functioning, Prospects (An Initial Evaluation)* (Athens: EETAA).

Tsoucalas, Konstantinos, 1987, *State, Society and Labour in Post-dictatorship Greece* (Athens: Themelio).

Velonias, Efthimios, 1987, 'Regional Administration/Local Government: The Existing Situation', *Dioikitiki Metarrythmisi*, 31–32 (July–Dec.) pp. 62–106.

Regional Planning and the Integrated Mediterranean Programmes in Greece

FOULI PAPAGEORGIOU
and
SUSANNAH VERNEY

I. INTRODUCTION

Special programmes to accelerate the development of the EC's Mediterranean regions had been in the air before Greek accession. However, it was the need to respond to 'the Greek problem' which supplied the political imperative for this idea to be reformulated as a concrete policy proposal.

Ten months after Greece joined the Community, the elections of October 1981 resulted in victory for Andreas Papandreou's PASOK. While by this time PASOK had considerably moderated the radical anti-EC platform it had adopted on its foundation in 1974, the party still had a strongly anti-EC image.[1] Although once in government PASOK could do little more than accept the *fait accompli* of membership, it had to justify this political shift on the EC by improving the terms of participation.

Thus in March 1982 the new Greek government submitted a Memorandum to the EC requesting special treatment for Greece because of its 'economic peculiarities'.[2] In its reply of March 1982, the Commission suggested that the Integrated Mediterranean Programmes (IMPs) could be the main instrument for meeting the Greek request.[3] When subsequently the proposed programmes became entangled in the EC's internal budget dispute, it was Papandreou's threat to veto Iberian accession unless the IMPs were approved,[4] which helped to propel the IMP negotiations to their successful conclusion with the passage of Regulation 2088 in June 1985. Domestically, the adoption of the IMPs was presented as a vindication of PASOK's EC policy during its first term in office (1981–85); it allowed a major turn-around in the Greek government's stance towards European Union in the summer of 1985.[5] Consequently, the IMPs acquired a particularly high profile in Greece, where they were seen not only as a Greek victory but also as a justification for Greece's continued membership of the EC.

Of the 6.6 billion ECU allocated to the IMPs to spur development in the EC's Mediterranean regions, half had been earmarked for Greece. But arguably of greater long-term significance than the provision of additional funding for Greek economic development was the programmes' introduction of the radically new concepts of *subsidiarity* (with implementation decentralized to the appropriate institutional level and not automatically allocated to the central bureaucracy) and *partnership* (with the national government having to share its responsibility for pursuing development programmes with local government officials and EC representatives through the formation of combined monitoring committees to oversee the IMPs). These concepts had particularly interesting implications in the Greek case.

The Greek political system has traditionally been highly centralized, with the distribution of personnel and offices, as well as the power to decide and implement policies, residing with the national government. It could be said that Greece has a maximum national and a minimal sub-national apparatus. While historically and culturally Greece has been regarded as consisting of nine geographical departments, these have never constituted a basis for administration. Instead, at the time the IMPs were first proposed, the only formal administrative structures below the central level were the 55 prefectures (or *nomoi*). The prefectures are run by government-appointed prefects who, since the early 1980s, have been flanked by consultative councils made up of appointed representatives of local government and interest groups. Meanwhile, politically, there have been only two levels of democratically elected government, at the national and local levels, with the latter fragmented into approximately 6,000 (mainly miniature) units.

But the concepts of subsidiarity and partnership on which the IMPs were based made it necessary to create sub-national units for planning and implementation above this first-tier local government level. For the purposes of the IMPs, Greece was divided into six areas, namely the Aegean islands, Attica, Central and Eastern Greece, Crete, Northern Greece, and Western Greece/the Peloponnese. (The seventh Greek IMP was a sectoral programme dealing with informatics and covering the entire national territory). The IMP regions were not given any political institutions or even any administrative structures apart from the monitoring committees set up to follow the progress of the IMPs themselves.

However, legislation introduced shortly after the submission of the first IMP, namely Law 1622/86 on 'Democratic Planning, Regional Development and Local Government', suggested some rethinking on the subject of regional structures. Law 1622 defined 13 administrative regions (*periphereies*),[6] which formed the basic unit for the IMPs' sequel, the Regional Development Plans (RDPs) under the Community Support Framework. Each region was to be headed by a government-appointed regional secretary, assisted by a skeleton staff of administrators recruited from the offices of the national administrative structure. Appointed regional councils were also established, under the chairmanship of the regional secretary. The councils have a mixed membership, including central state and local government representatives, and have been endowed only with planning responsibilities. Regional secretaries were first appointed in 1988 and the regional councils were convened soon afterwards. However, the planning role of the regional council and the identity of the region as a political and institutional entity has yet to be fully established. The regions are meant to act as 'watchdogs' over the regional budgets and to co-ordinate planning activities, but they do not as yet represent an administrative tier co-ordinating policies and administration between central government and the prefectures.

Nevertheless, in the Greek context, the very fact that the regions had been created at all constituted a considerable step forward. It would seem that the IMPs and the RDPs, conceived as economic development programmes, also represented, in effect, an example of a European Community financial 'stimulus' to promote the reform of sub-national governmental structures. Given the traditional reluctance of Greek governments to decentralize, these programmes appear to provide a good example of institutional reform being encouraged by Brussels, rather than emerging exclusively as the outgrowth of internal political processes.

II. THE STUDY

Thus, the introduction of these European Community development programmes seems in itself to have had an impact on the centralized Greek political system by necessitating the country's sub-division into suitable units for economic planning purposes. How far did the process of planning and implementing these programmes help to consolidate the concept of sub-national government in Greece? In what way and to what extent did they contribute to shaping a regional identity, and to awareness of what could and should be done at the local level to promote economic development and social change? What sort of relationship are the Greek regions developing with the EC? This article provides some preliminary answers to these questions by examining the early phase of IMP implementation. Our study is based on a series of 70 open-ended interviews, conducted between April and June 1989 with representatives of government ministries, public agencies and interest groups, which were either directly involved in the management of the programmes or were deemed to be important observers of the IMP process.

In conducting our research, we focused on two IMPs chosen to represent 'polar opposites'. Crete, the first IMP formulated not only in Greece but also in the whole Community, was considered to be a 'pilot' programme which revealed all of the shortcomings of the initial method and procedure in formulating the programmes. Lessons learned in putting together the Crete IMP were subsequently used to help draw up the other IMPs in Greece, Italy, and France. In contrast, Northern Greece had the reputation of being the best managed and most effective Greek IMP. The success of an IMP is measured by its rates of spending in relation to its yearly expenditure targets ('financial absorption rates' in the official terminology). During the first two years of operation, the Crete IMP had achieved an absorption rate of around 25 per cent while the rate for Northern Greece was over 50 per cent.

Seventeen interviews were conducted in Crete and 18 in Northern Greece. The 35 regional interviews were balanced by 35 interviews conducted in Athens, with members of the Interministerial Monitoring Committee which was responsible for the central co-ordination of IMP monitoring, and with representatives of national public agencies and interest groups involved in the IMPs either as 'implementation agencies' or as direct targets of IMP measures or sub-programmes. Our interviewees included three members of the Informatics IMP monitoring committee. However, because this programme covered the whole of Greece and therefore had no regional dimension, the information collected in these interviews has been utilized in this report only as an input in the discussion about motivation and work attitudes of members of the monitoring committees. The interviews completed were distributed as shown in Table 1.

The material collected in the interviews provides a rich and complex picture of the perceptions of some of the key people involved in the implementation of the IMPs. It supplies a background against which we can evaluate the programmes' role in regional development and the specific and more general shortcomings of the implementation process. The interviews provide two different perspectives – from the centre and from the periphery – which help to illuminate the differences of approach between these two levels as well as the relationship between them. In this article, the data collected during the interviews will be used, first, to assess the institutional framework and the administrative mechanisms which have been employed to implement the IMPs, and second, to discuss how perceptions of the single market and links with the EC are

TABLE 1

	Crete	Northern Greece	Central Administration
Monitoring Committee members	11	11	12
Other Interest Groups	2	2	10
Other Public Agencies	2	3	10
Official IMP Evaluator	1	1	-
Regional secretary	1	1	-
Informatics IMP	-	-	3
TOTAL	17	18	35

likely to affect the *modus operandi* of the local organizations as agents for regional development.

III. INTEGRATED PLANNING AND THE REGION

The role of the IMPs in regional development has been a matter of debate. The initial optimism and great expectations attached to integrated planning soon gave way to disappointment and frustration. The disappointment had two main causes. The first was the methods used by the central administration to compile the IMPs. The second was the Brussels-stipulated financing procedures. The IMPs were based on the *additionality* principle, according to which EC finance was complemented by national funding. All financial inputs, whether from the Greek government or from the EC, were channelled through the Greek Public Investment Programme. Moreover, most of the EC contribution was to be paid retrospectively, after the work had been completed. This meant that in the first instance, money had to be found from the national budget. The result was that the IMPs became dependent on central government financing. The linking of EC funds to the prior expenditure of national allocations caused considerable accounting problems for the Greek state and inevitably slowed down the entire IMP process.

Frustration grew soon after the implementation of the IMPs started. The allocation of responsibilities concerning the implementation of IMP actions was unclear, and relationships between central and local agencies became strained. Moreover, revisions or amendments to the programmes proved to be difficult to negotiate with Brussels and time-consuming to agree domestically.

Our study indicates that the issues of decision-making and implementation are of critical importance for both integrated planning and the establishment of a regional identity. The questions posed by the local authorities and interest group representatives did not only concern the degree of authority of the regions in the planning and financing of the IMPs. They went further, to dispute whether any significant degree of regional autonomy (or even effective development in line with local needs and aspirations) could ever be achieved under the present system of centralized decision-making and administration in Greece.

These concerns are well illustrated in our following discussion of four aspects of the IMPs: (a) the initial formulation of the programmes; (b) their financial management; (c) the allocation of responsibilities for implementation between the central and local levels; and (d) the revision process.

The Formulation of the IMPs

The first Greek IMP, for the island of Crete, was submitted to Brussels in August 1985. By December 1987, a little more than two years later, the contracts for all the Greek IMPs had been signed, detailing what were supposed to be fully integrated plans designed to spur regional development during the seven-year period between 1986 and 1992. The process followed in drawing up the six regional IMPs was more or less the same, although there was clearly a learning experience operating which meant the later programmes were better defined and more operational than the first ones. The 'pilot' programme for Crete was 'a plunge into dark waters', to quote a senior official from the Ministry of National Economy, as the concept of planning was still a novel notion for the Greek civil service.

Central economic planning was introduced to Greece in 1964, when the National Centre for Planning and Economic Research (KEPE) was established in its present form. KEPE was entrusted with the responsibility for formulating short, medium and long-term plans for economic and social development on behalf of the Greek government. From the beginning, the five-year plan was selected as the most suitable instrument for economic planning, serving the needs of the ministries involved in economic development and, in particular, the ministry responsible for drawing up the National Investment Programme (initially the Ministry of Co-ordination, subsequently renamed as the Ministry of National Economy).

The five-year plans produced by KEPE have often been accused of being a highly centralized 'exercise on paper'. However, one should not underestimate the problems of KEPE staff in gaining access to crucial information from central and regional government departments and the reluctance of ministries to make medium-term planning and policy commitments. During the 1980s, some attempt was made to decentralize the formulation of the five-year plans by inviting planning proposals from prefecture councils and local government authorities. This effort culminated in Law 1622/1986, which instituted systematic procedures for decentralized/democratic planning, but was never fully implemented, with the result that regional influence in the formulation of the five-year plans remained extremely limited. Morever, the concept of planning never really reached the civil service outside KEPE, and the implementation of five-year plans did not extend beyond the public works programmes included in them.

Other attempts at decentralized planning since 1981 included the 'Campaign for Urban Reconstitution through Town Planning' launched by the Ministry of Planning and the Environment in 1983. This covered practically all urban centres and was essentially an effort to establish integrated planning at the municipal level. However, the lessons learned from the Town Planning Campaign did not affect the process of IMP formulation. The information gathered and the proposals made in the context of dozens of town plans all over Greece were never used, even as an input for drawing up the IMPs. This was because the responsibility for IMP formulation lay with a different ministry, namely the Ministry of National Economy.

This phenomenon of 'watertight compartments' with little or no contact between them is endemic to the Greek public administration, and has deleterious effects on the state's capacity to engage in integrated planning. This naturally extended to the IMPs, where a typical complaint by our respondents concerned their lack of information about other agencies' participation in the programmes.[7] During the IMP formulation phase, the lack of formal mechanisms for the exchange of information and co-ordination of activities seriously affected the consistency, pragmatism and sometimes relevance of the programmes.

The absence of national sectoral planning has also been a problem. The IMP private investment measures provide a characteristic illustration. IMP subsidies to support private investment in industry or tourism could not be allocated on the basis of national development plans for these sectors, as such plans simply do not exist. Consequently, the success or failure of these measures was a matter of coincidence. For example, at the time of our study, the hotel investment measure of the Crete IMP was over-subscribed, although both public and private agencies representing tourism interests agreed that instead of more hotel beds, Crete urgently needed more tourist-related infrastructure (especially better airports). The opposite occurred in Northern Greece, where there was a need for more hotel beds, but where private interest in this sector lagged behind. On the industrial front, however, the Northern Greece IMP was over-subscribed, while in Crete the subsidies available for manufacturing had not been taken up by the local entrepreneurs. Drawing up integrated programmes at the regional level becomes extremely difficult when the central administration is not 'integrated' or co-ordinated in its planning and development activities.

The limited contribution allowed to local authorities or interest group leaders in the formulation of the IMPs was a major source of discontent in the regions. Responsibility for drawing up the programmes lay with the Ministry of National Economy. During the initial stages of the planning process, the Ministry asked for development proposals from government departments and central agencies, and also from the prefects. The latter were supposed to consult with local authorities and other agencies in their areas, but it seems that in most cases this did not occur in any systematic or uniform way. While each prefecture was provisionally allocated a quota of one billion drachmas to be distributed according to local priorities, in practice these quotas were often significantly exceeded. Moreover, many of the projects recommended were small-scale, local works, mostly having to do with the construction of local roads and school buildings.[8] These reflected the kind of infrastructure programmes that have been the traditional concern of the prefectures, but were not necessarily suitable for what were supposed to be integrated programmes to promote the overall development of the region. Because so many of the prefects' proposals were rejected by the Ministry of National Economy, the balance between 'regional' and 'central' projects often tipped to the detriment of the former.

In the end, the final draft programmes submitted to the EC were put together by the Ministry of National Economy, using a few simple rules. Their criteria judged measures according to the eligibility principles and cost limitations formulated by the EC, rather than making any serious attempt to assess the contribution that particular proposals might be expected to make to regional development. Perhaps this was only to be expected, given the lack of integrated planning experience in Greece and particularly the time constraints which the Ministry officials were operating under; moreover, a serious hindrance to any attempt at strategic planning in Greece is the general absence of reliable data. The overall result was that the IMPs were assembled at the central level in a somewhat piecemeal manner, instead of emerging as the product of an exercise in integrated planning, bringing together national and local policy-makers in trying to formulate a mutually accepted programme that would meet local development needs.

Practically all our respondents agreed that the outcome was far from perfect or even acceptable. However, the criticisms made by regional representatives had a different tint from those voiced at the centre. In Crete, over half our interviewees complained that their IMP lacked a strategic plan. To quote one respondent, instead of being an integrated development programme, it was 'an array of ad hoc investment projects with marginal socio-economic effect'. Also, essential infrastructure related to tourism and industry had been left out, while a vast number of small and unimportant public works projects had apparently been included at random. Similar but somewhat milder criticisms were made concerning the formulation of the Northern Greece IMP. In this case, our respondents stressed the lack of an overall conceptual framework, the absence of strategic sectoral planning (for example, in industry and tourism), and the insertion of the wrong priorities. A quarter of our respondents in Crete and a similar proportion in Northern Greece referred explicitly to what they deemed to be the hegemonic attitude of the Ministry of National Economy in planning and trying to control the detailed implementation of the IMPs.

Interestingly enough, many representatives of central agencies accepted these criticisms made by our regional interviewees, but commented that the regions lacked adequate administrative and financial monitoring structures to ensure efficient planning and implementation. This encapsulates the classic 'chicken-or-egg' decentralization dilemma. Central bureaucrats tend to argue that decision-making and policy implementation powers should not be decentralized until the sub-national levels of government can prove that they are able to assume these tasks successfully. However, it is hard to see how the regional administration can ever learn to formulate and administer policies effectively, unless the national government allows it the resources, personnel, and legal responsibilities to do so.

To sum up, although the IMPs were supposed to be an experiment in decentralized development targeted towards the stimulation of endogenous forces, they appeared to become an exercise in centralized control and the stifling of local efforts. Moreover, many national interest groups, such as the General Confederation of Labour, the Panhellenic Confederation of Agricultural Co-operatives and the Association of Greek Industrialists, also complained that they had not been consulted during the formulation of the IMPs, despite the fact that they represented crucial economic and social interests. This planning procedure, which allowed maximum control to the central government bureaucrats, undermined the possibility of using the IMPs to mobilize public opinion and to achieve social consensus around issues of development and planning.

The Financing of the Integrated Programmes

As mentioned above, the IMP finance is channelled through the Public Investment Programme of the Ministry of National Economy. The initial plan was to allocate two-thirds of the IMP budget to measures to be implemented by central agencies, while the remaining one-third would be managed by the prefectures (that is, the local branches of the national administration). However, comparisons of the six regional IMPs show that the ratio between central and local control of expenditures differed from one IMP to another. In Crete, the central agencies' share reached 85–90 per cent of the budget. This drastically affected the programme's effectiveness because it burdened the implementation of the IMP with the inflexible procedures and structures of the central bureaucracy and national accounting system. It appeared that nobody had foreseen at the planning stage that some of the IMP measures could never be implemented under this rigid top–down process, because the national agencies responsible for implementation of IMP measures and sub-programmes were in no position to commission the necessary studies or to appoint suitably qualified personnel to carry out the programmes.

A stunning example of the inflexibility of the national procedures was the a priori ban issued on all new appointments in the public sector as part of the government's austerity programme to limit the budget deficit. The ban was enforced without taking into account the commitments made under the IMP programmes. As a consequence, all of the IMP measures foreseeing the appointment by the national government of specialized staff were brought to a halt.

In contrast, the IMP measures financed and controlled by local agencies seemed to have a much better track record, both in spending the allocated funds and in producing reliable results. This suggests that greater decentralization of the budgetary allocation and responsibility for implementation would improve the speed and effectiveness of the programmes.

The Allocation of Responsibilities for Implementation

The allocation of implementation responsibilities between central and local authorities was also part of the IMP planning process. Often, the agency financing an IMP measure was not the one responsible for its implementation. In theory, according to the IMP contracts, implementation of all 'local' measures was the responsibility of the prefecture. Given that by its very nature almost the entire IMP project was to be implemented through local initiatives, the prefectures should thus have been informed about all the measures. In practice, if the central agency financing a measure was also responsible for implementation, it did not inform the prefecture about the progress of the measure. Thus, the most important entity of decentralized administration currently in existence – the prefecture – was not informed about, and had no control over, the implementation of those IMP measures in its area which had been allocated to central agencies.

This complex and paradoxical situation was underlined by the fact that, at the time our interviews were conducted, there were no plans to link the prefectures into the recently-established IMP computer system. This linked the regional offices of the Ministry of National Economy with the central administration in order to provide a flow of information about IMP progress. It seems the prefectures were simply not seen as essential recipients of the information service controlled by the Ministry of National Economy, even when this concerned measures being implemented in their areas.

Objectively speaking, the 55 prefectures are too small as entities to undertake all decentralized implementation. The solution would appear to be the co-ordination of implementation at the regional level. The 13 RDP Regions would seem to be the ideal level for planning and co-ordinating the implementation of development programmes (although not necessarily carrying out the implementation, which should be allocated to appropriate authorities at the central, and particularly the prefecture and municipal levels). The problem in Greece today is that the regional administration is not independent, and has very limited authority and resources.

The Revision of Plans

The ability to make revisions, if circumstances change, is an essential part of any planning process. It was perhaps especially necessary in the case of the Greek IMPs which were drawn up hastily, without previous planning experience or clear priorities.

The need for greater flexibility was clearly felt by all our regional respondents. However, the existing system allowed the regional monitoring committees no powers over revision. They could only make proposals to the central Interministerial Monitoring Committee, which in turn could only take decisions on amendments covering up to ten per cent of the IMP budget. More extensive revisions then had to be referred to Brussels, and reportedly took at least a year to be approved. Some of our respondents felt this process was unnecessarily unwieldy, particularly given that EC representatives were included on the regional monitoring committees anyway.

The revision procedure had proved frustrating not only for the regional representatives but also for the central administration. Even the staff of the Ministry of National Economy had tired of what one official described as the 'zigzag process' of revision proposals moving endlessly between the regional IMP committees, the national Interministerial Committee in Athens, and the EC bureaucracy in Brussels. The process was considered to be wasteful in terms of both time and effort.

Some members of the IMP committees spoke explicitly about the need for direct communication with Brussels. This would appear sensible and realistic in terms of improving operational efficiency. However, politically it is likely to prove extremely difficult in a country with such a strong centralist tradition. Like its counterparts in other peripheral EC states such as Portugal and Ireland, the Greek government seems to want to retain exclusive political control of all relationships with the EC. The monopoly of information is, of course, considered to be one of the essential characteristics of power.

IV. REGIONAL VS. CENTRAL IMPLEMENTATION AND THE MONITORING PROCESS

The implementation of each regional IMP was reviewed and supported by a monitoring committee, chaired by one of the regional secretaries.[9] The committees' members included the sub-programme managers; representatives of local interest groups (mainly chambers of commerce), local government, agricultural co-operatives, universities, banks, etc.; officials from at least two directorate generals from Brussels; and in the case of Crete, the prefects. The secretariat of each committee was made up of the sub-programme managers. The latter were civil servants, either on informal secondment from their ministry to the committee (as was the case with most of the sub-programme managers in Northern Greece in 1989); or serving part-time on the committee, while also spending time in their regular civil service jobs (as was the case with some of our interviewees in Crete). With the exception of the secretariat, all the other committee members were unpaid.

The monitoring committees had to meet every three months to review the progress of IMP implementation on the basis of the information collected by the secretariat. This information was then passed on to the central Interministerial Committee in Athens, in the form of a quarterly report. The regional monitoring committees were also supposed to be linked to monitoring committees at the prefecture level. But in practice these usually were not operational. We discovered in Northern Greece that even where they did exist, they had no co-operation or even communication with the regional monitoring committee.

The limited role of the regional monitoring committees was mentioned by about half our respondents in both Crete and Northern Greece as an important shortcoming in the IMP process. It was evident that this issue had caused frustration for many committee members, and it had even resulted in a resignation in Crete.

The IMP monitoring committees were not regarded as part of the civil service structure, and were not given any formal status in Greek law as either public or semi-public bodies. Nor had they been allocated any decision-making powers. They had no authority to apply sanctions against agencies which failed to meet targets or to provide information. Instead, their role was purely advisory. Their main job was to keep account of the 'absorption' or expenditure rate for the various IMP measures, and to register their physical progress (for example, how many kilometres of road had been built, or how many peach trees had been uprooted and replaced by new varieties). Although on paper the committees had the right to intervene and ask the implementing agencies to take special action if implementation was not going well, this did not seem to happen in practice. Members complained that their lack of more substantial powers meant the committees ended up looking at IMP implementation simply from an accountant's point of view; concentrating on technical details and missing strategic issues; and striving to increase the programme's financial 'absorption' rate without showing similar concern for its developmental aspects.

The committees' lack of formal status had left their secretariats burdened with problems. Although their members were supposed to go on location in order to actually see the progress of IMP measures and to offer advice, they were rarely able to do so, because they were not entitled to travel expenses.[10] This meant they were totally reliant on secondhand information about the progress of the projects, which they were not able to check for themselves. Consequently, the sub-programme managers were hardly 'managers' in the normal sense of the word. Several described themselves as 'telephone operators', trying desperately to extract information about the progress of IMP measures from central agencies and prefecture-level civil servants. Their informal status and ungraded positions as members of the secretariat made it particularly difficult for them to demand information in an official capacity. Rather, as they put it, they had to 'beg' for it. In this connection, several secretariat members referred with some bitterness to their relations with central agencies, and to the 'superiority-complex' of the Athens-based civil servants towards their provincial colleagues.

Both in Crete and Northern Greece, our interviewees stressed that the committees' informal status meant the secretariats were not able to obtain expert advice and technical support. This meant they were not able to buy essential equipment, including computers. Some respondents remarked on the generally negative attitude of the government bureaucracy towards new ideas and technology, and to the fact that the committees could not expect the central administration to help them in such matters. One example mentioned concerned the effort to establish computer links between the secretariat and the prefectures in Northern Greece. All requests had fallen on deaf ears.

On a personal level, practically all of our respondents from the IMP secretariats in Crete and Northern Greece had the same complaints concerning the insecurity of their positions in the secretariat, their loss of promotion opportunities (because many of them had left their formal posts), and the lack of financial incentives to compensate both for the above and for their commitment and hard work. Despite this, at the time of the interviews, both teams in Crete and Northern Greece had high qualifications, remarkable open-mindedness, and the will to be effective and innovative – all of which are very unusual characteristics in the Greek civil service. Apparently, the secretariat staff were among the best in their areas of specialization. In addition, it should not be overlooked that most of them were also politically committed to the governing party and to working for the success of the IMPs. This was particularly apparent in Northern Greece, where the secretariat was attached to a government department (the Ministry of Northern Greece).[11]

In relation to the functioning of the committees themselves, one of the innovatory aspects of the IMPs had been the concept of partnership. This meant EC officials were directly involved in the management of the programmes through their participation in the monitoring committees. The presence of officials from Brussels in committee meetings seemed to have operated in a dual manner. Where relationships between the regional IMP committees and central agencies (particularly the Ministry of National Economy) were strained and rather antagonistic, EC representatives often managed to defuse the situation and restore balance by operating as a *super partes*. Where the committee's relationship with the central administration was good, the committee members felt more confident in opposing the EC officials' strict interpretation of the dictates of the programmes. In either case, there was a general feeling among monitoring committee members that the opinions of the Greek and EC members of the committee did not carry the same weight, with the EC representatives considered to have more influence. This was criticized, on the grounds that the relationship was supposed to be one of partnership, and not of the subordination of the national and local levels to the EC. Some of our respondents also claimed that 'wrong decisions' by EC officials had often held back important changes to the programmes.

There had also been disagreements within each of the two regional committees we examined. Party political differences had occurred, but these generally appeared to be less significant than disagreements between the technocrats in the secretariat and the local politicians or interest group representatives. The former often referred to the parochial character which they complained the latter's presence gave the committee. According to the technocrats, the local government and interest group representatives often tried to secure funds for their constituencies or sectors, without taking an objective view of the various measures or of the needs of the programme as a whole. The interest group representatives, on the other hand, protested that there was never any opportunity at committee meetings to examine the various topics in depth, so that they had to take the secretariat's reports at face value. Some of them even suggested (although not very convincingly) that all committee members should become full-time employees and receive suitable renumeration to allow them to work seriously on proposals and to exercise real control over the secretariat. However, on the whole, the secretariat staff were praised by the other committee members for their commitment, hard work, and professionalism.

Despite the shortcomings in the operation of the regional monitoring committees, mainly stemming from their lack of authority, they seemed to have a positive image within the wider local communities, as indicated by the comments of local interest group representatives. More specifically, the monitoring committees were seen by our interviewees as mechanisms for social control, ensuring fair and honest implementation of the IMPs. They were also seen as a school for novel practices, such as time-scheduling, information monitoring, and eventually, planning – radical concepts in the context of the Greek civil service. The monitoring committee members and secretariat were described by several respondents as being 'as good as any European civil servants', which signified that they had acquired a 'European' attitude and style of work. The representatives of local agencies saw this as a first step towards the modernization of the Greek bureaucracy.

Local agency representatives also suggested that their own experiences with the IMP committees had offered them useful opportunities to practice better co-ordination (although it was generally admitted that this opportunity had not been fully exploited yet). They had also gained knowledge about negotiations and day-to-day relationships with the EC.

Indeed, the majority of our respondents in both Crete and Northern

Greece regarded IMP implementation as a useful learning experience. They expected the lessons to be utilized in the drawing up and implementation of the RDPs. The comment made by a prefect in Crete, that 'the IMPs were the school for the RDPs', echoed the attitude of most representatives of the public agencies or interest groups in both areas.

Moreover, the IMP process was seen as important in creating an 'identity' for its geographical area through increasing consciousness of local needs. The IMPs had raised in a more urgent form the question of a transfer of power from the centre to the periphery – that is, to a regional level of government. The implementation of the IMPs had yielded knowledge about the needs and procedures at the prefecture level; about the functioning of central and local agencies as implementation agents; and about relationships between the regional and central administration, and between the regions and the European Community.

In addition, three particular issues raised during our regional interviews merit further attention. First, the implementation of an integrated programme in practice requires an administrative reform of the civil service, to allow the introduction of real project managers at the implementation level. Second, a support mechanism is needed to distribute information to the public and to local agencies about the opportunities offered by the programmes, and to facilitate co-operation and co-ordination between agencies. During the initial phase of IMP implementation, a positive contribution in this direction had been made by EETAA (the Hellenic Agency for Local Government and Local Development), which organized meetings and seminars for public agencies and monitoring committee members. Third, local control at the implementation stage appears to be much more effective than central control, the latter being difficult due to current bureaucratic procedures and problems of physical distance. It is characteristic that in both Crete and Northern Greece, all the measures being implemented by prefectures were progressing well, while measures implemented by central agencies lagged behind. Indeed, some, including, for example, those under the jurisdiction of TAP (the Archaeological Fund of the National Tourism Organization), had not yet started.[12] It should also be noted that local authorities (that is, at the first-tier local government level) were less effective than the prefectures as implementation agencies. This was probably due to the fact that they did not possess either the prefecture's human and technical resources or its expertise in construction projects.

Comments made by central civil servants to a certain extent confirmed the complaints of our respondents in the regions. More than half of the central agencies (ministries and public sector organizations) did not seem to have a good relationship with the regional monitoring committees. The most usual complaint concerned the pressure being put on them to provide regular information on the progress of IMP measures. It should be noted here that monitoring and progress report writing is an unusual practice for the Greek civil service. One respondent, representing one of the largest public sector organizations in Greece, declared explicitly that the EC was 'unreasonable' to expect data on a quarterly basis. Other public agency staff, although willing to help, could not always comprehend the constant demands for information from regional monitoring committees.

However, this was not a uniform finding. In other cases, respondents remarked approvingly on administrative innovations which their organizations had introduced as a result of the IMP monitoring procedures. Most members of the Interministerial Monitoring Committee, as well as the civil servants from the IMP department at the Ministry of National Economy, spoke more positively than our regional interviewees had done about the partnership which was being developed with the EC. In general, civil servants in Athens seemed to feel more 'equal' to the EC officials who took part in monitoring committee meetings, than their provincial counterparts did.

Asked about the lessons learned from IMP implementation, half of the ministerial officials stressed co-ordination and co-operation between agencies as an important achievement. In the context of the 'watertight' government departments mentioned above, the existence of the Interministerial Monitoring Committee in particular was viewed as a positive development. Several of its members talked enthusiastically about the novel and valuable experience of exchanging information with other ministries involved in the programmes. They also suggested that this process of learning from the successes and mistakes of other sectors of the public bureaucracy should become a more generalized practice.

Interestingly, decentralization as a positive effect of the IMPs was mentioned by only two out of 20 national public agency officials and by one among ten national interest group representatives. Several interviewees from public agencies also referred to technical modernization of the public administration (for example, through the introduction of computers), better management, quicker procedures, and the introduction of a 'European' spirit of work. A few mentioned the increase in awareness concerning the need for planning and national policy. The rest could see no effect at all.

A notable finding was that, in contrast to our regional respondents, among the 35 officials interviewed in Athens only three referred to the IMPs as a useful experience for the drawing-up of the RDPs. This was a little surprising because at the time of the interviews, all the public agencies were in the process of compiling their own proposals for the RDPs. This seems to suggest that the IMPs had a deeper effect in the regions as an instructive planning experience than they had had in the centre.

V. EUROPEAN PROSPECTS AND REGIONAL LINKS

The future relationship of the Greek regions with the EC will depend to a considerable extent on regional agencies beginning to 'think European'. Our study suggests that in 1989, eight years after Greece's EC entry, this process was still at a very early stage. While the Community was generally viewed in a positive light, there seemed to be a lack of awareness about the possibilities which accession had opened up at the European level. As a rule, contacts with the EC did not seem to be extensive, systematic or co-ordinated.

While all of the regional interest group representatives we interviewed expressed an interest in establishing EC links, most were not sure how this could take place. About half were running Social Fund-supported training programmes for their members, and thought of these as 'their link' with the EC. Also, a fair number stressed access to information about EC programmes and European agencies as the first step towards establishing a link with the Community. All of the regional interest group representatives voiced their frustration over the lack of access to EC information, and pointed out that although their groups' headquarters in Athens had often developed contacts with the EC and a system of information exchange, this knowledge was not passed down to the sub-national level. Moreover, we did not come across a single regional agency which was participating in a European consortium or network. Indeed, the notion of the European network was not familiar to people at the local level. This did not mean the idea was unattractive. When asked explicitly whether they would be interested in participating in such an initiative, our respondents replied affirmatively. Meanwhile among the interest group representatives at the regional level, one-third expressed an interest in joining a European network, while the rest thought this could be a job for their headquarters in Athens.

Only three years before the magic date of '1992', the representatives of public sector agencies at the sub-national level did not seem to have a clear notion of what the single market would mean for them. Instead, discussion of the country's future EC role almost invariably led to the suggestion that Greece should get more money. In contrast, the question of their European prospects after 1992 was of concern to all the professional groups contacted. The respondents voiced worries about increased competition from Europe and felt that Greece was not prepared for full integration. But most also expressed optimism over the benefits of opening up a wider market for their products. Those concerned with tourism and agriculture in particular were concerned about the lack of adequate transport and communications infrastructure and regretted the fact that the IMPs had not improved the quality of airports and roads in preparation for the single market. This issue appeared to be equally important in both Crete and Northern Greece, and may well reflect the sentiment in other Greek regions.

At the central level, our interviewees had a somewhat clearer idea about Greece's prospects within the EC. We found there were notable differences in perceptions of the EC among different types of agencies. The ministries in general took a pecuniary view, tying their EC prospects with increased EC funding. Almost half of the ministry officials referred to the positive effects of the IMPs in terms of the 'Europeanization' of the Greek administrative system, and commented that national integrated programmes would allow Greece to take more effective advantage of EC funds. One-third felt their own field of responsibility (for example, environment, transport, education, culture) should be made a higher priority, while the rest either hoped for more EC money in general, or wanted the Community to put more pressure on Greece to achieve its development objectives in a more efficient manner.

In contrast, representatives of agencies from the wider public sector tended, on the whole, to connect their future EC prospects with their participation in European organizations and with the establishment of closer links with similar agencies in EC countries.[13] Half of these respondents referred to European links as a means of increasing the competitiveness and scope of their organizations. Two members of our sample were completely pessimistic about any possibility of co-operation with non-Greek partners in mutually beneficial programmes.

National interest group representatives had a rather confused perception of networking at the European level, although many of them referred to the need to safeguard the professional interests of their members as their prime concern in relation to the single market. One-third of this group clearly voiced their worries about 1992; the rest referred to the need to establish links and co-operation with similar European agencies. Two-thirds of the Athens-based interest groups we contacted had already established such links, while the remaining one-third had attempted to do so without success. Links which had been established included both participation in European organizations which act as EC 'social partners' (such as COPA, the Committee of Agricultural Organizations in the EC, and the ETUC, the European Trade Union

Confederation), and bilateral links with similar national organizations in other Community member states.

It was striking that none of our 35 Athens interviewees referred to the role of the regions in relation to Greece's European prospects and the single market. Although it was clear that our regional respondents looked to the centre for guidance, information, and contacts with the EC, it seemed that the centre was not willing and often perhaps was not capable of providing a link with the Community on behalf of the regions. As some of our Cretan respondents said, direct contact with Brussels would not only solve many bureaucratic problems which have slowed down the implementation of the IMPs, but it could also start a flow of information between the EC and the regions which could motivate regional organizations and interest groups to start thinking about European Community links and co-operation.

VI. CONCLUSIONS

The region as a political and administrative entity is still a very new institution in Greece. Neither the six IMP regions nor the 13 RDP regions were delimited on the basis of tradition or cultural identity. Instead, their boundaries were the result of political compromise and, especially in the case of the RDPs, were often unrealistic in dividing geographic entities. Thus the regions are currently in search of an identity; it remains to be seen whether European Community development programmes can provide a regional 'identity card'. This would certainly be facilitated if the regions were to be allocated responsibilities for physical, economic and social planning and allowed to follow autonomous policy-making procedures; if formal mechanisms could be established at regional level for inter-agency co-ordination in the drawing up and implementation of plans; and if the regions were allowed to establish formal direct links with the EC bureaucracy in Brussels. So far this has not been the case. Our examination of the first phase of the IMPs suggested that by 1989, decision-making and co-ordination procedures and general expertise in integrated planning had not been securely established at the regional level.

However, a start had been made in this direction, and our research indicated that there had been some positive effects on the functioning of both central and regional administration. Although the change was not dramatic, there had clearly been an alteration in the style and attitudes of many programme participants. Overall, by 1989 there was a perceptible difference in climate in comparison to 1985, when the first IMP had been drawn up. Experience in IMP implementation had given the regional bureaucracy a certain amount of self-confidence, and provided valuable lessons for developing the subsequent RDPs. Thus by 1989 when the RDPs were being compiled, there was already an awareness of the need for planning and the effective management of programmes, and experience had been gained in monitoring and day-to-day handling of implementation procedures.

An important improvement in the formulation of the RDPs was that initial responsibility for drawing up each of the draft programmes lay with the relevant regional secretary and the regional office of the Ministry of National Economy. In cases where the regional secretary took an active interest in the formulation of the RDP, exercised the right to hold regional conferences and other public consultation and information meetings, and utilized people with IMP-gained experience, the results were closer to an integrated plan than had been the case with any of the IMPs.

However, final control over the programmes was exercised by the Ministry of National Economy on the basis of its five-year plan, and following the elections of June 1989, the regional secretaries, as party political appointees, were all replaced. As is the rule in Greece, most of the new incumbents ignored the work of their predecessors. Moreover, the uncertain situation created by three successive parliamentary elections in ten months, with the consequent high turnover of political personnel, increased the authority of the central civil servants at the expense of the temporary political appointees in the regional administration. Thus the eventual outcome was reminiscent of the IMP process in that the final plans were drawn up by officials in the Ministry of National Economy. Instead of becoming strategic plans for development, setting priorities and connecting them with specific actions for implementation, the RDPs, like the IMPs, were essentially a list of proposals compiled by the prefectures on the basis of the demands of the local authorities and other agencies in their constituencies.

The problems of RDP formulation highlight the need to make the regional authorities more independent of central government, preferably through direct elections. As long as the leadership careers of regional administrators depend on their role as obedient servants of the centre, they can never become effective exponents of regional and local interests. Essentially, all the limitations of the IMP process detailed in our article resulted from the Greek administration's attempt to run regional programmes without devolving any substantial powers to the regional level. Although the IMPs were regional programmes in name, in practice a sizable component was centrally planned and centrally implemented. The degree of regional control was frustratingly small, as exemplified by the regional monitoring committee's lack of power to authorize revisions or to take action in the case of 'problem' agencies. The procedures followed with the IMPs undermined their functionality and meant EC development funding was not being put to the best possible use. This weakened Greece's overall development effort and thus its prospects of convergence with the economies of the other EC member states.

This does not mean there are no grounds for optimism. On the positive side, no matter how imperfectly formulated and implemented the IMPs and RDPs were in practice, they had stimulated the introduction of regional structures and promoted the idea of regional programmes as a feature of Greek national development planning. Moreover, this article, based on data gathered in 1989, can only be an interim report on the timid decentralization process which the IMPs and the RDPs appear to have stimulated in Greece; a follow-up study will clearly be desirable. It is possible that as such regional programmes progress, they will begin to acquire their own momentum, with the operational needs of an efficient planning and implementation process bringing about a gradual 'silent revolution' in centre–periphery relations. However, our basic conclusion points to the need for significant political change if the Greek region is ever to become really meaningful as an effective planning and development unit.

NOTES

1. On the evolution of PASOK's EC policy, see Kevin Featherstone, *Socialist Parties and European Integration: A Comparative History* (Manchester: Manchester University Press, 1988), pp. 170–90, and Susannah Verney, 'From the "Special Relationship" to Europeanism' in Richard Clogg (ed.), *Aspects of Greek Politics and Society in the 1980s* (London: Macmillan, 1993, forthcoming).
2. The Memorandum has been published in English in *The Greek Review*, 17 July 1982. For analyses of the Memorandum, see *Epitheorisi ton Evropaikon Koinotiton*, Vol. 3, No. 2 (April–June 1982) and Achilleas Mitsos, *He elliniki viomichania sti diethni agora* (Athens: Themelio, 1989), pp. 394–412.
3. See Commission of the European Communities, 'Greece in the European Community: Assessments and Proposals', COM(83)134 final, Brussels, 29 March 1983.
4. At the Dublin summit in December 1984.
5. At the Milan Council in June 1985, Greece had voted against convening the Inter-Governmental Conference (IGC) which drew up the Single European Act. However, only weeks later, the Greek Government changed its mind and decided to participate in the IGC. In the interim, not only had the EC approved the IMP Regulation, but also PASOK had won a second electoral victory which greatly increased its margins for manoeuvre.
6. The 13 development regions were defined as Attica, Central Greece, Central Macedonia, Crete, Eastern Macedonia, Epirus, the Ionian Islands, the North Aegean islands, the Peloponnese, the South Aegean islands, Thessaly, Western Greece, and Western Macedonia.
7. Indeed, it was striking that a number of the representatives of agencies from the wider

public sector (that is, generally not including government ministries) had never seen copies of the complete programmes, and consequently had no clear overall conception of what they entailed.

8. It was typical that although school buildings were not eligible for inclusion in the IMPs, many prefects had incorporated them in their proposals.
9. With the exception of Crete, all the IMP regions cover two or more of the development regions created under Law 1622/1986, and therefore fall within the administration of several regional secretaries.
10. Several respondents in fact claimed to have financed such trips out of their own pockets.
11. In contrast, in Crete the secretariat was linked to an administrative department, that is, the regional office of the Ministry of National Economy.
12. This agency had particular problems, many of which stemmed from its dependence on the Ministry of Culture, which meant its IMP measures had to surmount not one, but two layers of central bureaucracy.
13. Only one asked for more EC money, while two felt Greece needed to change its policies in relation to the European Community.

Portuguese Regionalism in the Transition from the *Estado Novo* to the Single Market

WALTER C. OPELLO, JR.

I. INTRODUCTION

The purpose of this article is to report the results of research carried out on sub-national government in Portugal and the role that it can play in accelerating the transition to the internal market. Fieldwork was done in Portugal in the late spring and early summer of 1989, during which period interviews were conducted, sites visited, documents collected and examined, and surveys carried out.[1] These surveys were done using Portuguese versions of two questionnaires that were slightly modified to solicit answers to questions on sub-national government structures and performance that were appropriate to the Portuguese. Questions were also designed to elicit opinions from elected public officials as well as private interest group leaders about issues of European integration and the prospects of creating a regional governmental structure for continental Portugal.

The article begins with a discussion of Portuguese regionalism before and after 25 April 1976. The results of the surveys are next presented in two sections, one section reports the respondents' assessment of the functioning of the regions and the other, their views about the future of the regions in the context of 1992. The article concludes with an analysis of the policy areas local officials and private interest group leaders would support as part of future Community inter-regional initiatives and co-operative programs.

II. PORTUGUESE REGIONALISM BEFORE AND AFTER THE OVERTHROW OF THE *ESTADO NOVO*

The history of Portuguese regionalism is essentially the history of the way Portugal has been internally organized from its inception. Portugal's First Republic (1919–26) was replaced in 1926 by a military dictatorship which evolved over the next years into a civilian, authoritarian corporatist regime controlled by Antonio de Oliveira Salazar who, after serving as minister of finance, was appointed prime minister in 1932.

The year after being appointed prime minister, Salazar promulgated a new constitution for his regime, which be began to call the New State (*Estado Novo*).[2] Based on corporatist principles, Salazar's new constitution gave considerable attention to local government, which was seen as one of the building blocks of his system. Salazar did not, however, make any changes in the subdivision of Portugal into districts, counties, and parishes. Each parish was administered by a board (*junta*) made up of a variable number of members depending upon the size of the local population. The members of these boards were to be elected from heads of households but in practice were appointed by the mayor (*presidente*) of the municipal chamber (*câmara municipal*). The municipal chamber administered both urban and rural areas of the county. Theoretically, the mayor was elected but in practice was, along with the other members of the municipal chamber, appointed by the civil governor (*governador civil*) of the district in which the county was situated. Finally, the civil governors of the districts were appointed by the minister of internal administration. The day-to-day routine of providing local administration was principally in the hands of the mayors. The civil governors were to see to it that the municipal chambers in their districts carried out assigned administrative tasks and could dismiss those local officials who failed to do so.

In 1936 a new administrative code was promulgated which regrouped the districts into a new provincial structure. Five new provinces were created and the districts rearranged and two new provinces were created on the Atlantic islands: the Azores and Madeira. Of the four levels of territorial organization specified by the 1936 code (province, district, county, and parish) the most important for the day-to-day provision of local governmental services was the county. No governmental structures were ever created at the provincial level and the districts were restricted to oversight responsibilities. The 1936 code, therefore, theoretically granted municipal chambers and parish boards extensive decisional authority and responsibility. In practice, however, this authority and power was nullified by the extremely limited financial resources made available to local authorities which made them almost totally dependent upon the central government. During the dictatorship, there was, in effect, no local policy-making process. Decisions concerning local matters were taken by the national government and handed down to the municipal chambers and parish boards as directives and administrative decrees. Local politics during the dictatorship was, therefore, minimal and trivial because the municipal chambers and parish boards were little more than administrative agents of the national government.[3]

The most significant feature of the *Estado Novo* was its bureaucracy and the preponderance of technocrats in the policy-making process. This feature, coupled with older absolutist tendencies inherited from previous history, created in Portugal a deeply entrenched, all-powerfull national government which overwhelmed local authorities and constrained and frustrated all dissent and political opposition.[4] Becoming increasingly frustrated by having to fight a ten-year long unwinnable war against liberation movements in Angola, Mozambique and Guinea (Bissau), the army of the dictatorship was gradually transformed from a reliable instrument of the *Estado Novo* to one which increasingly began to contemplate overturning the government in order to avoid the disgrace and dishonour of defeat in Africa.[5] On 25 April 1974 the military overthrew the *Estado Novo* and launched Portugal's present democratic regime.

After a two-year period of exception, a new constitution was promulgated by the constituent assembly. A significant feature of this document was its call for the regionalization of Portugal's governmental system. Regionalization was seen by Portugal's new democratic elites as the solution to two serious problems facing the fledgling democracy. The first was the need to decentralize and democratize the highly centralized and bureaucratized state apparatus built up over the nearly half century of the *Estado Novo* dictatorship. Creating regional governments was a way of decentralizing that apparatus and making it more responsible to democratic decision-making by creating a functioning level of government between the centre and local authorities. This would move government closer to the people, diffuse bureaucracy and increase the degree of citizen participation in the policy-making process.[6]

The second problem was and still is today the need to deal with Portugal's economic and social underdevelopment as well as the severe geographical inequalities which exist in the country, especially between the Atlantic littoral and the interior. Portugal's historical pattern of economic and social evolution has produced extreme disequilibrium in terms of population densities, infant mortality rates, literacy, energy consumption, industrialization, income per capita, and access to social and medical services between the Atlantic coastal zone, where Portugal's population is concentrated in two major urban conurbations, Lisbon and Porto, and the hinterland and Atlantic islands, which are increasingly deserted and devoid of productive economic activity.[7]

The Constitution enshrines three types of regions: autonomous, administrative, and planning. The autonomous regions are constitutionally similar to Italy's 'special' regions (for example, Sicily and Sardinia) which because of their separation from the mainland and unique economic and political conditions have been granted a special measure of independence. As the Azores and Madeira are separated from continental Portugal and have manifested a desire to be more independent of Lisbon,[8] each archipelago was designated an autonomous region and has functioned as such since 1976.

The Constitution (Articles 227–236) gives the autonomous regions the power to legislate in all matters of local interest; to exercise their own executive authority; to collect and spend their own revenue; to draw up a regional development plan; and to control the disbursement of all funds made available by the national government for local social and economic development. Each island region has been empowered to elect its own executive (*presidente*) and unicameral legislature (*assembleia regional*).

Despite the extensive grants of power and authority to them, the regions are not, however, sovereign. Each region has assigned to it a representative of the national government, the minister of the Republic (*Ministro da República*), who co-ordinates the activities of the national government's ministries located in the region and who must countersign all legislation passed by the regional assembly. The Minister of the Republic may veto bills and send them back to the regional assembly as well as refer those deemed unconstitutional to the Constitutional Tribunal. The Minister of the Republic may also dissolve a region's organs of government should they be found to be engaging in activities contrary to the Constitution.

The administrative regions, which have not yet been created, would replace the district level of local government. The Constitution (Articles 225–265) requires all administrative regions to be created simultaneously but only after a favourable vote of a majority of the counties that would be contained in the proposed regional area. The governments of the regions would be empowered to direct the region's public services and co-ordinate the activities of their municipal executives. Each region would be expected to prepare its own regional development plan and participate in the national planning process. The administrative regions would have two political organs: a regional assembly (*assembleia regional*), which would be constituted by members directly elected from among the registered voters residing in the region as well as members chosen by an electoral college made up of the region's municipal assemblies, and a regional executive (*junta regional*), which would be chosen by the regional assembly from among its own members. Each region would have assigned to it a representative of the government selected by the cabinet (*conselho de ministros*) who would co-ordinate the activities of the government's ministries in the region.

Despite the almost universal agreement among Portugal's new democratic political class that the administrative regions are absolutely necessary to reduce centralization and territorial disequilibrium, their creation has been delayed principally because of intense disagreements about what criteria ought to be used to delineate their boundaries. Since the promulgation of the constitution in 1976 a running debate has been conducted by politicians, academics, and technocrats in the press and at conferences about how many administrative regions ought to be created and where their boundaries ought to be drawn. Although a number of regionalization plans have been proposed, there is a certain similarity among them because the planners tend to use, more or less, the same technical criteria to delineate the regions: river basin ecology, history, and socio-cultural characteristics. Thus, most regionalization plans are variations on one of the earlier proposed. For example, the plan which was put forward by the Ministry of Internal Administration during the sixth provisional government (1975) carves mainland Portugal into seven administrative regions, five of which would be drawn to encompass the coherent geographic and socio-economic entities created by Portugal's five principal river basins, and two of which would encompass the metropolitan areas of Lisbon and Porto in order to deal which the special problems caused by such large conurbations and high population densities.

There is another factor which must be mentioned to explain the failure of Portugal's new democratic political class to create the regions called for in the Constitution. This factor is political. All Portuguese governments since 1976, no matter their political coloration, have looked upon regionalization with mixed emotions. They know, on the one hand, that the regions are necessary to solve the problems of centralization and asymmetry but, on the other, they fear the political opportunity creating the regions might make for the opposition. Politics in Portugal is still too much an either/or proposition for a government to contemplate creating new bastions of power for the opposition to conquer.

The failure to create the administrative regions means that on the mainland the system of districts, counties, and parishes established during the *Estado Novo* dictatorship is still in place. It has been, however, democratized by grafting on to each level an elected legislature and by requiring that the executive of each be accountable to that legislature. Each of Portugal's 4,183 parishes now has a unicameral assembly (*assembleia de frequesia*) the size of which varies with the number of resident registered voters in the parish. The executive of the parish (that is, the *presidente de junta* and *vogais*) whose size varies with the size of the parish, is chosen by the assembly of the parish to whom it is constitutionally responsible. Each of the 305 counties has a unicameral assembly (*assembleia municipal*) composed of the parish presidents within the county as well as an equal number of citizens elected at large. The executive of the county (that is, the *câmara municipal*) is elected directly and, like the parish executive, its size varies with the number of registered voters in the county. The mayor (*presidente da câmara*) is the individual heading the electoral list which receives the highest vote. The mayor is the administrative officer at the local level and as such supervises local government employees, convenes and presides at meetings of the executive, and represents the county at the district and national level. All local government officials are elected simultaneously for three years terms.[9]

The additions to the structure of local government have made the policy-making process at that level much more democratic, but many problems remain. The system is still too centralized, and parish and county executives still act, for the most part, as local administrators for the national government, which must still ultimately approve their activities. Mayors are still more responsible to the civil governor rather than to their assemblies. Moreover, despite the passage of a new local finance law in 1979 which provides local authorities with substantial grants of unrestricted revenue, local governments are still quite dependent upon the national government for money to pay for local projects.[10]

The planning regions called for in the Constitution (Article 95) represent the continuation of the development of such regions begun during the waning years of the *Estado Novo*. In 1966 due to the pressure from technicians who recognized the need to regionalize the planning process, the Division of Regional Planning (*Divisão de Planeamento Regional*) was created within the Directorate of Planning Services (*Direcção de Serviços de Planeamento*), which was then attached to the Prime Minister's secretariat. When the Third Development Plan (1968–73) was drawn up in 1967 it was organized in terms of five planning regions. In 1969 five corresponding regional planning committees (*comissões de planeamento regionais*) were created in order to implement the Plan's regional development projects and to prepare the Fourth Plan. These committees for the first time conducted systematic studies of the problems of regional development and provided technical assistance to local governments. The Fourth Development Plan promulgated in 1973 gave considerable attention and resources to the five planning regions. During the early months of 1974, before the *golpe*, the regional planning committees were transferred to a newly created Secretariat of State for Planning (*Secretariado de Estado do Planeamento*) which was situated within the Ministry of Finance and Economic Coordination. Although planning had begun during the *Estado Novo* it was, however, not very successful. The regional planning committees were short of qualified staff; the plans they drew up were frequently unrealistic; and there was no participation of the citizenry in the planning process.[11]

After the overthrow of the *Estado Novo* in April 1974, the regional planning committees were transferred to the Ministry of Internal Administration (*Ministério da Administração Interna*) and in 1977 they were replaced by Regional Coordinating Committees (*Comissões de Coordinação Regional: CCRs*), one for each planning region on the mainland. The CCRs were given the responsibility for coordinating the technical, financial, and administrative support for local governments and devising and executing regional development plans. The CCRs were composed of representatives from groupings of counties, the directors of the region's technical assistance offices (*Gabinetes de Apoio Técnico: GATS*), and by representatives from the regional offices of the ministries of the national government.[12]

The accession of Portugal to the EC on 1 January 1986 has further solidified the process of regionalization, especially with regard to planning. Accession has meant that Portuguese planners must respond and conform to EC planning standards and directives which, as laid down by the Regional Policy Committee, are designed to reduce socio-economic disequilibria as well as prevent new ones appearing within the Community. As a result of the criteria selected by the Community in identifying underdeveloped regions, Portugal was successful in having its entire geographical space declared underdeveloped and therefore falling within the guidelines for designating the country as an Objective 1 area.

The Portuguese proposal for the allocation of the Structural Funds set aside for Objective 1 areas was formulated in March 1989. The five-year plan or the Community Support Framework (CSF) for Portugal is intended to be simultaneously a national and regional development plan. It presents Portugal's regional development strategy within the context of the overall request for development assistance from the Community. The CSF (1) summarizes Portugal's national and regional socio-economic situation; (2) describes the development strategy to be used to resolve problems identified; (3) indicates the regional development priorities for which financial assistance from the Structural Funds is requested; and (4) specifies which entities of the Portuguese government will implement projects funded. The plan is organized sectorially as well as regionally. It follows the five mainland planning regions used in earlier plans (Norte, Centro, Lisboa e Vale do Tejo, Alentejo, and Algarve) as well as the autonomous regions of the Azores and Madeira in allocating financial resources. It also identified sub-regions such as the Vale do Ave, Vale do Tejo, the Alto Minho, Pinhal Interior and trans-regions such as the Raia Central, Regiões Fronteiriças, Sotovento Algarvio, and the Peninsula de Setúbal, for which special development projects have been identified.[13]

The CSF was prepared under the auspices of the Secretary of State for

Planning and Regional Development (*Secretaria de Estado do Planeamento e do Desenvolvimento Regional*). The drafting was done by a working group headed by the Director-General of Regional Development and composed of the directors of the regional services of various government ministries, representatives from the CCRs of the five planning regions, the directors of planning from the autonomous regions of Madeira and the Azores, and the Director of the Central Planning Department. The Director-General of Regional Policy from the EC Commission was also a regular participant in the meeting of the group. After elaboration by this group, the CSF was negotiated with the EC by Portugal's Ministers of Foreign Affairs and Planning. The regional aspects of the plan will be implemented and evaluated by the CCRs, directors of planning from Madeira and the Azores, as well as various local authorities.[14]

Portugal has chosen to use the great bulk of its 1989–93 financial allocations for projects designed to improve its transportation and communications infrastructure. The emphasis on transportation and communication is necessary in order to enhance the accessibility of Portugal's market to the markets of the broader Community as well as to develop Portugal's own peripheral zones, especially the area along the frontier with Spain and the archipelagoes of Madeira and the Azores. Therefore, many of the plan's projects are for the construction of highways and bridges as well as the improvement of ports, railroads and airports. About sixty per cent of the funds requested by the plan are earmarked for such infrastructure development.[15]

Although the desire to create administrative regions on the mainland has not been fulfilled, the realization of the planning regions has proceeded apace. This is, no doubt, due to the fact that the planning regions were in place before 25 April 1974 and were not potential bastions of power for political opponents. The Constitution contemplates a role for the administrative regions in the planning process (Article 258) through the elaboration of their own plans as well as participating in the elaboration the national plan. This is the procedure presently employed on the part of the two autonomous regions.[16]

III. ASSESSMENT OF REGIONAL FUNCTIONING

In order to assess the functioning of the regions and to shed light on the kinds of regional interactions, common regional programs, and complementary regional policies which would be appropriate for the next stage of EC integration from the point of view of Portuguese elected officials and interest group leaders, a survey of such individuals was conducted. The instruments used to assess these points of view were based on a standard questionnaire prepared by the project director. The major difference between Portugal and some of the other countries included in the project for study was the absence of functioning regional government, except the two autonomous regions of Madeira and the Azores. This meant that there was no single region of sufficient size to provide an adequate universe of elected regional governmental officials and interest group leaders to ensure a sufficient rate of return to meet the sample size that would permit any reliable generalizations. The strategy of sampling only the autonomous regions was rejected because the combined universe of elected officials and interest group leaders on the islands was too small. It was also rejected because it was thought that, owing to strong regionalist sentiments, the sample would be too biased in favour of regions and not reflect opinions about regionalism among officials and leaders throughout Portugal.

As the mayors of the counties are the key elected officials in the Portuguese scheme of local government, the decision was taken to direct the questionnaire designed for politicians to the entire universe of these 305 individuals. In addition, the same questionnaire was sent to the 104 deputies of the assemblies of the autonomous regions. The questionnaire for interest group leaders was sent to the presidents of all 243 regional commercial, agricultural, fishing, industrial, and labour groups in Portugal. The total sample was, therefore, 95 elected officials and 59 interest group leaders. The background characteristics of the respondents are given in Table 1.

The Portuguese version of the questionnaires was designed to take into account the fact that the administrative regions did not yet exist on the mainland. The respondents from the mainland were therefore instructed to answer questions in terms of the particular region (Norte, Centro, Lisboa, e Vale do Tejo, Alentejo, and Algarve) in which they were situated. Those respondents located on Madeira and the Azores were, of course, instructed to answer in terms of their particular autonomous region.

In order to find out how both groups of respondents assess the functioning of the regions on policy-making and implementation, they were asked a series of questions designed to determine their general disposition toward the regions, either planning or autonomous. The first question in this regard asked respondents to indicate their degree of satisfaction with the way their region functions in terms of a number of aspects relevant to the policy-making and implementation process. The results for both groups of respondents for this question are displayed in Table 2. The data reveal that both groups of respondents tend to be quite

TABLE 1

BACKGROUND CHARACTERISTICS OF THE RESPONDENTS

Characteristics	Elected officials		Interest Group Leader	
Region	N	%	N	%
Acores	20	22.1	4	6.8
Madeira	10	10.5	3	5.1
Norte	23	24.2	19	32.2
Centro	18	18.9	12	20.3
Lisboa e Vale do Tejo	11	11.6	12	20.3
Alentejo	11	11.6	6	10.2
Algarve	2	2.1	3	5.1
Age	N	%		
30-39	21	22.3		
40-49	43	45.5		
50-59	26	27.5		
60-69	3	3.3		
Education	N	%		
Primary	3	3.2		
Secondary incomplete	7	7.4		
Secondary complete	24	25.3		
University incomplete	10	10.5		
University complete	51	53.7		
Profession	N	%		
Manual worker	2	2.1		
Technician	3	3.2		
Elected Official	3	3.2		
Civil servant	17	18.4		
Military	1	1.1		
Businessman	4	4.2		
Bank worker	13	13.7		
Farmer	1	1.1		
Lawyer	12	12.6		
Physician	5	5.3		
Teacher/Professor	22	23.1		
Accountant	2	2.1		
Engineer	6	6.3		
Political Party	N	%		
PSD	49	51.6		
PS	28	29.5		
CDS	6	6.3		
PCP	10	10.5		
MDP	1	1.1		
PRD	1	1.1		

dissatisfied with the functioning of their regions with respect to the aspects of policy-making listed. On average, 74.6 per cent of elected officials and 79.4 per cent of interest group leaders indicated that they were either not or little satisfied with regional functioning. Of the two groups of respondents, the percentages displayed suggest that interest group leaders are somewhat more dissatisfied with regional functioning than elected officials. The respondents appear to be somewhat satisfied with only two aspects of regional functioning: the ability to propose projects for elected officials and co-ordination with local government for interest group leaders.

TABLE 2
DEGREE OF SATISFACTION WITH REGIONAL FUNCTIONING (%)

	Elected Officials (N=95)				Interest Group Leaders (N=59)			
	Satisfied				*Satisfied*			
Aspect	Very	Some-what	Little	Not	Very	Some-what	Little	Not
Programmatic choices	0.0	16.0	55.3	28.7	0.0	12.3	66.7	21.1
Planning capacity	0.0	16.1	61.3	22.6	0.0	19.0	51.7	29.3
Project management	3.2	22.3	58.5	16.0	0.0	14.0	57.9	28.1
Implementation time	2.1	21.3	53.2	23.4	0.0	7.1	41.1	51.8
Preparation of personnel	6.4	36.2	51.1	6.4	0.0	8.8	57.9	33.3
Coordination with local government	5.4	19.6	54.3	20.7	3.5	26.3	43.9	26.3
Availability for consultation	2.8	296	42.3	25.4	0.0	22.0	32.0	46.0
Ability to spend	0.0	10.2	60.2	29.5	0.0	11.5	42.3	46.2
Quality of political class	2.2	27.8	58.9	11.1	0.0	12.5	57.1	30.4
Use of university research	1.1	13.6	53.4	31.8	1.9	18.5	37.0	42.6
Ability to propose at national level	13.0	35.9	45.7	5.4	0.0	18.2	45.5	36.4
Mean	3.3	22.6	54.6	20.0	0.5	15.5	48.6	30.8

The data in Table 2 allow the conclusion that both groups of respondents are quite dissatisfied with the way their regions are functioning with respect to various aspects of policy-making and implementation. This conclusion is reinforced by the frequencies of responses to three additional questions along these lines put to the interest group leaders. One question was: 'In your interest sector, the most important policy initiatives come from which level of government, local, regional, or central?' The frequencies of responses were: central government level, 35.6 per cent; regional level, 32.2 per cent; and local level, 23.7 per cent. These responses show that the regional level is perceived to be nearly as important as the national level of government as a source of policy initiatives despite the fact that governmental structures for policy-making and implementation do not exist. What does exist, though, at the regional level is the planning offices of the national ministries, and the answers might be reflecting the overall influence that local officials perceive as emanating from this level. The answers to two additional questions – 'How much impact does the regional government/CCR have on the interest of your organization' and 'Is the impact of the regional government/CCR positive?' – suggest that, despite being an important source of policies relevant to the respondent's groups, the regions do not have much impact on those interests and what impact they have is not positive. Fully 84.8 per cent of the respondents indicated that the impact of the regional government/CCR was either not significant or slightly significant and 61.5 per cent judged what little impact the regions/CCR had as being negative.

What explains the negative orientations of the respondents towards the functioning of their regions? The most obvious explanation is that the regions in reality do not function well owing to the fact that they are relatively new entities on the archipelagoes of Madeira and the Azores and have not been put in place on the mainland. Another explanation might be negative orientations toward the idea of regions in the minds of the respondents. That is to say, perhaps local politicians and interest group leaders do not believe that regionalization is a good idea in the first place and this inclines them to be negatively disposed toward the regions independent of their actual functioning.

In order to measure their disposition toward regionalization, interest group leaders were asked '... do you think that the idea of creating autonomous and administrative regions is a good or bad idea?' By very large majorities (79.3 per cent and 84.7 per cent) the respondents indicated that creating the autonomous regions was a good idea and creating the administrative regions on the mainland would be a good idea. In addition to this question, both elected officials and interest group leaders were asked to indicate which level of government (local, regional, and national) ought to have primary responsibility in a variety of policy areas. The responses to this question are presented in Table 3 and reveal that the respondents prefer the region as the appropriate level of government for most of the policy areas listed. These data indicate that the respondents not only think that the idea of creating regions was a good idea but that the regions ought to have responsibility for most policy areas. It follows, then, that the dissatisfaction expressed above concerning the current functioning of the regions does not derive from any negative orientations held by the respondents toward the idea of regionalism *per se*.

TABLE 3
LEVEL OF GOVERNMENT APPROPRIATE TO VARIOUS POLICY AREAS (%)

	Elected Officials (N=95)				Interest Group Leaders (N=59)			
Area	State	Region	County	Shared	State	Region	County	Shared
Health	23.7	60.2	12.9	3.3	44.1	47.5	8.5	0.0
Agriculture	6.4	78.7	10.6	4.3	12.1	81.0	6.9	0.0
Police	31.5	26.1	39.1	3.3	32.8	22.4	43.1	1.7
Environment	7.4	34.0	48.9	9.6	15.3	35.6	49.2	0.0
Primary education	3.2	29.8	63.8	3.2	22.0	30.5	47.5	0.0
Secondary education	14.9	63.8	17.0	4.3	25.4	45.8	28.8	0.0
University	44.6	47.8	1.1	6.5	40.7	52.5	6.8	0.0
Industria-lization	5.3	70.2	18.1	5.5	5.2	69.0	24.1	1.7
Foreign trade	54.3	40.2	1.1	3.3	50.8	42.4	5.1	1.7
Artisanry	1.1	20.4	73.1	5.4	3.4	32.2	62.7	1.7
Credit	16.0	60.6	16.0	7.4	33.9	49.2	16.9	0.0
Scientific research	55.3	39.4	5.3	0.0	39.0	52.5	6.8	1.7
Taxes	31.2	36.6	22.6	9.7	44.8	29.3	25.9	0.0
Transportation	9.6	60.6	24.5	5.3	13.8	48.3	36.2	1.7
Employment	77.4	19.4	1.1	2.2	64.4	30.5	3.4	1.7
Public works	21.3	58.5	17.0	3.2	28.8	47.5	20.3	3.4
Cultural affairs	4.3	38.3	48.9	8.5	3.4	37.3	57.6	1.7
Urban areas	1.1	24.5	71.3	3.2	5.1	28.8	66.1	0.0
Mean	22.7	44.9	27.4	5.0	26.9	43.5	28.7	0.9

The data in Table 3 also show a considerable agreement between the two respondent groups in terms of which policy areas ought to be the responsibility of which level of government. For example, both local politicians and interest group leaders strongly agree that the region is the most appropriate level of government for the policy areas of agriculture and industrialization. They also agree, but less strongly, that the region is most appropriate for the areas of health, secondary education, credit, transportation, and public works. Both groups of respondents also strongly agree that the most appropriate level of government for the policy areas of primary education, artisanry, cultural affairs, and urban areas is the county (*município*). The two respondent groups also agree, but less strongly, that the county is the most appropriate level of government for the allocation of responsibilities in the areas of environmental protection and policing. Both local elected officials and interest group leaders strongly agree that the central government is the most appropriate level of government to deal with foreign trade and employment policy. Finally, both groups view the central and regional governments as needing to share responsibility for the policy areas of university education, scientific research, and taxes.

In sum, the results of the survey presented thus far show local elected officials and interest group leaders to be very favourably disposed toward the regions, even though they are not seen to be functioning satisfactorily. The question now arises: Are there any differences among the respondents in terms of location? That is, do respondents from the Azores and Madeira which have been operating as autonomous regions since 1976 evince stronger regionalist sentiment and greater satisfaction with regional functioning? To find out, elected officials were broken down into regional categories (Norte, Centro, Lisboa e Vale do Tejo, Alentejo, Algarve, Madeira, and Açores) and their responses to the questions about regional functioning were tabulated with these categories. The results of this analysis, which can be seen in Table 4, show that there is a tendency for elected officials from the Azores and Madeira to be very or somewhat satisfied with the functioning of the regions than are respondents from continental regions, with the exception of those from the Norte region who seem to be as satisfied as their island counterparts. Respondents from the Centro, Lisboa e Vale do Tejo, Alentejo, and Algarve regions on the whole tend to be little or not satisfied with regional functioning.

What explains these different patterns of responses? The fact that the pattern of satisfaction-dissatisfaction for the Norte region is very similar to that of the Azores and Madeira militates against the possibility that the answer has to do with the latter two being autonomous regions while the former one is only a planning region. The patterns may in fact be a reflection of the territorial distribution of the bases of support for Portugal's main political parties. It is well known to specialists of Portuguese affairs that the Atlantic archipelagoes and the north of Portugal are strongholds of the Social Democratic Party (*Partido Social Democrata: PSD*) and the Christian Democrats (*Partido de Centro Democrático Social: CDS*) while the south, especially the Alentejo, is the bastion of the Communist Party (*Partido Comunista Português: PCP*) and its ally the Popular Democratic Movement (Movimento Popular

TABLE 4
DEGREE OF SATISFACTION WITH REGIONAL FUNCTIONING, BY REGION (%)

	REGION						
Degree of satisfaction	Azores	Madeira	Norte	Centro	Lisboa V.Do Tejo	Alentejo	Algarve
Very satisfied	5.0	8.0	3.0	1.0	0.0	3.0	0.0
Somewhat satisfied	20.0	35.0	32.0	17.0	13.0	11.0	5.0
Little satisfied	61.0	42.0	49.0	57.0	54.0	54.0	36.0
Not satisfied	14.0	10.0	15.0	24.0	33.0	32.0	59.0

TABLE 5
DEGREE OF SATISFACTION WITH REGIONINGAL FUNCTIONING, BY PARTY (%)

	PARTY							
Degree of satisfaction	(Left)	MDP	PCP	PRD	PS	PSD	CDS	(Right)
Very satisfied		0	0	1	1	3	2	
Somewhat satisfied		0	10	13	16	29	30	
Little satisfied		82	30	43	61	52	54	
Not satisfied		18	60	43	20	15	14	

Democrático: MDP). Support for the Socialist Party (Partido Socialista: PS) and the Party of Democratic Renewal (*Partido Renovador Democrático: PRD*) tends to be concentrated in Lisboa and Porto as well as in the Centro region. The differences in evaluation of regional functioning may, therefore, be reflected in the party affiliations of the respondents.

In order to find out, the responses to the question about regional functioning for local elected officials were tabulated with their political party affiliation. These calculations, which can be seen in Table 5, reveal a strong and clear tendency for PCP, MDP, PRD and PS elected officials to be consistently dissatisfied with the functioning of their regions. Elected officials of the PSD and CDS, while on the whole dissatisfied, were much more likely to express satisfaction with at least some areas of functioning. Therefore, it is entirely conceivable that the consistent expression of dissatisfaction by officials of the PCP, MDP, PRD, and PS is a reflection of political opposition to the national government which is in the hands of the PSD rather than unhappiness in an objective sense with regional functioning. It is also conceivable that Madeira and Norte do objectively function better because the national government is responding more adequately to its strongest constituency. In any case, there is no doubt that region/party affiliation in some mix tends to some degree to colour an elected officials evaluations of regional functioning.

IV. INTER-REGIONAL CO-OPERATION

Now that evidence has been presented which establishes that local elected officials and interest group leaders view the region as the most appropriate level of government for carrying out policy in many areas as well as the fact that they do not see the regions (planning or autonomous) as functioning very satisfactory, a discussion of how the respondents see the regions with respect to the advent of the unified market in 1992 is in order.

The first question put to the respondents along this line was: 'is your region well prepared ... for the coming of the unified market in 1992?' Table 6 shows that by large majorities both local elected officials and the leaders of interest groups are of the opinion that their regions are poorly prepared for the unified market. This assessment is only slightly less pessimistic on the part of the interest group leaders whose percentages of response show a tendency to more often judge their regions to be at least somewhat prepared or well prepared in the various structures. For these respondents, their region's university system and level of associationalism are perceived to be somewhat prepared for the challenges of the unified market. For the elected officials, port facilities, social and health services, and university systems are seen to be at least somewhat ready for 1992. It should be noted that neither group of respondents judge any structural aspect of their regions to be adequate for the challenges of 1992. These findings are not at all surprising given the results observed above with respect to the respondents' assessment of the functioning of the regions. The regions are seen as not only functioning badly but poorly prepared for the coming of unified market and the increased competition from the rest of Europe.

What do the respondents see as the likely consequences of 1992 on policy in their regions? In order to find out both local officials and interest group leaders were asked whether certain situations would arise as a result of the creation of the unified market. Table 7 presents the fre-

TABLE 6
LEVEL OF STRUCTURAL PREPARATION FOR 1992 (%)

	Elected Officials (N=95)			Interest Group Leaders (N=59)		
		Prepared			Prepared	
Structure	Well	Samewhat	Poorly	Well	Somewhat	Poorly
Small/medium enterprises	0.0	8.5	91.5	0.0	10.7	89.3
Port facilities	2.3	40.2	57.5	3.5	24.6	71.9
Air communication	0.0	30.4	69.6	5.2	31.0	63.8
Road network	0.0	34.0	66.0	3.4	34.5	62.1
Railroad network	0.0	7.4	92.6	4.1	20.4	75.5
Farms	0.0	4.3	95.7	1.7	17.2	81.0
Social services	2.1	37.2	60.6	3.4	32.8	63.8
Health services	1.1	42.6	56.4	3.4	20.7	75.9
University system	0.0	52.2	47.8	5.3	49.1	45.6
Associationalism	1.1	23.4	75.5	8.6	41.4	50.0
Skills of labour force	0.0	12.8	87.2	6.9	37.9	55.2
Industrial/tech. innovation	0.0	9.6	90.4	6.9	25.9	67.2
Industrial restructuring	0.0	6.4	93.6	3.4	27.6	69.0
Functionality of urban areas	1.1	24.7	71.3	5.3	35.1	59.6
Utilization of historical/ environment	2.2	34.4	63.4	6.9	39.7	53.4
Commercial network	0.0	24.7	75.3	6.9	31.0	62.1
Mean	0.6	24.7	74.5	4.7	29.9	64.8

quencies of response to this question in terms of a set of possible consequences. It is readily apparent from the table that the high degree of congruence observed in previous tables between both groups of respondents for functioning of the regions and level of structural preparation is repeated. The general pattern of congruence between both groups is disturbed only in two situations: confusion of functioning among levels of government and employment. On these two situations the frequencies are reversed with interest group leaders much more often indicating that confusion of functioning among levels of government and unemployment

TABLE 7
PROBABLE CONSEQUENCES OF 1992 (%)

	Elected Officials (N=95)		Interest Group Leaders (N=95	
Consequence	Will happen	Will not happen	Will happen	Will not happen
Access to new markets	80.6	19.4	83.1	16.9
Less of regional identity	16.1	83.9	20.7	79.3
Stimulation of techn. innovation	89.2	10.8	87.9	12.1
Confusion of functions	40.9	59.1	62.1	37.9
More competition	92.6	7.4	98.3	1.7
Stimulation of instit. renovation	96.8	3.2	84.5	15.5
Worsen situation in less developed areas	63.0	37.0	61.0	39.0
Improve social services	73.9	26.1	68.4	31.6
Retard decision making process	66.0	34.0	71.9	28.1
Adoption of new environm. standards	91.5	8.5	79.7	20.3
Increased unemployment	40.0	59.6	55.9	44.1
Access to new financial markets	86.2	13.8	80.7	19.3
Restructuring of commercial network	90.2	9.8	79.3	20.7
Reconversion of agricultural product.	89.1	10.9	84.7	15.3
Modernization of regional administr.	93.6	6.4	73.7	26.3
Concentration of Industry	47.8	52.2	53.4	46.6
Improvement of living standards	81.5	18.5	73.7	26.3
Mean	72.5	27.5	66.9	33.1

will happen and elected officials much more frequently indicating that these will not happen as a consequence of 1992.

These two situations aside, both groups of respondents concur that positive consequences such as access to new markets, stimulation of technological innovation, stimulation of competition, improved social services, the adoption of new environmental standards, increased access to financial markets, the restructuring of commercial distribution networks, the stimulation of agricultural reconversion, the modernization of local administration, and the improvement of the standard of living as well as negative consequences such as the worsening of conditions in the less developed areas, the retardation of the decision-making process, increased costs of production, and the concentration of industry will occur. Interestingly, neither group sees the loss of regional identity as a consequence of greater EC intervention.

In order to learn the best way for the EC to interact with regional authorities in light of 1992, the respondents were asked a series of questions designed to determine what type and level of trans-regional co-operation they would favour after that date. The first question along this line was the level of intervention that the EC ought to take in a list of policy areas? The frequencies of response for this question are given in Table 8 which reveals that both local elected officials and interest group leaders strongly favour an increase in EC intervention in their regions for the various policy areas listed. The data presented show that of these two groups the interest group leaders were by a slight margin more inclined toward an increase in intervention than were elected officials. They were especially keen on increased EC intervention in the areas of environmental standards enforcement, financial support for projects in less developed areas, promotion of technological innovation, and the promotion of immigrant integration. Elected officials were strongly in favour of increased intervention in the areas of support for projects in less developed areas, scientific research, promotion of technological intervention, and promotion of immigrant integration. The only policy area where both groups favored a diminution of intervention by the EC was in the area of controlling the circulation of immigrants. This result is not surprising considering that Portugal has been traditionally a country of high emigration.

The second question in the series put to the respondents asked them to indicate how important they thought that certain policy instruments already present in a number of federal systems would be necessary for the EC to possess in managing the course and consequences of the unified market after 1992. The results of this question are displayed in Table 9. The data presented reveal that both groups of respondents are of the

TABLE 8
DEGREE OF INTERVENTION BY EC AFTER 1992 (%)

	Elected Officials (N=95)			Interest Group Leaders (N=95		
Policy Area	Increase	Same	Diminish	Increase	Same	Diminish
Enforcing environmental standards	75.5	18.1	6.4	89.8	5.1	5.1
Evaluating regional investment projects	45.2	29.0	25.8	50.8	33.9	15.3
Evaluating district investment projects	24.5	35.1	40.4	49.2	32.2	18.6
Financing projects for less developed areas	92.6	3.2	4.3	89.7	6.9	3.4
Monitoring financial markets	67.4	27.2	5.4	65.5	31.0	3.4
Orienting scientific research to Europe	81.5	14.1	4.3	77.2	19.3	3.5
Promoting technological innovation	89.2	10.8	0.0	91.5	8.5	0.0
Formulating guidelines for vocational education	64.9	22.3	12.8	63.8	29.3	6.9
Monitoring the labour market	63.0	31.5	5.4	70.7	22.4	6.9
Controlling the circulation of immigrants	20.7	25.0	54.3	42.1	21.1	36.8
Promoting the integration of immigrants	78.7	14.9	6.4	77.2	17.5	5.3
Coordinating foreign trade	55.6	24.4	20.3	60.3	24.1	15.5
Mean	63.2	21.3	15.5	69.2	21.4	9.4

opinion that all of the various types of interventions listed are either necessary or indispensable. The percentage of responses suggests that, of the two groups, interest group leaders on average see such interventions as not only necessary but indispensable. This is the case especially for European-level environmental, labour market, and telecommunications agencies and a European administrative court. Although elected officials view most of the types of intervention as necessary, they tend to see at least two as indispensable: a Euro-environmental agency and European-programmes for sectoral intervention. The percentages indicate that only the European CONSOB (for example, a European equivalent of the US

TABLE 9

DESIRABILITY OF VARIOUS TYPES OF EC INTERVENTION AFTER 1992 (%)

Type of intervention	Elected Officials (N=95)			Interest Group Leaders (N=59		
	Indispensable	Necessary	Not necessary	Indispensable	Necessary	Not necessary
Central European Bank	26.1	62.0	12.0	31.0	55.2	13.8
Euro-environmental agency	42.6	55.3	2.1	55.0	44.8	0.0
Euro-programmes for sectoral intervention	44.7	51.1	4.3	39.7	60.3	0.0
Euro-agencies for interregional cooperation	24.5	66.0	9.6	32.8	55.2	12.1
Postgraduate Euro-diplomas	28.7	52.1	19.1	39.7	48.3	12.1
Euro-administrative court	38.7	47.3	14.0	51.7	32.8	15.5
Euro-agency to monitor labour market	21.3	67.0	11.7	50.0	41.4	8.6
Euro-CONSOB	20.2	58.5	21.3	31.0	50.0	19.0
Euro-conference of regional presidents	39.4	51.1	9.6	39.7	50.0	10.3
Offices for regions in Brussels	34.0	50.0	16.0	41.4	43.1	15.5
Euro-telecommunication agency	37.6	58.1	4.3	50.9	45.6	3.5
Mean	32.5	56.0	11.5	42.0	47.9	10.0

Securities and Exchange Commission) and postgraduate diplomas were viewed as somewhat not necessary by elected officials. Interest group leaders felt that the Euro-administrative courts, the European CONSOB, and offices for regions in Brussels were not necessary.

The third question in this series asked the respondents to indicate the level of desirability of certain common initiatives that could occur among regions of different European countries in the context of the unified market. The frequencies of responses for this question are presented in Table 10. They reveal that, like the results displayed in Table 9, both groups of respondents in general viewed the common initiatives as

TABLE 10
DESIRABILITY OF VARIOUS TYPES OF INTERREGIONAL INITIATIVES (%)

Type of initiative	Elected Officials (N=95)			Interest Group Leaders (N=59)		
	Indispensable	Necessary	Not necessary	Indispensable	Necessary	Not necessary
Lobby of regions at EC Commission	25.6	54.4	20.0	14.3	58.9	26.8
Formulation of development projects	47.3	47.3	5.4	43.1	55.2	1.7
Cultural-tourist exchange programs	37.6	62.4	0.0	54.4	45.6	0.0
Plans for applied research	31.2	67.7	1.1	43.1	56.9	0.0
Policies to protect environment	61.3	38.7	0.0	66.7	33.3	0.0
Promotion of products/services	33.0	58.2	8.8	39.7	55.2	5.2
Strengthen regional airline service	44.1	51.6	4.3	56.9	37.9	5.2
Training of civil service personnel	49.5	43.0	7.5	44.8	48.3	6.9
Promoting of joint-ventures	23.7	73.1	3.2	46.6	50.0	3.4
Integrated programmes for neighbouring regions	38.7	58.1	3.2	48.3	48.3	3.4
Mean	39.2	55.5	5.3	45.8	49.0	5.2

necessary or indispensable. Again, interest group leaders tend to view these instruments as indispensable while elected officials more frequently see them as only necessary. Interest group leaders see common regional environmental protection policies, cultural/tourist exchange programmes, and strengthening regional airlines as especially indispensable. The percentages of response for this question show that elected officials concur on the indispensability of one of these common regional initiatives: environmental protection policies. The only type of common regional initiative to receive significant not necessary responses from both groups of respondents is the regional lobby at the EC Commission.

In sum, the data presented in Tables 6 to 10 suggest that both elected officials and interest group leaders view their regions as woefully prepared for 1992. Both groups of respondents believe that there will be many consequences for the regions once the unified market comes into existence. None the less, both groups of respondents were favourably disposed towards increased EC intervention in various policy areas and see various type of interventions and regional policy initiatives as not only necessary but indispensable for the regions in the context of the unified market. It should be noted that tabulations between the responses to the questions concerning the level of preparation for and consequences of 1992 and the region and political party affiliation of the respondents did not reveal any variation. Thus, region/party affiliation seem only to affect the respondents' evaluation of regional functioning not their expectations about 1992.

CONCLUSIONS

The present analysis shows that Portugal is at present in a transitional period between the old model of the centralized states as represented by the *Estado Novo* and a new regionalized form of state organization. There is a diffused desire on the part of local politicians and interest group leaders for a full implementation of the articles in the Portuguese Constitution that foresee the creation of full-fledged regional governments capable of engaging in policy-making and implementation. The European Commission has tried to nudge Portugal in the direction of implementing its constitutional provisions for the region through the insertion of a regional level component in the Community Support Framework. However, up until now the Portuguese government has limited the participation of the regional level to the planning regions and the structure of the national ministries.

The data presented above show that local elected officials and interest group leaders in Portugal are receptive to such efforts. Once the administrative regions are in place, the EC could and should work to enhance the preparation and training of regional administrative personnel, especially those concerned with planning and project management.

The preferred content of the framework for inter- and trans-regional co-operation from the point of view of the Portuguese respondents can be inferred from the data presented in Tables 8, 9 and 10. Of the policy areas, types of EC intervention and inter-regional initiatives listed in these tables, 60 per cent of both groups of respondents either wanted an increase in or found necessary the following intervention/initiatives: (1) enforcement of environmental standards; (2) financing less developed areas; (3) monitoring financial markets; (4) orienting scientific research towards Europe; (5) promoting technological innovation; (6) guidelines for vocational-technical education; (7) monitoring labour markets; (8) integration of immigrants; (9) coordination of foreign trade; (10) central

European bank; (11) Euro-environmental agency; and (12) agency for inter-regional co-operation. All of these initiatives can be taken by the Commission from the top and can be imposed, once they are transformed into regulations and directives, on the member states. However, these initiatives do not create any space for a bottom-up approach which is a fundamental aspect of the demand for regional reform in Portugal.

The answers to the questionnaires collected within Portugal show that there is also a strong desire to gain decision-making autonomy *vis-à-vis* the central government. It is true that the central government administrative apparatus is at times efficient and has shown an ability to administer EC policies at the national level in an effective manner, but the Portuguese experience has also shown that the strong national approach imposed on the local choices for development strategies has limited the ability of local areas to find their market niches in the production of goods and services. Once the major infrastructure projects are in place, will the centre insist on deciding where and what products will be produced by Portuguese manufacturers and service providers? The experience of other countries along the Mediterranean rim, such as Spain and Italy, has shown that these decisions are more appropriate for local officials in collaboration with entrepreneurs, but to take these decisions local officials need the institutions and resources and legal/political autonomy to make and implement decisions. Without such a structure, such decisions will remain centred in Lisbon and therefore weaken Portugal's opportunity to take full advantage of the unified market.

NOTES

1. Administrative support was provided by the Instituto de Ciências Sociais (ICS), Universidade de Lisboa. The author would like to express his appreciation to the Institute's director, A. Sedas Nunes, for putting the ICS at his service for the duration of the project as well as to Paul Autunes Ferreira for his able research assistance.
2. For a good overview of Salazar's regime consult Howard J. Wiarda, *Corporatism and Development: The Portuguese Experience* (Amherst, MA: University of Massachusetts Press, 1977).
3. Joyce Fiestenberg Riegelhaupt, 'Peasants and Politics in Salazar's Portugal: The Corporate State and Village "Non-politics"', in Lawrence S. Graham and Harry M. Makler (eds.), *Contemporary Portugal: The Revolution and Its Antecedents* (Austin, TX: University of Texas Press, 1979), pp. 163–73.
4. Lawrence S. Graham, *Portugal: The Decline and Collapse of an Authoritarian Order* (London and Beverly Hills, CA: Sage Publications, 1975), pp. 17.
5. On the *golpe de estado* and subsequent events see Douglas Porch, *The Portuguese Armed Forces and the Revolution* (Stanford, CA: Hoover Institution Press, 1977); Rona Fields, *The Portuguese Revolution and the Armed Forces Movement* (New York: Praeger, 1976).
6. *Livro Branco Sobre Regionalização* (Lisboa: Secretaria de Estado da Administração Regional e Local, 1981): 25–36.

7. In 1985, the Atlantic coastal area which accounts for only 25 per cent of the national territory contained more than 70 per cent of the population and produced about 85 percent of the GDP. Lisbon has 36 per cent of the country's population.
8. During the period of exception after the 1974 *golpe* two separatist movements appeared on the islands: The Madeira Liberation Front (*Frente de Libertação Madeirese: FLMA*) and the Azorian Liberation Front (*Frente de Libertação Açoriana: FLA*) which sabotaged government buildings and actively sought to detach the Azore from Portugal and make them a protectorate of the United States. See Tom Gallagher, 'Portugal's Atlantic Territories: The Separatist Challenge', *World Today*, 39 (Sept. 1979), pp. 353–9.
9. See Walter C. Opello, Jr., 'The Second Portuguese Republic: Politico-Administrative Decentralization Since April 25, 1974', *Iberian Studies, 7* (Autumn 1978), pp. 43–48 for details.
10. See Walter C. Opello, Jr., 'Local Government and Political Culture in a Portuguese Rural County', *Comparative Politics, 13* (April 1981), pp. 271–89.
11. Jorge Gaspar, 'Regional Planning, Decentralization and Popular Participation in Post-1974 Portugal', *Iberian Studies 5* (Spring 1976), pp. 31–2.
12. Ernesto V.W. Figueiredo, *Portugal: Que Regiões* (Braga: Instituto Nacional de Investigação Científica, 1989), p. 39.
13. Secretaria do Estado do Planeamento e do Desenvolvimento Regional, *Portugal: Plano de Desenvolvimento Regional, 1979–1983* (Lisboa, 1989).
14. Ibid.
15. Ibid.
16. The Constitution has been revised twice since it was promulgated in 1976, the first time in 1982 and the second in 1989. The 1976 and 1982 versions clearly state that the area of the administrative regions will conform to those of the planning regions. The 1989 version is mute on this point.

Regions and the European Community: A Comparative Analysis of Four Spanish Regions

FRANCESC MORATA

I. INTRODUCTION

The political transition in Spain from authoritarianism to democracy was characterized by the need to find a solution to the permanent crisis of the old centralist state – that is, to provide a positive response to the historical claims for regional autonomy on the part of Catalonia and the Basque country. The dual consensus reached across the ideological spectrum and the centre-periphery cleavage helped to establish the political autonomy for these two regions. The aspirations for regional autonomy was enshrined in the 1978 Spanish Constitution, and the extension of regional government to the other 15 regions in Spain constituted the only compromise possible at the time on the issue of decentralization. Spain's entry into the European Community was also seen as the final step in a political and social process which had started after the death of Franco and which effectively put an end to the country's isolation from developments taking place in the rest of Europe.

Nevertheless, as for other regionalized member states, Spain's entry into the EC has created problems of a political and institutional nature which highlight the shortcomings of the 1978 constitutional agreement on the regions. Despite this, European integration and devolution are not contradictory phenomena. Instead, from a number of perspectives they are part of a complementary and increasingly interdependent processes. The interconnection between the two processes will be illustrated through the use of data collected as part of a cross-national project looking at the role of regions in the European Community in preparing for the opening of the single market at the end of 1992.

The work in Spain was carried out using two samples of political (elected members of the regional assemblies) and socio-economic elites (representatives of regional interest groups) in four regions (Andalusia, Catalonia, Galicia and Valencia) that represent various levels of economic development and political colorations characteristic of regional politics in Spain.[1] We will also examine the attitudes of the regional respondents toward the creation of new Community initiatives and policy structures that could increase the power and range of Community actions in the post-1992 context.

A Brief History of Spanish Regional Institutions

The Spanish Constitution is a hybrid system which is neither federal nor regional but based on the principles of the 'unity of the Spanish nation' and the 'autonomy of the nationalities and regions which constitute it'. Due to the Constitutional Pact, the unitary-autonomy conflict expresses itself in the difficulty faced by the parties in reaching satisfactory agreements on the organization of the nation–state. The complex and ambiguous nature of the division of power between the central and regional institutions has been a source of constant controversy and had led to many cases being taken to the Constitutional Court.

In principle the creation of an Autonomous Community (AC) at the regional level does not depend on the Spanish Parliament but on the representative territorial assembly which is responsible for formulating a Status of Autonomy. The various regional statutes are legally protected against future change and hence have a similar standing to the Constitution in establishing the distribution of power.

Statutes fall into two categories which reflect two different ways of reaching autonomy: special and general. The first category covers the three historical national minorities (the Basque country, Catalonia, and Galicia) with the addition of Andalusia for political reasons. These four regions have 'full' autonomy statutes which must be ratified by referendum.

The second category is a transitional category: after a five-year period the autonomous authorities can request wider powers to obtain 'full' autonomy (this has already happened in some cases). The Spanish parliament can transfer legislative and executive functions without any statutory reform.[2] Thus the Spanish system – which was initially heterogeneous – in fact tends toward greater homogeneity based on the full autonomy of the regions.

Devolution also presumes the existence of an institutional and administrative organization. The Constitution establishes three kinds of institutions: a legislative assembly elected by universal suffrage; a government council headed by a president; and a high court of justice. The distribution of functions is based on two lists linked to the forms of autonomy. The Autonomous Communities can take on the following functions: organization of regional administration; local administration (some minor functions); territorial planning (urban planning, housing, public works, environment, etc.); and social services, culture and economic policy (tourism, small trades and industry, agriculture and fishing, communication and development).[3]

However, the real limitation to devolution relates to the central state functions.[4] The legal provision is rather ambiguous and has given rise to numerous legal conflicts and the intervention of the Constitutional Court, either at the request of the central or regional governments. It is a highly complex system based on shared and concurrent powers. In the majority of cases the Constitution attributes the 'basic legislation' or 'basic norms' relating to governing functions (banking and credit facilities, health, education, planning, employment, transport, environment, mass media, local government, etc.) to the central state institutions. Nevertheless, the limits between the two powers are rather unclear. Thus, the institutional actors at the centre and periphery often operate unilaterally invading each other's competences.

The Spanish system only partly follows the logic of the German 'executive federalism' in which the *Länder* have a double function, namely the planning and enforcement of *Länd* regulations and the implementation of federal legislation and policies. According to the Spanish Constitution, central controls are only allowed when regions carry out functions previously transferred or delegated by central institutions. At the same time, the latter maintain some of their executive functions within the regions, which thus provides them with a bureaucratic territorial apparatus.

With regard to the federal tradition, the Constitution established several institutional mechanisms to ensure the representation of regional interests at the national level. Some members of the Upper Chamber (*Senado*) are directly elected by territorial parliaments and these can also deposit bills in the Lower Chamber (*Congreso*).

Finally, regions enjoy autonomy according to the principles of co-ordination with state finance and inter-regional solidarity. The regional financing system is broadly based on shared central revenues, regional tax revenues and contributions from a shared cooperation fund (*Fondo de Compensación interritorial*).

Current Practice: Shortcomings and Conflicts

The implementation of the new state can be divided into three main phases: 1978–81; 1981–83; and 1983–89.[5] The first phase coincides with the application of the constitutional measures, the subsequent approval of the Autonomous Statutes for national minorities and the establishment of their representative institutions. During this phase proposals for political reorganization implicitly referred to in the Constitution had considerable backing. Pressure from the nationalistic parties – often backed by the Communist and Socialist left – offset the centralizing inertia of the governmental Centre Democratic Union (UCD) party, conditioned by its commitment to economic and bureaucratic elites traditionally belonging to the centre.

The second phase began with the failed *coup d'état* which led to the resignation of Prime Minister Suarez and the internal destruction of the UCD in favour of a more conservative right. The political crisis led to the so-called autonomous agreements between the UCD and PSOE (Socialist Party), which in turn led to an attempt to carry out an indirect constitutional reform by the means of a 'law harmonizing the autonomous process'. Even though the law was rejected by the Constitutional Court in 1983 as unconstitutional, following a great political and legal debate, the motives which inspired it continued to dominate central government's behaviour, even after the election victory of the PSOE in 1982.

The third phase was characterized by the institutionalization of the Autonomous Communities and the confirmation of the PSOE's absolute majority in the 1986 general elections. In the 1983 regional and local elections, the PSOE became the dominant political force in twelve regions, whilst in 1984, nationalist parties consolidated their hegemony in the Basque country and Catalonia. Conflict and tension arising from opposition to devolution, on the one hand, and struggles for further autonomy on the other characterized centre–periphery relations during this time. The most significant effect was the clear Socialist loss of support in favour of regional parties and the political right in the 1987 regional elections, compensated by its participation in coalition governments in the Basque country and Galicia. The debate was centred on four main questions: the definition of central–regional powers, the reform of the central administration, the distribution of central financial resources, and the lack of co-ordination.

Definition of central–regional powers: The ability to form a majority government freed the PSOE from the obligation of having to negotiate the laws defining the functions and powers of the regions (for example, administration, electoral system, civil servants, university, health). These laws considerably reduced their range of powers forcing the Constitutional Court to intervene. At the same time, the central government has not hesitated in opposing regional legal arrangements when these were considered to encroach on central competences. By 1990 these controversies had generated around 800 legal disputes and reflected a high degree of conflict. The decisions of the Constitutional Court, however, have tended to preserve the intervening powers of the central institutions. Moreover, a number of regional authorities see the 1985 Local Government Act, which established the province as the second level of local administration, as a threat to the process of decentralization. The 1985 Act allows central government to transfer grants and other resources to provincial and local councils as a means of implementing national policies and by-passing the regional level of government.

Reform of the central administration: According to the Constitution and Statutes, the regions are the main administrators of public services, but a real central administrative reform has not yet taken place.[6] The number of civil servants continues to increase as the size of the central government increases.

The heterogeneous powers of the Autonomous Communities allows the central government to maintain a central bureaucratic apparatus with executive functions which affect only some of the AC but helps to justify the existence a broad territorial administration (central government delegates, provincial governors and ministerial agencies). The bilateral government negotiation with each of the 17 regional actors is bureaucratic and time-consuming.

The tendency of the central government to cut regional functions is seen in the reduction of services and resources transferred, which in turn affects the new administrative framework. The fragmented devolution has had an immediate impact on regional administrations. The regions have chosen the easiest way out: the reproduction of the inherited structures. Moreover, resistance to transfer by central bureaucratic elites has led the new authorities to employ staff from the local administration or the private sector, often with a partisan point of view.

The distribution of financial resources: The legal development of the Constitution established – with the exception of the Basque country and Navarra[7] – a provisional financial system for the AC based on the evaluation of the central services devolved to the new administrations, the product of transferred taxes and the Shared Cooperation Fund. The first mechanism required the formulation of a very complex method of evaluation and the establishment of 17 bilateral commissions to estimate the annual cost of transferred services. In fact, the combination of both elements has allowed central authorities to decide the amount of matching revenues according to central budget priorities. At the same time, the

AC must avoid creating their own financial resources if they do not want to play the role of tax collectors. The cooperation fund (30 per cent of central budget investments) has failed in the double function of reducing territorial disparities and providing financial investments for all regions. In these circumstances, the new authorities had no other option than to run into increasing indebtedness (15 per cent of total expenditure in 1990).

The new finance system – effective from 1987 to 1991 – was the result of a difficult commitment which has already been called into question. The most important innovations concerned the division of the cooperation fund into two independent blocks (less developed regions and more developed regions) and the prospects for permanent participation in some central revenues. Nevertheless, the AC continued to be financially irresponsible and the block grants were still excessively high. In 1990 the participation of regional authorities in total public expenditure rose to 22 per cent, which represented 32.6 per cent of total public investments.

Lack of coordination: Despite appearances, the Spanish Constitution does not facilitate the effective integration of regional concerns in the formulation of central policies. In contrast to Germany and like Italy, regional interests are almost excluded from the central legislative process. The Senate is, in fact, a non-specialized chamber elected on a majority basis at the provincial level, where national parties dominate. Only 20 per cent of the senators are elected directly from the regional parliaments. This situation weakens institutional cohesion, leads to centrifugal tendencies and, in short, undermines the decentralized system's ability to function.

As for the formulation and implementation of public policies, state programmes have tended to ignore or give low priority to the needs of regional authorities (for example, reindustrialization or reconversion for sectors in crisis), and the role of the sectoral conferences institutionalized since 1983 is in no way comparable to that of similar bodies in Germany. The bodies in Spain barely facilitate the exchange of information on decisions already adopted unilaterally or negotiated without the existing procedures (for example, the new financial arrangement).

Effective coordination is the result of the political bargaining which has dominated the devolution process, allowing short-term political calculations to prevail over the need for rationality and efficiency. The highly complex nature of these administrative workings reveals some characteristics common to decentralization: diachronicity, fragmentation, central interference, absence of a clear model of public administration and, hence, constant political conflict.

None the less, the model of intergovernmental relations has substantially changed since 1982. Firstly, the PSOE's control of central institutions has led, in effect, to an identification of party interests with state interests. The same applies to the regional administrations governed by nationalist forces. This combination allows us to put forward the hypothesis of two intergovernmental policy-making styles. The first (of partisan inspiration) characterizes the relations between central government and the regions under Socialist control. Co-ordination is fundamentally based on hierarchical relations or internal party negotiation. Conflict erupts in response to power struggles and not because of different conceptions of the institution's role. These regions are not well placed to put much pressure on central government.

The second style corresponds to the relations between Madrid and the AC governed by nationalist forces, particularly Catalonia, or right-wing parties. Here, the behaviour of the actors, based on political antagonism, has until 1991 been basically reactive, oscillating between the constitutional management of conflicts and hard bargaining until a bilateral agreement is reached. In the end, one-sided attitudes (partisan exploitation of confrontation, mutual distrust and political victimization) have tended to dominate the common values and interests that could promote consensus and co-operation. The only relevant exception has been the Basque country where there was a government coalition between Socialists and nationalists (PNV) forces from 1987 to 1990. Tension related to terrorism and the implications for the Basque PSOE in government have generated a relatively effective model of intergovernmental relations characterized by political exchange (ideological concessions for political administrative and financial resources and institutional collaboration).

Reforms

The urgent need for reform is becoming increasingly evident. Until now, lack of consensus had led to the constant postponement of decisions. However, the electoral losses suffered by the PSOE in the October 1989 general elections and the importance of the single market have facilitated the dialogue with the nationalist and centralist forces. 1991 was important in initiating a series of discussions. First, a global agreement has to be reached which will satisfy the claims of the less autonomous regions and bring them up to the same level as the others.[8] Second, and as a result of the first condition, negotiations started in order to find a concrete definition of the financing system. Third, most of the parties share a desire to broaden the system of territorial representation in the Senate and to revise the existing mechanisms of inter-governmental co-operation. The outcome will automatically be the reform of the central administration in order to avoid conflict and overlapping functions.

II. THE REGIONS, THE STATE AND THE EUROPEAN COMMUNITY

As has been noted elsewhere, Spain's entry into the EC has had institutional and political consequences.[9] As in the other decentralized member states, the transfer of sovereignty has had special effects on the constitutional position of the regions which, in contrast to the central government, do not participate directly in Community decision-making. Regional authorities have insistently claimed the right to intervene in decisions affecting them. Nevertheless, despite progress in some areas, this objective has not been met. The Spanish policy style in the Community clearly reflects the deficiencies of the centre-periphery system of relations.

The Impact of the European Community

European integration involves a commitment by the member states to create and develop a supranational system, whilst preserving their constitutional structures.[10] In the case of member states with regional structures this logically means the involvement of sub-national authorities in policy-making in areas which affect them. Nevertheless, comparative analysis shows that preserving internal balance depends more on political negotiations and intergovernmental co-operation than on constitutional interpretation.[11] After 1986, most of the Spanish regions claimed the right to participate in Community decisions, although no formal agreement had been reached with the central authorities. In this article we will here evaluate the institutional and politico-administrative impact of Spanish entry into the EC, and go on to examine the most recent central government proposal for regional participation.

The transfer of powers caused by EC membership has meant a substantial reduction of regional decision-making powers in many sectors (agriculture, industry, economic planning, territory, transport, research, environment and consumer rights). According to the internal distribution of functions, the regions should implement Community decisions in the above sectors. However, despite the coercive power of the central institutions to ensure regional duties,[12] the procedural requirements are unable to guarantee the execution of European norms according to plan. Until now, there has been only conflict on this subject, notably in 1989 when the Canary Islands government initially refused to implement the customs tariffs reduction foreseen in the accession treaty. Political negotiation facilitated the resolution of the controversy. On the other hand, conflict between central government and the regions arise when both consider themselves competent to enforce EC norms.

At the regional level, responses to integration have been relatively uniform despite the absence of any mechanism for horizontal coordination. Following the example of the German *Länder*, Catalonia, the Basque country, Galicia, Murcia, the Canary Islands and Valencia have set up offices in Brussels which provide information services and contacts with the EC administration. In general, there have been attempts to adapt current norms to Community law. Above all, the functional and organizational changes refer to the management of the Structural Funds and the corresponding programmes. The criteria are relatively homogeneous: the Ministries for Economy, Agriculture, and Employment, assisted by inter-ministerial committees, are responsible for the co-ordination, evaluation and implementation of projects. The integration of interest groups in the implementation of EC policies through information and consultation procedures is seen as a political priority by most of regional administrations.[13]

Since Spain's entry into the EC in 1986, there is still no institutional agreement to regulate regional participation in Community decision-making. In contrast to the situation in Germany and Belgium, participation of the Spanish regions via the Senate is, for obvious reasons, not feasible. Faced with pressure from the regional authorities, at the end of 1985 central government presented a proposal for an 'agreement on cooperation in matters of Community affairs'. This was immediately rejected by Catalonia and the Basque country as anti-autonomist in nature.

The second proposal, launched in 1986, also came to a standstill. This was a proposal based on the system in force in Germany from 1980 to 1986. It provided for the transfer of all information affecting regional domains. The sub-national authorities would inform the central government of their policy criteria with a view to forming the 'state will', and forcing the executive to incorporate them, 'if possible' into the Spanish position, providing they were compatible with the 'general interests of the state and the process of integration'.

In order to make the procedure operational, a proposal was made to constitute a regional committee which would co-ordinate and co-operate with the central authorities through the AC. In addition, the committee could propose the designation of an 'observer' and an 'extra observer' for the regions permanently representing Spain in the EC, with diplomatic status under the jurisdiction of the Spanish ambassador. The functions of the observers would include sending reports and documents to the regional committee. In their capacity as members of the Spanish delegation, both observers could attend meetings of EC committee and working groups 'expressing opinions coinciding with those of the official delegation'. Besides the technical shortcomings of the proposal (two observers for seventeen authorities seems inadequate) the main problem is that the most powerful regions want their representative to have a greater degree of autonomy with respect to the official representation.

The central government's refusal to accept this request has effectively blocked the signing of the agreement. The only effective arrangements reached until now refer to some basic principles and practical aspects. The first item includes the mutual compromise to respect the internal distribution of functions and the loyalty to the Constitution in matters dealing with the EC. Second, in May 1990 both authorities decided to establish a computer data base, linked to the Secretary of State for the EC, which provides Community information to regional governments.

Participation in the ERDF

In 1986 – prior to the reform of the Structural Funds – participation in regional Community policy brought with it the formulation of the first Spanish regional development programme (RDP) which included the RDP formulated by the 17 regions. The study was co-ordinated by a regional planning committee together with representatives of the various administrations. The Spanish government's final proposal to the Commission introduced important changes to the regional programmes, both in the selection of assisted areas and in financing priorities. One year later, the regions were able to present and oversee their own projects, which represents around 30 per cent of granted aid.

Since the introduction of the 1988 ERDF regulation, the preparation and supervision of the regional programmes has come under the jurisdiction of the public investment committee, an informal co-ordinating body of the central administration in which all the regions are represented. The regions have intervened in the formulation process but not in the final decision. Just as the Community regulation provides for the presentation of specific plans for the regions included in Objectives 1, 2 and 5b, the central government opted instead for the presentation of three global plans for the three Objectives. The implication is that the procedure does not permit a sufficient regional input and contradicts the principles of reform, according to which the regional level constitutes the nucleus of preparation, co-ordination and execution of Community national, regional and local intervention.

The presentation of a unique plan for each Community Objective area is probably in response to the government's desire to have a broader operational margin in order to decide on the territorial allocation of the resources which depend on the central administration (60 per cent for Objective 1 regions, 40 per cent for Objective 2 areas), In any case, the adoption of new regulations and the negotiations of the Community Support Framework (CSF) for Spain has facilitated direct contact between the Commission and the Spanish regions. These have held meetings with Community officials with a view to establishing the CSF and defining the criteria for using the appropriate resources by means of 'operative programmes'. The main problems occur over the distribution of resources between levels of government.

Previously, regional access to the ERDF was coordinated by participation in the Internal Cooperation Fund (30 per cent). Nevertheless, technical problems have made it advisable to cut off both funds. As a result of direct negotiation with the Commission, the regions in Objective 1 areas will manage 33.8 per cent of the resources allocated during the period 1989–93, while 7 per cent will be allocated to local authorities. Similarly, regions in Objective 2 areas will manage 50 per cent of their funds while the rest will be distributed respectively to the municipalities (10 per cent) and central government (40 per cent).

III. THE SELECTION OF RESPONDENTS

In Spain, regional disparities are a fundamental obstacle to the creation of the social and economic cohesion set out in the Single European Act. These are very intense among the 17 regions, of which nine fall into Objective 1 areas, and seven into Objective 2. Population and surface area of both types of measure represent 80.2 per cent and 85.1 per cent of the total in Spain. In 1987 Spanish per capita GDP was equivalent to 67.9 per cent of the average for the four major member states.

Internal territorial imbalances are also acute: between the industrialized North and the agricultural South and between the more accessible and populated West and the East which has a weaker infrastructure and is removed from the great axes of economic development.

We have chosen for sampling four regions from the territorial, socio-economic and political point of view: Andalusia, Catalonia, Galicia and Valencia. The four occupy one-third of the total surface area with a population of almost 20 million. Moreover, three of them are border regions: Catalonia with the French Languedoc-Roussillon and Andorra; and Galicia and Andalusia with Portugal. These characteristics constitute an extra element of interest in the EC perspective.

Interviews were conducted with 200 regional representatives (half of the total) distributed according to political and territorial representation and 100 'regional observers' (Chambers of Trade and Industry, Unions, general and sectoral entrepreneurial organizations, professional corporations, public agencies, cultural and environmental associations, local government lobbies at regional level, and others). These 300 interviews represent an overall representative sample of regional political leaders and interest group officials in the country. Both samples were interviewed using a structured questionnaire that was devised in collaboration with the project leader in order to guarantee a certain amount of homogeneity with the questions and sampling procedure used in the other Objective 1 countries covered by the study.

Before analysing the samples we will look briefly at the main economic problems and the institutional features of the four regions.

Andalusia is the most populated and extensive of the four regions with 6.8 million inhabitants over an area of 87,262 sq. km. It has a standard rate of economic productivity equivalent to 78 per cent of the Spanish average, with a high percentage of the population employed in agriculture and a high level of unemployment (*ca.* 29 per cent). The main obstacle hindering economic development is the low level of labour force skills, and a low level of private management ability. The lack of diversification of the productive system is worsened by dependency on external technical and energy resources and by the shortcoming in the network of commercial structures. The low level of income generates a low saving capacity, and hence a low level of productive investment. These territorial problems are aggravated by the high level of regional deficit for expenditure on public infrastructure, etc.

Catalonia is the region with the second highest population: six million inhabitants over 32,00 sq. km. It is a mainly industrial region which generates nearly one-quarter of the Spanish industrial product, with a clear predominance of small and medium-sized industry. However, the industrial crisis between 1976 and 1985 has meant a drastic loss of employment in the sector (nearly 300,000) and the proportional increase of unemployment, especially in the Barcelona area. The main difficulties facing the region are: the low level of technological investment and hence a low level of productivity; the lack of dynamic sectors; the shortcomings of the distribution sector; and the excessive concentration of population and productive activity in metropolitan Barcelona. In addition, there is a clear need for investment for environmental protection.

Galicia has a population of 2.85 million over an area of 29,500 sq. km. It is a rural region where the primary sector (agriculture) employees 45.6 per cent of the active population (the equivalent for Spain is 17 per cent) generating only 11.4 per cent of GRP. Industrial activity is largely based on fisheries and some large industries and only employs 22 per cent of the active population. The service sector is underdeveloped and not linked to other productive sectors. Galicia suffers from serious problems of inadequate internal and external communication links which worsen the fragility of the productive structure and the low level of social mobility.

The last region in our sample, Valencia, has 3.73 million inhabitants over an area of 23,305 sq. km. It generates an average income similar to the Spanish one. The major sectors are agricultural export (40 per cent from the Spanish ones) and manufacturing, based on small and medium-sized traditional industry. The main problems are unemployment (19 per cent), regional energy dependency, scarcity of public works and infrastructure, in addition to problems of pollution, soil erosion and shortages of water resources.

Of the four sample regions, three (Valencia, Andalusia, and Galicia) are Objective 1 regions. Catalonia is included in the Objective 2 areas. During the last five years, Catalonia and Valencia have demonstrated a turnaround in the economic activity and are among the most dynamic regions in Spain.

The results of both set of interviews with regional politicians and interest group leaders (that is, the 'regional observers') in the four regions will be discussed on the basis of five major concerns for the development and affirmation of the regional institution in Spain: regional performance, centre-periphery relations, political life, regional political system, and the role of the European Community.

IV. SUCCESSES, FAILURES AND REGIONAL PERFORMANCE

The evaluation of regional institutions often assumes a partisan colouration, but there are also broad areas of agreement among respondents at the regional level. The data in Table 1 show that there is a high level of consensus among the respondents in evaluating the success and failures of the regional government. First of all, there is a strong agreement in support of the need for strengthening the regional institutions. This is true in all of the regions, particularly in Catalonia and Andalusia where there appears to be a higher degree of satisfaction with self-government among the political elite. The development of a nationalist cultural identity and the process of 'linguistic normalization' (establishment of formal and actual linguistic parity for regional languages *vis-à-vis* Spanish) are emphasized in Catalonia and Galicia together with the introduction of a regional television channel. The regions' economic policies are considered to be quite successful by observers in Galicia and Valencia, while their counterparts in Andalusia stress the region's success in territorial planning in opening up the region to the outside through a significant strengthening of the road and communications systems.

TABLE 1
ASSESSMENTS OF THE SUCCESSES AND FAILURES OF THE REGIONAL GOVERNMENT

	Catalonia		Andalusia		Galicia		Valencia	
	Obs. %	Pol. %	Obs. %	Pol. %	Obs. %	Pol. %	Obs. %	Pol. %
SUCCESSES								
-Self-government	38.0	31.0	23.0	60.4	25.0	43.2	10.0	44.7
-Culture, language, national-regional identity	36.4	40.8	7.7	-	7.7	38.0	21.0	15.8
-Mass media	6.9	28.2	-	-	-	10.8	-	-
-Economic and financial policy	-	-	-	19.6	37.5	5.4	63.2	48.6
-Territorial policy	-	17.0	19.2	24.2	19.2	11.4	-	-
-Education and research	-	17.2	-	9.4	-	46.0	15.8	10.8
-Foreign policy	41.4	8.4	-	-	-	-	-	-
-Environment policy	-	-	19.2	-	-	-	-	-
FAILURES								
-Institutional-administrative inefficiency	24.1	18.3	27.0	26.4	-	24.3	26.3	19.0
-Lack of competences	13.8	18.3	-	17.0	-	46.2	-	-
-Agricultural policy	-	-	34.6	45.2	50.0	-	42.1	10.8
-Intergovernmental relations	-	13.0	-	10.2	11.5	10.8	-	19.0
-Lack of consensus	20.0	21.1	-	11.3	-	-	-	10.8
-Social policy	13.8	-	-	24.5	-	-	21.0	16.2
-New territorial setting	13.8	24.0	-	-	-	32.4	-	-
-Territorial policy	-	-	-	-	34.6	17.1	26.3	-
-Financing system	-	13.0	-	-	-	16.2	-	-
-Environment policy	13.8	13.0	-	-	-	-	-	-
-Health service	-	10.2	27.0	20.8	-	-	-	-
-Industrial policy	-	-	-	11.3	11.5	14.3	-	-

In Catalonia the observers stressed the importance of the region's 'foreign policy' (that is, in attracting investments, tourism, and political contacts from the rest of Europe). Economic policy and environmental initiatives registered a strong positive response in both Valencia and Andalusia.

On the negative side, institutional and administrative inefficiency is most frequently cited as a shortcoming in all four regions, particularly in Catalonia and Andalusia. On this point, the influence of partisan opinions among the political elite is balanced out by the views of the regional observers. The problem particularly affects the general shortcomings of the public administrative system (lack of reform, bureaucratization, etc.).

Agricultural policy (Andalusia and Galicia), fisheries and territorial

TABLE 2
LEVEL OF DISSATISFACTION WITH REGIONAL ACTIVITIES

	Catalonia		Andalusia		Galicia		Valencia	
	Obs. %	Pol. %	Obs. %	Pol. %	Obs. %	Pol. %	Obs. %	Pol. %
Dissatisfied with:								
-Utilization of research facilities	94.4	81.7	88.0	71.7	96.0	78.4	100.0	73.7
-Time necessary to implement measures	85.7	71.4	100.0	77.4	92.3	71.3	94.4	65.4
-Coordination with local government	90.0	59.2	92.0	50.2	73.7	72.9	72.2	63.9
-Ability to propose at national level	66.7	51.5	92.0	55.8	100.0	72.9	82.2	69.4
-Project feasibility	75.0	53.5	92.0	43.4	88.0	54.1	83.4	55.3
- Planning capacity	53.9	49.3	84.0	32.0	84.6	48.6	94.4	39.5
-Ability to spend	92.8	57.9	76.0	41.5	59.6	50.0	73.7	44.8
-Programm. choices	53.5	41.4	72.0	34.6	61.5	72.2	72.2	36.9
-Preparation/commitment of personnel	57.1	55.7	68.0	65.0	61.5	54.0	78.9	44.7*
-Quality of political class	46.4	22.8	84.0	30.8	86.0	51.3	73.7	23.7*
-Availability for consulting	10.7	51.4	48.0	35.8	61.6	54.1	47.4	44.7

* somewhat satisfied

investments (Galicia), health services (Andalusia) and the environment (Catalonia) are the most criticized sectoral policy areas. The lack of policy-making powers and financial resources is a source of concern in Catalonia where the new local territorial structure (that is., relations with local government) has come under heavy criticism from central government. This item may be linked with the perceived lack of political consensus and the increased conflict present in inter-governmental relations linking the region with central government as much as some local government institutions.

On the other hand, in Andalusia and Valencia the opposition points to the excessive dependence on central government. The evaluation of satisfaction (or in our case, dissatisfaction) with the current level of regional performance allows us to measure more accurately the actual nature of the success and failures accumulated by the Spanish regions during the first decade of operation.

The view of the regional observers is that dissatisfaction with regional government performance is rather high in all regions. In fact, Table 2 shows that dissatisfaction is much higher among the observers than among the politicians.[14] The most dissatisfied observers are to be found in Galicia and the least in Catalonia. Observers tend to be less unhappy in general with the region's 'availability for consultation' and 'ability to spend', but there are significant variations. In Catalonia the observers are definitely unhappy with the region's utilization of research facilities, co-ordination with local government, and ability to spend but are, in contrast, quite happy with its availability for consultations and overall quality of the political class. The latter, instead, is placed into question in all of the other three regions by about two-thirds of those interviewed.

With regard to the answers to the question of whether the regional government has had a positive impact on the activities of the interest group, only a clear majority of respondents in Catalonia express the view that the region is important for the regional interest organizations. In Andalusia the opinions are evenly balanced. Catalan observers gave very positive response on the impact of regional government in terms of satisfaction, whereas their counterparts in Galicia and Valencia consider it to be quite negative.

Despite the dissatisfaction with the day-to-day operations of the regional governments, the process of devolution has more supporters than opponents. The most favourable opinions are registered in Catalonia, Galicia and Valencia, and less so in Andalusia. This is related to the evaluations of the process of regional institutionalization. The institutionalization of the region has been deemed to have brought more good than bad in Galicia and especially in Catalonia where 96 per cent of the respondents expressed an overall positive evaluation of the decentralization process. A large minority (43 per cent) in Valencia expressed the most negative opinions while the largest bloc of sentiment considers it to have brought both good and bad results in Andalusia.

The political elites show a rather clear disagreement over regional performance, even though opinions tend to correspond to partisan cleavages. This is particularly clear in Andalusia given that the dominant political force governs with a very comfortable majority. Great importance is therefore attached to the unanimous or almost unanimous negative perceptions of 'time necessary to implement', 'use of facilities' and 'ability to propose at the national level'. 'Coordination with local authorities' (apart from Andalusia), as well as 'preparation and commitment of regional personnel' (except Valencia) and 'project feasibility' (apart from Andalusia) are strongly criticized. Opinions are strongly positive on the 'quality of the political class' (with the surprising exception of Galicia), 'planning capacity' and 'ability to spend' (with balance in

TABLE 3
PREFERENCES FOR INCREASES IN REGIONAL POWERS BY SECTOR

Increased regional powers in:	Catalonia		Andalusia		Galicia		Valencia	
	Obs. %	Pol. %	Obs. %	Pol. %	Obs. %	Pol. %	Obs. %	Pol. %
Artisanary	96.4	100.0	100.0	97.8	100.0	94.4	100.0	97.3
Cultural affairs	100.0	100.0	91.3	95.7	100.0	100.0	88.9	97.3
Agriculture	96.6	97.0	87.0	95.7	100.0	100.0	77.8	94.6
Urban areas	100.0	92.5	78.3	86.4	70.8	100.0	100.0	100.0
Education	100.0	98.5	78.3	95.7	91.7	100.0	78.9	94.6
Health	100.0	100.0	47.8	91.3	87.5	100.0	94.1	97.3
Environment	89.7	95.5	82.6	83.3	88.0	88.9	89.5	95.6
Industrial develop.	96.4	88.2	65.2	85.4	87.5	86.5	84.2	91.9
Transports	86.2	97.0	78.3	87.8	80.0	100.0	77.8	83.8
University	93.1	98.3	52.2	85.1	91.7	97.3	78.9	97.3
Employment	96.4	94.0	78.3	80.9	84.0	89.2	83.3	97.3
Public Works	96.4	98.5	60.9	91.3	80.0	91.9	83.3	80.7
Scientific research	79.3	91.2	60.9	86.7	54.2	78.4	61.1	81.1
Taxes	74.1	83.1	47.8	55.9	72.0	74.2	52.6	60.5
Credit	66.7	78.3	52.2	43.5	52.2	70.3	31.6	62.2
Foreign Trade	74.1	76.5	30.4	29.8	45.8	86.5	52.6	56.8
Police	85.7	86.8	56.5	39.1	34.8	55.6	47.4	51.4

Galicia). The most remarkable differences among regions are over 'programmatic choices', 'availability for consultation' and 'planning capacity' for Andalusia and Valencia.

When the respondents were asked whether they would like to see an increase in regional powers, the overwhelming majority responded affirmatively. Table 3 demonstrates that respondents in Catalonia were the most enthusiastic in widening the powers of the region, and only one-quarter of the observers and even fewer of the politicians had any doubts that taxes, foreign trade, credit, and scientific research maybe should not be devolved to the region. Interviews in Andalucia found a lack of full support for devolution in the additional areas of health and the university system. Otherwise, the amount of support for devolution was uniform

TABLE 4
CHARACTERIZATION OF REGIONAL POLITICAL LIFE

The politics of this region are more ______ than the regional average in Spain:	Catalonia		Andalusia		Galicia		Valencia	
	Obs. %	Pol. %	Obs. %	Pol. %	Obs. %	Pol. %	Obs. %	Pol. %
Modern	86.2	92.8	13.0	28.5	4.0	13.5	50.1	70.2
Consensual	31.0	28.1	43.4	25.0	16.0	21.6	50.0	32.4
Honest	52.2	47.9	4.3	47.0	0.0	32.4	27.8	49.4
Stable	75.8	83.1	52.4	77.6	12.0	16.7	22.0	78.3
Programmatic	28.6	32.4	4.3	34.7	0.0	10.8	5.6	45.9
Productive	51.8	63.4	8.7	34.7	0.0	22.2	34.4	79.2
Unitary	10.7	19.7	17.3	22.9	4.0	2.8	11.1	18.9
Autonomous	86.0	86.0	4.3	24.5	4.2	11.1	5.6	43.2
Democratic	-	50.7	-	70.3	-	51.3	-	81.0
Pragmatic	-	33.7	-	32.6	-	59.5	-	37.8
Rightist	-	47.9	-	4.1	-	35.1	-	2.7
Centrist	-	43.7	-	4.1	-	43.2	-	18.9
Leftist	-	8.5	-	87.7	-	21.6	-	78.4

and strong in all other areas (for example, cultural affairs, artisanry, agriculture, urban areas, environment, employment, etc.)

Contacts between observers and political elites at the regional level are more occasional than regular or formal, while relations with national, local and – in particular – regional civil servants appear to be more formalized. The regional political elites establish relations according to their public or party activity. They maintain weekly contacts with voters, parliamentarians from their own party and other parties and, less frequently, with regional and local political leaders. They meet representatives of regional and local groups, members of parliament from other parties, and regional and local civil servants on a regular basis. Contact with the president of the region, members of other regional assemblies, national civil servants, representatives of national interest groups and national party leaders are less frequent. Finally, there is little or no evidence of a stable relation with national leaders from other parties, central government delegates, national ministers and under-secretaries.

Table 4 presents data on how the interviewees characterized the political life and style of our four regions. The results show that the four regions are quite distinct from each other. Catalonia is considered to be modern, stable, and autonomous in its political activity, but it is also characterized as non-consensual, non-programmatic and non-unitary in nature. The politicians are split in characterizing its ideological characteristics. They are evenly split in characterizing the region as democratic, pragmatic, and rightist.

Andalucia and Galicia are reported not to be modern, honest, programmatic, unitary, and autonomous. Valencia falls somewhere in the middle between these two polar opposites, however it too is characterized by the observers as non-programmatic, non-autonomous, and not stable.

There is just a certain agreement in qualifying the regions as more clientelistic than programmatic, parochial rather than unitary, and conflictual rather than consensual (the latter with the exception of observers from Andalusia and Valencia). Only Catalan and Valencian respondents – overall political elites – consider their region's political life to be modern. Conflict dominates the Catalan and Galician systems. Paradoxically, in the other two territories, consensus behaviour finds more supporters among the observers and much less support among the political elites.

Responses may reflect the different position of both groups in the political process, but ideological views abound. Nevertheless, in general the political elites consider the regional political style as more pragmatic than the average, especially in Galicia. This is true whatever the dominant political tendency: centre-right in Catalonia and Galicia; centre-left in Valencia; and centre-left in Andalusia. In all four regions, particularly in Valencia and Andalusia, political life is considered more democratic than the regional average in Spain.

Catalan political life is viewed by both sets of respondents as being honest, whereas the opposite view is expressed by observers in Galicia, Valencia and Andalusia. As expected, political stability is particularly high in regions governed by an absolute majority (Catalonia and Andalusia), while Galicia and Valencia are characterized by instability, showing a very strong discrepancy among the views of both groups. One can detect internal coincidences in qualifying the region as 'productive' (Catalonia) or 'rather unproductive' (Galicia).

With regard to the issue of whether the regions are 'autonomous' or subordinate' *vis-à-vis* the centre, the first term covers most of the opinions in Catalonia and the least in Andalusia and Galicia. These views remain independent of political colouration and reflect an objective reality. The views of observers and political elites also vary widely in

Valencia due to the fact that the majority party is alone in expressing the view that the region is somewhat autonomous from the centre.

V. REGIONAL POLITICAL ELITES AND THE POLITICAL SYSTEM

After having asked questions on the nature of the regional institutions and policies, the interview turned to cover the issues of the nature and activity of the regional political class. The purpose of these questions was to measure the degree of institutionalization that regional political actors (members of the regional government as well as party elites) had achieved in our four regions. It is difficult to imagine how the regional institutions in Spain can achieve a significant level of decision-making autonomy if the regional political class is not autonomous from its counterparts at the national level. In other words, regional autonomy is not only derived from legal, constitutional arrangements but it is also based on a certain self-conception of the political life and political autonomy of the region from dictates originating from the centre.

Most of the political elites interviewed in our survey combined representative and party activity at the local and regional levels. A significant minority (30 per cent) also carry out a professional activity. Commission meetings, contacts with voters and other legislative activities appear in this order in the regional representative's personal agenda.

The priorities in the activities as a regional representative expressed by the respondents in Spain only partly correspond to the traditional conceptions of representation. The deference of 'the less protected' is cited as the primary priority, followed by the discussion and improvement of legislation, the protection of general interests, and finding the solutions of socio-economic problems. The second set of answers points to the promotion of the party struggle, the defence of regional interests at the national level, and the management of the regional administration.

In asking the respondents to reflect on the power relationships within their parties in the selection of members of the regional government, selection of candidates in regional elections, and how to vote on issues in the regional parliament – the overwhelming response was that the regional party leaders had the most influence. Nevertheless, the influence of individual politicians on the choice of priority issues was deemed to be very important in all four regions. Half of the respondents estimate that the influence of central government on regional government behaviour is very important. This perception is particularly high in Andalusia, Valencia and Galicia, where the PSOE governs alone or in coalition at the regional level. Among the regional political figures which are attributed a high degree of influence are the regional president (*ca.* 60 per cent), and other regional government leaders (ca. 43 per cent). This perception is coherent with the 'presidentialism' or emphasis on strong executives which characterizes regional government in Spain.

A great degree of influence is also attributed to regional party leaders, the media, private interests and local leaders. A low to medium degree of influence is attributed to individual members of the regional assemblies, national ministers and members of the central parliament, as well as trade unions, agricultural associations, local leaders, senior civil servants and state agencies. The clergy, central government delegates and civil governors are considered to have very little influence in regional affairs.

There is a strong belief in Spain that traditional party loyalty is the first factor conditioning voter choice. This reflects a high perception of the consolidation of the sub-national, regional party system. The second determining factor is considered to be the candidate and the third the regional party leader. The fourth factor – the national party leaders – is not really considered to be important because of the weight of regional parties in the four regions, especially in Catalonia and Galicia. Finally, electoral programmes at the regional, local and national level rank as less important factors. Thus, in both regional government decisions as well as in regional party matters regional level leaders are considered to have the most power, reflecting the high level of institutionalization achieved by the Spanish regions in a relative short period of time.

While more than half of those interviewed considered that there existed a high level of trust among politicians in regional assemblies, a broad majority characterized the activity of the regional assembly as containing a higher degree of conflict than cooperation. This opinion is particularly widespread in Catalonia and Andalusia.

The political attitudes of the respondents reflect the political composition of regional assemblies and many times the political affiliations of the respondents. When asked their level of support for a series of issues and institutions, the regional politicians expressed their highest level of support for the concept of federalism and for trade unions (66 per cent), along with the Federation of Cities (*Federación de Municipios y Provincias*) (*ca.* 58 per cent), small merchants (57 per cent) and PSOE (*ca.* 52 per cent).

Low levels of support were expressed for the CDS, the national centrist party of the former Prime Minister, and the major banks where Spain's economic power is concentrated (4.5 per cent). On the other hand, the national entrepreneurial organization (CEOE), the right-wing *Partido Popular* (PP), the Spanish Communist Party (PCE), rightist ideology and the clergy account for less than 17 per cent of support. Below average levels of support were expressed for nationalists (40 per cent). Apart from Catalonia, where nationalist feelings are predominant irrespective of party loyalty, these scores seem to correspond to the electoral weight of both options in the other three regional assemblies.

The Spanish political class is relatively young as more than 55 per cent of its members were born after 1944, and of these 42 per cent were born in the period between 1944 and 1951. This fact along with the recent establishment of democracy implies that in almost all cases political participation dates from the end of the 1970s or the beginning of the 1980s.

The sample shows a high correlation between party and public position. More than half the regional representatives are also members of regional party secretariats or committees. There is also a significant number of regional party secretaries and members of national party executives and committee. Almost one-quarter of the respondents holds local or provincial party office. The political curricula show that for a majority of the regional politicians the move to the regional assembly starts with an experience in local government.

The above statement is coherent with the evolution of public offices. More than half of the legislators have held municipal or provincial office in the period between 1979 (first local elections) and 1983 (second local elections). Moreover, a great number have held both representative and executive office (mayor, town or provincial councillor).

There is also a clear tendency towards a professionalization of the political class in the regions. In Catalonia most of the politicians were re-elected. In Valencia, Galicia and Andalusia there has been very little turnover in members of the assembly. Almost half of the representatives report that they are 'professional' while the rest consider themselves to be 'semi-professional' politicians. There is no room for amateurs in regional politics.

VI. THE ROLE OF THE EUROPEAN COMMUNITY

Given the consolidated nature of Spanish regional politics, we will now turn to a consideration of the impact that the creation of the single market after 1992 will have on the region. As stated above, in Spain regionalism and European integration developed as parallel phenomena and have significantly influenced each other as they proceeded down the road of development. The creation of the single market will not only influence national economic and social policies, it will also have a significant impact on the regions.

TABLE 5
EVALUATION OF THE ADEQUACY OF SOCIO-ECONOMIC STRUCTURES FOR 1992

	Catalonia		Andalusia		Galicia		Valencia	
	Obs. %	Pol. %	Obs. %	Pol. %	Obs. %	Pol. %	Obs. %	Pol. %
Railroad network	86.2	91.2	75.0	79.2	100.0	94.6	89.5	88.5
Road network	55.2	41.2	84.6	64.2	100.0	94.6	94.7	69.2
Health service	85.0	73.5	92.0	64.2	93.4	86.5	78.0	53.8
Social service	81.0	69.1	91.0	69.8	85.3	67.6	76.7	61.5
Urban areas function.	58.6	55.2	70.8	73.6	75.0	56.0	84.2	80.0
Level of technological innovatio n	58.6	42.4	92.0	80.8	69.6	83.8	78.9	65.4
Skill level of labour force	60.7	23.5	84.6	79.2	60.9	62.2	73.7	50.0
Commercial network	50.0	45.6	72.0	64.0	81.8	81.1	55.6	61.5
Level of asociationalism	34.5	25.4	60.0	75.0	75.0	78.4	57.9	61.5
Structure of small-medium sized indus.	46.4	25.0	87.0	80.0	66.7	74.3	52.9	42.3
University system	93.1	53.0	92.0	50.9	45.8	45.9	63.2	38.5
Air communications	79.3	73.5	41.7	49.1	41.7	40.5	57.9	57.7
Utilization of historical/environ. res.	34.5	28.4	60.0	28.8	54.5	54.1	66.7	73.1
Industry restructur.	17.9	15.2	54.2	53.8	77.3	64.9	36.8	23.1
Port system	46.4	43.3	56.0	47.2	43.5	37.8	42.1	19.2

Among the observers there is little doubt that the region does not have an adequate socio-economic structure to meet head-on the challenge of the single market in 1992 (see Table 5). In all of the regions the respondents are rather negative on the adequacy of the region's railway and road transport networks, health and social services, the functionality of urban areas and the levels of technological innovation and labour force skills. We should note the unanimously negative responses of the respondents to the first two items in Galicia. Political elites and observers agree – although the former are less pessimistic – with regard to the inadequate levels of technological innovation (Catalonia), the skills of the labour force (Catalonia and Valencia), the structure of small and medium-sized enterprises (Valencia), the utilization of historical-environmental resources (Andalusia), and the port system (Andalusia). Andalusia registered the highest level of negative judgments on the adequacy of its social services (health and social services), with the only, partial, exception being the perceived adequacy of the air transport system. In Galicia respondents gave quite positive responses to the nature of the port system, university and air transport.

These positive attitudes were spurred by the importance of the fishing industry, the recent creation of three universities, and the need to compensate for the shortcomings of the territorial transport system. In Valencia the restructuring of the steel industry and the port system have brought about satisfactory solutions. Lastly, as expected, Catalonia presents the highest level of economic adaptation to the exigencies tied to the realization of the single market in some of the key sectors concerned with industrial restructuring, the tertiary sector, the structure of SMEs (the most dynamic ones) and the use of historical-environmental resources for tourism. Only one region, Catalonia, registers positive responses on levels of associationalism: the tradition of associationalism in Catalonia may explain the higher level of administrative and economic performance found in that region.

Both regional observers and political elites have a clear idea of the impact that 1992 will have on their associations (see Table 6). The impact is judged to be very positive in all matters affecting economic development. An increased level of unemployment is not considered likely, even though observers in Catalonia, Andalusia and Galicia believe that production costs will increase. According to the regional politicians, 1992 will lead to the modernization of the regional administration. Significantly, all observers disagree on this point.

There is general agreement as to the likelihood of institutional renewal, the adoption of new environmental standards and the improvement of social services. No loss of regional identity is anticipated. Nevertheless, both sets of respondents feared the confusion of functions between the different levels of administration, or even some kind of slow down in the decision-making process, especially in Catalonia and Galicia.

Andalusian and Galician observers are more worried about the deterioration of conditions in the country's less developed areas.

There is almost unanimous agreement among the respondents, as reported in Table 7, on the need to extend EC powers. In other words, the Spanish regional respondents feel that the Community ought to increase its economic powers in all areas, particularly in the financing of projects for less developed areas, the promotion of technological innovation and the evaluation of regional investment projects. Observers and politicians agree that financing a European defence policy should remain the same, and that there should be a high level of immigration control for non-EC countries.

TABLE 6

ANTICIPATED IMPACT OF THE SINGLE EUROPEAN MARKET

	Catalonia		Andalusia		Galicia		Valencia	
	Obs.	Pol.	Obs.	Pol.	Obs.	Pol.	Obs.	Pol.
Will bring:	%	%	%	%	%	%	%	%
More competition	96.6	98.6	76.9	94.2	88.0	89.2	89.5	94.7
Access to new markets	93.1	98.6	80.8	94.3	88.5	97.3	94.7	94.7
Technological innovation	100.0	95.8	73.1	94.3	92.0	86.1	84.2	97.4
Restructuring of commercial distribution networks	96.6	98.6	84.6	76.0	100.0	95.0	94.0	98.0
Provide access to new financial markets	96.6	93.0	76.9	90.6	92.3	91.9	94.7	89.5
Reconversion of agricultural production	88.6	91.2	89.2	86.8	93.7	89.2	90.5	89.5
Concentration of industry	93.1	93.0	80.8	69.8	76.0	83.8	73.7	81.6
Increase unemployment	17.9	13.0	38.5	24.5	41.7	30.6	26.3	31.6
Increase production costs	57.1	50.0	65.4	38.5	37.5	32.4	63.2	42.1
Adoption of new environmental standards	96.6	92.9	79.2	82.4	78.3	89.2	84.2	97.4
Improvement in social services	74.1	90.1	50.0	78.8	36.0	88.9	52.6	81.6
Worsen situation in disadvantaged areas	41.4	44.3	53.8	42.3	52.0	62.2	52.6	28.9
Confusion of functions	82.8	54.3	84.0	59.6	72.0	64.9	76.5	57.9
Institutional renewal	75.9	77.5	53.8	84.3	72.0	66.7	72.2	65.8
Slow down decision-making process	53.6	51.4	73.1	38.5	70.8	62.2	35.3	47.4
Modernization of regional administration	46.4	63.2	48.0	63.5	32.0	72.2	31.6	65.8
Loss of identity	7.1	16.9	26.9	25.0	19.2	13.5	29.4	23.7

TABLE 7
ASSESSMENT OF THE EXTENSION OF EC POWERS

More powers should be allocated to the EC to engage in the:	Catalonia		Andalusia		Galicia		Valencia	
	Obs. %	Pol. %	Obs. %	Pol. %	Obs. %	Pol. %	Obs. %	Pol. %
Financing of projects in underdeveloped areas	96.6	98.6	100.0	100.0	100.0	91.9	94.4	89.5
Promotion of technological innovation	100.0	97.2	92.0	98.0	95.8	94.6	89.5	81.6
Evaluation of regional investment projects	85.7	87.1	84.0	90.4	87.5	81.1	83.3	68.4
Formulating guidelines for vocational training	89.7	85.9	92.0	92.2	66.7	81.1	84.2	64.9
Control over the enforcement of environ and urban planning standards	86.2	80.0	78.0	92.2	76.4	77.8	62.2	68.4
Euro perspective for scientific research	79.3	87.1	84.0	94.2	65.2	77.8	83.3	63.2
Foreign trade coord.	77.8	87.1	84.0	84.3	78.3	63.9	83.3	59.5
Promation of immigrants integration	70.4	78.6	79.2	80.0	63.6	86.8	73.7	50.0
Monotoring of labour market	85.7	81.7	84.0	92.2	47.8	81.1	73.7	60.5
Monitoring of financial markets	66.7	54.3	72.0	66.7	68.2	61.1	55.6	45.9
Emigration control from non-EC states	48.1	54.9	66.7	48.1	43.5	27.0	57.9	35.1
Finance eurodefence policy	25.0	35.2	58.3	34.6	21.7	35.1	36.8	34.2

The creation of Community policy instruments are welcome in all cases (see Table 8). Regional respondents believe that an Euro-environmental agency, European communications body, and the ability of the regions to establish their own offices in Brussels are indispensable. A Central European Bank, programmes, agencies or consortia for regional co-operation, together with a European administrative court and the conference of regional presidents are highly desirable.

It is rather difficult to differentiate between politicians and observers or between regions on these matters. The observers in Galicia and observers and political elites in Valencia express, in general, the lowest preferences for a European environmental agency, Euro-administrative

TABLE 8
EVALUATION OF EC POLICY INSTRUMENTS

	Catalonia		Andalusia		Galicia		Valencia	
	Obs. %	Pol. %	Obs. %	Pol. %	Obs. %	Pol. %	Obs. %	Pol. %
Central-federal bank	96.6	98.6	88.4	98.1	100.0	100.0	100.0	91.0
Telecommunications agency	93.1	98.5	96.0	100.0	100.0	97.1	100.0	97.3
Environmental Agency	96.6	100.0	100.0	100.0	100.0	97.3	77.0	97.3
Agency to monitor labour market	96.4	100.0	95.8	100.0	100.0	97.3	100.0	91.9
Common programmes for transregional sectoral policies	93.1	97.1	93.1	100.0	100.0	91.7	100.0	88.9
Interregional euro-consortia	96.4	95.6	92.3	92.5	100.0	94.6	100.0	81.1
Administrative Court	96.6	95.7	96.2	97.2	94.4	88.9	94.4	75.7
Agencies for inter-regional cooperation	93.1	94.6	88.5	96.2	90.9	94.6	94.1	69.4
Post-graduate euro-diplomas	85.7	95.7	91.7	96.1	71.4	94.6	88.2	89.2
Conference of regional presidents	96.6	97.2	91.7	92.5	95.5	100.0	71.1	73.0
Representation of regional assemblies	89.3	97.1	76.0	96.2	95.5	100.0	66.7*	94.4
Offices representing the regions in Brussels	96.6	97.2	84.0	89.2	90.9	100.0	88.9	86.1
Control of firms and banks	86.2	94.4	88.3	90.4	63.6	80.6	66.7	91.9

(*) only 'desirable'

court and agencies for interregional cooperation, conference of regional presidents, post-graduate diplomas and control of firms and banks.

The regions are ready to support common initiatives which promote horizontal relations (see Table 9). There is general agreement with the need from a European rather than national perspective to protect the environment, to formulate and implement development projects, plans for applied research, integrated programmes for border regions and policies to improve interregional communications. At the same time, the respondents express a clear wish to build cultural-tourist exchange programmes or activities, promote products and services or joint ventures, strengthen regional air services and training civil service personnel. The idea of a regional lobby in Brussels in generally welcomed.

TABLE 9
COMMON REGIONAL INITIATIVES

	Catalonia		Andalusia		Galicia		Valencia	
	Obs. %	Pol. %	Obs. %	Pol. %	Obs. %	Pol. %	Obs. %	Pol. %
Policies to protect the environment	100.0	100.0	100.0	100.0	100.0	97.3	100.0	100.0
Cultural-tourist exchange programmes	96.6	100.0	100.0	100.0	100.0	97.3	100.0	100.0
Plans for applied research	93.1	98.1	100.0	100.0	100.0	97.3	94.4	100.0
Formulating development programs	96.6	98.5	92.3	100.0	100.0	94.5	94.4	100.0
Integrated programmes for contiguous border regions	96.6	98.5	96.0	98.2	100.0	100.0	100.0	88.0
Activities to promote products and services	93.1	94.0	100.0	98.1	91.3	94.5	94.4	100.0
Promoting joint-ventures between industries	92.9	97.0	96.0	98.2	89.5	94.5	100.0	100.0
Increase of inter-regional rail-road communications	96.6	98.5	100.0	98.0	91.3	94.5	100.0	96.0
Training civil servants	89.3	94.0	92.3	94.3	86.4	94.5	88.9	96.0
Strengthen regional air-line services	96.6	95.5	92.3	92.5	86.4	94.5	72.2	100.0
Lobby in the EC Commission	86.2	79.1	72.7	52.0	85.0	77.1	81.0	63.7

VII. CONCLUSIONS

Regional devolution and Spanish entry into the EC are two important aspects of Spanish institutional and political life during the 1980s. The problem is, however, how to make the two compatible. The transfer of internal competences to the Community has taken place at a time when the new territorial structures were as yet not firmly established and when there were marked differences in the distribution of political power, which in turn gave rise to permanent conflicts between centre and periphery.

These political and administrative shortcomings *vis-à-vis* social demands and Community challenges necessitate a review of political attitudes, and – in particular – of the style of intergovernmental relations, with the aim of increasing coordination and cooperation. The sample of regional respondents interviewed in this study show that regional level political systems have become well established in Spain during the last two decades. Cultural and linguistic cleavages have been added to ideological ones, particularly in the case of the national minorities in Catalonia and Galicia.

The interviews point to the existence of a regional elite which is highly professionalized and with a tendentiously pragmatic and rather anti-centralistic behaviour. On the whole, the regional elite is reasonably satisfied with the activities of the region, despite the persistence of ideological differences. The importance of the existence of trust among political opponents is a recognized fact, and there is a strong consensus that the regional executive must not be strengthened at the expense of the powers of the regional assembly.

Despite differences in perception, both observers and political elites stress the inadequacy of regional socio-economic structures and the rather negative performance of their administrations. In any case, there is a general agreement in favour of increasing regional powers at the expense of the central government. Respondents have high hopes for the implementation of the single market, but they are somewhat concerned about its political and administrative consequences. Preferences about the new role of the EC cover all suggested areas, particularly those of economic development, the promotion of technological innovation, and other sectoral policies. The same positive attitude is evident in the use of new sectoral or regional EC instruments.

Lastly, all propositions related to the promotion of trans-regional co-operation receive a high degree of support. In short, respondents in Andalusia, Catalonia and Valencia see the increasing powers of the EC as linked to the needs of the single market. Instead of seeing the creation of the single market as a risk, they regard it as a chance to develop their own potential and to establish European trans-regional networks.

NOTES

1. Interviews were carried out from May to September 1989 with respondents.
2. This took place in the Canary Islands and Valencia.
3. Section 148.2 of the Spanish Constitution.
4. Section 149.1 of the Spanish Constitution.
5. J.M. Valles and M. Cuchillo, 'Decentralization in Spain: A Review", *European Journal of Political Research* (1988), p. 395.

6. J. Tornos (ed.), *Informe sobre las Autonomias* (Madrid: Civitas, 1988), pp. 121–31.
7. Section 155 of the Spanish Constitution.
8. The Spanish case illustrates the fact that when a certain level of autonomy is granted the natural progression at the regional level is to increase it while at the national level the tendency is to decrease it.
9. F. Morata, *Autonomia Regional i Integraciò Europea* (Barcelona: Institut d'Estudis Autonòmics, 1987), pp. 219–31.
10. D. Dagtoglou, *La nature juridique de la Communauté Européenne*, in Commission des Communautés Européennes (ed.), *Trente ans de Droit Communautaire* (Bruxelles: Office des Publications des Communautés Européennes, 1985).
11. R. Hrbek and U. Thaysen (eds.), *Die deutschen Lander und die Europaischen Gemeinschaften* (Baden Baden: Nomos, 1987).
12. Ministerio de Economia, 1989.
13. J. Molins and F. Morata, 'Spanish lobbying in the European Community', Paper prepared for the ECPR Workshop, Essex, 23 March 1991.
14. This difference in views can be attributed to the partisan affiliation of many of our political respondents.

The Regional Reform in Italy: From Centralized to Regionalized State

ROBERT LEONARDI

I. INTRODUCTION

The decentralization of power from national to regional and local government has been much discussed in recent years as part of the debate on institutional reform and the impact of the European Community on member states. As is evident in other contributions to this volume, decentralization has become a dominant theme in previously centralized states. Apart from such instances of regime crisis and transformation (for example, Soviet Union and Yugoslavia), the question that needs to be asked within the context of the European Community is whether the regionalization of traditionally centralized nation–states leads to a decline in economic efficiency and rationality or whether economic performance is enhanced by the creation of intermediate forms of institutional arrangements.

This article wishes to analyse the issue by examining one of the first extensive examples of political decentralization in the 1970s: the regionalization of Italian government over the last two decades. The analysis will show that decentralization of unitary states is not a 'linear' process that develops over time in an even manner through a clean qualitative leap from one system of institutions to another. On the contrary, the implementation of the regional reform in Italy took place (and is still taking place) in 'cycles' characterized by periods of rapid change that are followed by moments of retrenchment and stagnation. Thus, it is approproiate to study regionalization in Italy as a longitudinal process that develops over time based on the alignment of internal political and economic pressures as well as stimuli impacting on the country's institutions from the outside.

The history of regional reform in Italy can best be described as a protracted political struggle between the supporters of the centre versus those of the periphery. From its birth in 1860 the Italian nation–state has been structured along unitary-centralized lines, but after the Second World War attempts were made to insert into the Republican Constitution a new conception of a unitary-centralized state based on a system of regional governments at the sub-national level. This struggle for regionalization of decision-making caused much controversy in the Constituent Assembly because a regional system meant a transfer of power from the national bureaucracy and a completely new way of managing power that was quite different from the model adopted by the Liberal and Fascist state systems.

Regional governments were established in 1970, a full set of administrative functions was passed to the regions in 1972, and a full-fledged devolution of powers was carried out in 1977. Why did these changes finally become possible in the 1970s while for 20 years they had been systematically and successfully repulsed by the country's rulers? The answer will be provided through an analysis of the political developments and socio-economic change that have characterized Italy in the post-war period.

Before beginning the analysis, some initial concepts and terms need to be clarified. First, the term 'decentralization' is used to mean the overall ideal or goal to be pursued in the restructuring of the state apparatus; the concept is embodied in Article 14 of the Italian Constitution that states 'the Republic is divided into regions, provinces, and communes'. The implementation of the goal of decentralization requires the fulfillment of numerous objectives of institutional change – among which are new political institutions, new relations among the political forces, the integration of new economic and social actors, and affirmation of a new set of values. 'Devolution' is defined as the transfer of power to the regional level of government as one of the specific objectives which is central to the process of decentralization. Devolution refers to the change in the distribution of political and administrative decision-making power in favour of the regions and, therefore, of the new regional political institutions.

For analytic purposes, it is useful to distinguish two aspects of the process of decentralization: devolution of authority from the centre to sub-national units and utilization of that authority effectively by the newly empowered units. Devolution and utilization are, of course, intimately related: both in the obvious sense that what is not devolved cannot be utilized and in the somewhat less obvious sense that the pace of devolution is likely to depend on the effectiveness with which existing grants of authority are utilized. Nevertheless, this distinction is important theoretically, since devolution and utilization are likely to be affected by different variables. In particular, uniformly delegated powers might be utilized with widely varying degrees of success in different regions or localities. Such, in fact, has been the experience of Italian regional government.

The process of devolution of decision-making powers means in general rather than formal terms increased autonomy for the sub-national units of government. Autonomy refers to the capacity for discretionary decision-making on the part of sub-national governmental bodies that is unhindered by external control. In formal terms, inter-governmental autonomy is affected by such factors as the legal and constitutional framework, the administrative framework (administrative controls, delegated functions, personnel patterns, and so on), and financial provisions for supporting regionally determined policies. But these factors – laws, rules, and money – are significant, not as absolute constraints on regional autonomy, but rather as resources in the endless, intricate bargaining that lies at the core of intergovernmental relations everywhere.

II. THE REGIONS AND THE NATION-STATE, 1861–1970

When the Italian nation-state was being created from a congeries of city-states and imperial remnants between 1860 and 1870, serious consideration was given to the establishment of relatively autonomous regional governments. In 1861 a proposal by Cavour, Farini, and Minghetti expressed the conviction that the regions represented the historical and natural reality of the nation. As Luigi Farini wrote:

> ... the Italian provinces are naturally and historically arranged in larger centres that have had and still have reasons to exist within the organism of Italian life. These centres contain ancient traditions founded on various natural and civic conditions; Italian politics which was divided among various communes and republics in the Medieval period found in these centres the initial forms and discipline of a State ... I believe that we have to take into consideration the existence of these centres above the province and below the conception of the State ... The political unit that we have to establish must be neither the product of an abstract conception nor an arbitrary solution. It must represent those effective natural and historical conditions that exist, and it must take into account those centers of moral suasion which exist and which, if they were suppressed, could bounce back and become dangerous. But if legitimately satisfied, they could contribute admirably to reenforce the nation. If we want to accomplish an efficacious decentralization and give to our country the institutions that it merits, then we must in my opinion respect the natural component parts of Italy.'[1]

But on 3 January 1862 Bettino Ricasoli, the Minister of the Interior, withdrew the 1861 proposal to create a regional system at the sub-national level, and the idea of regionalism was definitively discarded with the passage of the provincial and communal law, n. 2248, of 20 March 1865 that created a centralized state structure. A number of Italian historians have asked why the Kingdom of Italy chose the Napoleonic model after unification: Why did men, who were believers of ideas that were nurtured by a deeply imbedded mistrust of Jacobinism that circulated in moderate political circles up to the time of the Restoration, once in power meticulously retraced the steps of the path against which they had written, continued to write, and would in the future write learned pages?[2] The most reasonable response was that, at the time, the fears of disintegration of the new nation–state and of the rise of radical democratic forces at the local level – for example, in Lombardy and Tuscany along with a few centres of the South – prevailed among the leaders of the Kingdom of Italy and made them adopt the Napoleonic pattern of thoroughgoing centralization.

It could be argued that the idea of regionalism that was propounded by Carlo Cattaneo and others became the victim of the primary objective of state-building – that is, the centralization of control over the distribution of resources, the creation of a uniform national system of law and public order, and the emergence of a national political class – which, accordingly, required in the opinion of many of the political leaders a strong, centralized state.[3]

Only after the Second World War with the emergence of democratic politics and a grassroots revulsion against the over centralization of the Fascist regime did strong regionalist sentiments resurface. In that historical period the creation of a regional system of government was made feasible by the opening up of the political system to a diverse variety of social groups on the heels of the Resistance movement which assumed the contours of a national liberation struggle. The practical ramification of the Resistance period was to bring into the political process a large number of Catholics, Communists, Socialists, and lay political forces which had historically been kept out of the system. In this perspective, the Resistance completed that process of nation-building that was begun in the 1860–70 decade. In this radically different political context the ideal of a regionally decentralized state corresponded to the need to democratize the Italian state system. As Michèle Monaco has written, '[In the post-WWII period] the regional problem emerges from the conviction that a well-functioning state requires the creation of a decentralized rather than a centralized structure.'[4] Thus from the beginning, the movement for decentralization had two goals that were inextricably linked: the rationalization and reorganization of the national bureaucracy and the devolution of decision-making and administrative powers to the regions and other units of local government for the purpose of promoting democratization of the political process, administrative efficiency, and socio-economic development.

Nevertheless, during the Constituent Assembly debate (1946-1947) it was clear that the major parties disagreed about how much power should be given to the regional governments. Consistent with the decentralized traditions of the earlier Catholic Popular Party and convinced that the Left would play a predominant role in the control of national government power, the Christian Democrats (DC) became the leading exponent of allocating to the regions a major role in the areas of economic and social policy-making – for example, in industry, commerce, finance, public health, and education.

Other parties favourable to the regions were the PRI, the Action Party, and a minority of Liberals led by Luigi Einaudi. Among the Socialists, important expressions of support for regionalism came from Adriano Olivetti and Emilio Lussu. The Communists, through predominantly centralist in orientation, did support the strong sentiment for regional autonomy that dominated Sicily and Sardinia. The Left voted as a block in support of the regional reform when the issue came up for a vote in June 1947.

The powers earmarked for the regions were spelled out in Article 117 of the Constitution, which empowered the regions to decide matters dealing with city and provincial government, local police, fairs and markets, public works projects and aqueducts, ports, mineral waters, quarries, hunting and fishing, agriculture, and artisanry. In subsequent articles (118 to 133) the Constitution provided the skeletal framework for regional government structures, spelled out their component parts (Article 121), defined their financial sources (Article 119) and relations with local governments (Articles 118, 130, and 133), and stipulated the nature of central government authority over the regions (Articles 123–127).

The Constitution also made the distinction between five regions (Sicily, Sardinia, Val d'Aosta, Trentino-Alto Adige, and Friuli-Venezia Giulia) that were allocated 'particular conditions of autonomy' and whose special statutes (thus the designation of 'special' regions) were to be adopted separately through specific pieces of national legislation. The special regions represented areas where separatist sentiments were strong – that is, Sicily, Val d'Aosta, and Trentino-Alto Adige – or in which there were particular border, language, or ethnic problems. Four of the 'special' regions were established by 1949 while the fifth – Friuli-Venezia Giulia had to wait until 1964.[5] The statutes of the other 14 regions (which in 1959 became 15 through the separation of Molise from Abruzzo) representing 85 per cent of the population were to be implemented according to uniform criteria. There was to be no differentiation of powers among these 'ordinary' regions.

The Constitution left many gaps to be filled by subsequent legislation. These problems were supposed to be resolved by a number of 'transitional norms' (*disposizioni transitorie*) that would come into effect with the Constitution (1 January 1948). One of these dispositions – the VIII – called for the holding of regional elections one year after the Constitution was adopted and another specified that national legislation would provide for the transfer of both personnel and functions to the regions.

Taking into consideration the regional provisions in the Constitution and the transitional disposition, it is clear that the founding fathers of the Italian Republic expected a quick and thorough transfer of powers to the regional level, but the attitude in favor of regionalism on the part of the ruling party – the DC – had radically changed in the 1947–48 period. The wartime alliance between Left and Centre succumbed to the pressures of the cold war and the bitter electoral campaign of 1948 and so did any chance for the implementation of structural reforms in the near future.[6]

The creation of a national system of regional governments became one of the major casualties of the increasingly polarized nature of the Italian scene. Once the parties of the Left were excluded from the national government, Alcide DeGasperi and other members of his centrist government openly opposed any restructuring of the national bureaucracy and the transfer of power to the sub-national level that might be used by the Left in areas where it was the dominant political force – for example, in the central Red Belt – to undermine national programmes. Piero Calamandrei denounced 'the majority's obstruction' of precise constitutional provision based on partisan political motivations.[7] As a result, the Italian Constitution's provision was allowed to remain dormant for over twenty years.

The government made more headway on the matter of defining the structure of regional government. On 10 February 1953 the government's proposal was transformed into law n. 62, more popularly known as the 'Scelba law' after the Minister of Interior, Mario Scelba, who piloted the bill through the legislative process and made sure that if the regions ever came into existence they would be under the tight reign of the central government. Nine years passed before another government undertook to propose any kind of legislative initiative on the matter of regional reform. Only with the coming into existence of the 'opening to the left' experience in 1960 – that is, Socialist party entrance into the governmental coalition – did the problem of regional reform appear as an important political issue.

As part of the government's renewed interest in the regions, the Third Fanfani government (1960–62) set up the Tupini Commission on 19

August 1960 to provide an estimate of how much a regional reform would cost. One of the strongest arguments used against the creation of the regions in the late 1940s and 1950s had been their cost. The argument went that given the pressing needs for national reconstruction the country could ill afford to use scarce resources to create another enormously expensive level of government. Once the Tupini Commission released its report, the Fanfani government introduced bills in Parliament to amend the 1953 Scelba law, provide a financial underpinning for the regions, develop framework laws for important policy sectors, identify regional boundaries, and transfer central bureaucratic personnel to the regional level.[8]

Despite the intentions of Fanfani, the initiatives never received sufficient attention from the bulk of the DC because the party considered the Fanfani initiative more as window dressing to appease the Socialists rather than as concrete commitments designed to produce immediate results. Strong pressures from the Right in Parliament and from within the DC finally forced Fanfani to drop his plans and eventually resign as Prime Minister.

The subsequent first Aldo Moro government (1963–64) returned for another financial estimate. (Studying the problem was one effective way of postponing implementation of regional reform until conditions were more favourable.) In 1966 the Carbone Commission produced an estimate that a 'minimalist' – partial transfer – implementation of the regional reform could cost the Italian state approximately 193 billion lire while a 'maximalist' – full transfer – one would come close to 500 billion lire.

Armed with this information the third Moro government (1966–68) felt that it was in a position to counter the objections of the Right and planned to proceed with the introduction of legislation calling for regional elections. This commitment was helped by the stance taken by the Communist leadership in the Chamber of Deputies. In December 1966 Pietro Ingrao announced his party's support of the government's proposed regional election bill. For the first time since the initiation of the centre–left coalition, the Communists joined in support of a major government reform bill, thus assuring a wide base of parliamentary support for regional government. In this manner it became much harder for opponents to regionalism in the government coalition to 'snipe' at the bill and prevent its implementation.

The regional election bill was finally introduced in Parliament on 10 March 1967. Proponents of the reform argued that, entirely apart from the constitutional mandate, regionalism was desirable as a remedy for the sclerosis and debilitating clientelism of the central bureaucracy, as a response to demands for more popular involvement in public affairs, and as a means for implementing economic planning and accelerating the development of backward regions. In essence, the rationale for regional decentralization was founded on the need to make room for local initiative and control in regional political affairs and policy-making. Many in the country, and especially in the Centre and North, were becoming increasingly uncomfortable with a policy process that stifled local initiatives and effectively routed all local decisions through the bureaucracy and politicians in Rome.

Another development that spurred regionalization was the rapid expansion of the Italian welfare state that had been in full swing during the 1960s. Given that the bureaucratic structure had not been rationalized or even adequately 'mechanized' (that is, introduction of a stable body of personnel with mechanical skills such as typing, etc.), the Italian administrative apparatus could not manage in an effective manner a growing list of welfare state programs. Without change, the state was on the brink of functional over-load and administrative paralysis. Opponents replied that regional decentralization was a costly experiment that would further fragment the already fragile structure of decision-making authority in Italy, expand opportunities for corruption and inefficiency, and even widen the North–South gap in socio-economic development.

Despite the longest filibuster ever mounted in the Italian Parliament, the proponents had the votes, and on 17 February 1968 the bill passed both houses with the support of the Christian Democrats, Socialists, Republicans, Communists, and Social Proletarians to become law n. 104. Opposed to the measure were the parties of the Right: Liberals, Monarchists, and Neo-fascists. The law provided for the election of regional councils based on universal suffrage, the use of proportional representation in allocating seats and the province as the electoral district from which to select candidates running on party lists, and the holding of regional elections at the end of 1969, which was later on moved by legislation to 1970. One day later, law 249 was passed which provided for an overall reform of the state bureaucracy in preparation for the implementation of regional decentralization.

III. THE TWO APPROACHES TO DECENTRALIZATION, 1970–77

Once the regions came into existence through the holding of elections of representatives to the new regional council, the devolution of powers to the regions from the national government was not by any means automatic. The process had to be mediated through a long series of political and administrative decisions that during the following seven years would develop along two basic lines of approaches to decentralization. The first approach (implemented between 1970 and 1972) was dominated by national governmental and administrative elites. The second approach (1973–77) was controlled by Parliament. A comparison of these two approaches will highlight the difficulties in following a purely 'administrative' or government-dominated approach to decentralization. Subsequent events have shown that even the second politically-oriented approach may prove to be less than satisfactory for the pro-regionalist forces unless the decision-making process to decentralize is associated with the implementation process that the initial decisions to decentralize are in fact fully carried out. Regionalization is by its very nature a political as well as administrative restructuring of unitary states. Therefore, to be successful the process requires careful political as well as administrative control.

At the beginning of 1970 the government set out to introduce two bills that would implement the regional reform. The first, law n. 281 of 16 May 1970, spelled out the financial resources to be provided to the regions, set out that Parliament would pass 'framework' legislation establishing the parameters for regional legislative activities, and allocated to the government the responsibility for preparing the decrees transferring to the regions' their constitutional administrative responsibilities. The second law, n. 775 of 28 October 1970, obliged the government to formulate decrees for the purpose of reforming the national bureaucracy. The elections of representatives to the fifteen newly created regions took place on 7 June 1970, but the regions had to wait until 1 January 1971 to enter into operation with a skeletal organizational structure and personnel. On paper, at least, Italy had a regional structure at the beginning of 1971.

The implementation of the 1970 legislation proved to be less than satisfactory for the regions. No provisions were made for the enactment of framework laws specifying the boundaries within which the regions were authorized to act. The specification of the administrative functions to be devolved was left up to the national bureaucracy to decide, since each ministry had to draw up its own devolution decrees. Moreover, the financial arrangements kept the regions closely tied to the wishes and procedures of the central government. In essence, the regions remained tied to the 'rulebook' and the 'pocketbook' managed by the central government.

Augusto Barbera has observed that after two years of activity it was clear that the regions were heavily conditioned by the power of the central authorities.[9] In addition, the decisions issued by the Constitutional Court in those first years contributed to the limitation of regional autonomy. The 1972 decrees that were to complete the transfer of powers to the regional level proved to represent a severe limitation of regional autonomy. They left the regions and exponents of regional reform very embittered. It was clear that the government had undertaken to transfer only bits and pieces of central administrative functions while the large part of decision-making powers remained with the national authorities.

In essence, the 1972 decrees emasculated the regions and cast them into the framework of 'super-provinces', subordinate administrators of the nationally determined policies. The effects of the economic crisis of the early 1970s (1974 oil shock and the development of double-digit inflation) and the decrease in funds available to local government accentuated the need to reform local government finances for the purpose of allocating to local authorities the responsibility of remaining within the confines of their locally generated resources and budgetary projections. However, in direct contrast with the intentions of the regional reform but in line with the spirit of the 1972 decrees, the government undertook in 1972–73 to change the structure of local government finances.

Instead of transferring more responsibilities to local government bodies in the collection and management of tax revenues, the government moved in the opposite direction: it centralized all taxing powers and made local government almost completely dependent on 'derived' or 'transferred' revenues. The change in the structure of local taxation powers made it increasingly difficult for the regions and all other types of local governments to prepare realistic three-year spending programmes and investment budgets as called for by subsequent legislation (that is, law 335/1976) or manage their yearly budgets in an effective and rational manner. In the 1980s Aldo Aniasi, the former Minister for the Regions, identified the reorganization of financial arrangements between the state and the regions as one of the steps necessary for placing the regions on a sound and responsible financial footing. However, the growing financial crisis of the Italian state during the 1980s made tax reform a low priority issue at the national level. To continue financing the public deficit (in 1991 it was estimated at ten per cent of GDP), the Italian national authority felt that they needed more rather than less revenue.

When the regions opened for business on 1 April 1972 with less than the full powers that all of them had expected, the optimism among the advocates of regionalism did not cease. The chilling effect of the restrictive interpretations by the Constitutional Court in 1972 drove home the message that the regional reform could not be implemented 'against the state through legal means'.[10] Quickly thereafter, the regions moved their attention from the legal/administrative to the political front in the attempt to expand their powers.

In these early years Italian regionalists interpreted their vocation in almost Messianic terms. As Percy Allum writes of this period, 'the hopes of the regionalists were centred essentially on the belief that the creation of politically autonomous regional governments would be responsible for a radical social and political renewal of the country'.[11] The lack of a full realization of the regional reform provoked a counterattack by the regionalist forces. The fact remains, though, that the creation of the new regional institutions – even in this weakened form – significantly changed the political dynamic of devolution. By coming into existence the regions changed the political landscape in Italy in a number of fundamental ways:

a new level of government with substantial powers in the fields of agriculture, transportation, public works, urban and regional planning, social and health services, tourism, vocational education, and environment was put into place and significantly compromised the centralized political and administrative process that had ruled Italy for 25 years after the end of the war;

a new level was created in the political system. Regional party structures that had only been allowed to develop in the special regions were now given free reign to evolve and create an intermediate level of party office and political career structures between the national and local levels;

a new dynamic developed in the formation of regional economies and endogenous forms of industrial structures through the introduction of decision-making powers and financial allocations in the areas of regional planning, artisan trades, industrial parks, development agencies, vocational education, and advanced services for industry. On the basis of regional economic policies the country witnessed the emergence of the 'third Italy' and a differentiated *Mezzogiorno*:[12]

a new attitude toward the political culture that has emphasized regional identity and culture and the emergence of regionalist parties and political programmes;

a new distribution of power among the parties that permitted parties long excluded from the control of power – for example, the Communists – or new parties such as the Greens to participate in regional government coalitions; and

a new structure for interest groups and voluntary associations that stressed the regional *vis-à-vis* the national and local components of organizational structures.

After the issuing of the 1972 decrees, a few of the regional leaders, cultural figures, jurists, and politicians reacted by creating a 'regionalist front' that could more effectively press national decision-makers for a more advanced form of regional decentralization. The regional governments of Lombardy, Emilia-Romagna, and Tuscany were particularly active in this period. The former was favoured to lead the regionalist front due to its dynamic socio-economic fabric, quality of leadership, and availability of resources. Emilia-Romagna, since the end of the war, had performed a vanguard role for the Left in experimenting with new policies at the local level. A parallel move in the direction of greater regional autonomy was also taken by the new 'players' created by the regional reform – that is, the Interparliamentary Commission for the Regions.[13]

In September 1973 the Interparliamentary Commission began a series of hearings to obtain the views of the region on the future of the reform. The strong regionalist tone of the hearings had a clear impact on the first draft of the bill presented to the Senate which constituted a major shift in content of the delegation of authority that the government was asking.

Pressure began to mount at the beginning of 1974 on the members of the Senate committee (that is, First Commission on Constitutional Norms and Local Government) assigned the task of redrafting the *legge delega* as well as within the ranks of the governing parties to bring about a full transfer of powers to the regions. The draft produced by the First Commission received widespread support when it was voted on 26 July 1974. The government did not assume a direct role in the discussions on the contents of the new bill and gave the Senate Commission a free reign. The 1974 Senate bill had the earmarks of the law that was eventually to become the watershed legislation of 1975 – that is, 382 –,[14] and it had already moved beyond the subject matter of the initial controversy – bureaucratic reform – toward the goal of an organic transfer of regional powers.

It was in the course of the debate in the Chamber that the separation of the two issues of regional decentralization and bureaucratic reform once again took place. This time, in contrast to the 1970 legislation, the government was not able to allocate the task of paring down the central bureaucracy's power to that same bureaucracy: the Chamber of Deputies insisted on maintaining parliamentary oversight of the process by specifying that the government had to get the approval of the Interparliamentary Commission before it could turn its proposals into law. It was felt that this innovation would keep the subsequent formulation of the executive decrees on a highly political plane, where regionalist forces could bring their maximum strength to bear and prevent the decrees from being manipulated at the administrative level by the bureaucracy. Control of the arena for decision-making was correctly seen by the regionalists as a key to the political dynamics of devolution. As a direct consequence of this change in political climate, on 22 July 1975 Parliament passed law n. 382 that codified all of the sentiments for a more thorough regional reform that had been building up since 1973. Law 382 was passed with the support of all of the parties with the exception of the Right.

Within the regional institutions the impact of the 1975 elections served to change the way of conceiving regional alliances and policy formulation – i.e., almost the creation of a second 'constituent' phase – where once again the emphasis was on consensus building and a lowering of the distinction between the majority and minority forces in the council. The PSI no longer felt bound to the existing governmental formula at the national level and opened negotiations to enter into governmental alliances with the Communists in a number of regions – for example, Emilia-Romagna, Piedmont, Lazio, and Liguria – where the two parties had not previously shared power. The DC, in turn, responded by opening the distribution of council posts and the formulation of regional policies to both the PSI in areas where it had enjoyed absolute majorities – Molise and Veneto – and to the PCI in traditional centre-left regions – that is, putting into practice a DC version of the 'giunte aperte' (open giuntas) advocated previously by the PCI. The course of political events at the regional level could not but have an influence on the national debate on the regional reform, and they were immediately evident in the qualitative leap represented by the nature of law 382.

Massimo Severo Giannini described law 382/1975 as a new form of law: 'it is a law that interprets and integrates the Constitution' rather than an ordinary formulation of national policies affecting specific sectors.[15] The uniqueness of the legislation lay in its prescribed 'methodology' for interpreting the meaning and intent of the relevant constitutional provisions, in spelling out the process to be followed in formulating the legislative decrees, and providing for a diversity of consultations in coming up with the final version of the decrees. As was required by one of the constitutional transitory dispositions, law 382 delegated to the government the responsibility of completing the devolution of power in accordance with the following criteria: (1) all powers attributed by the Constitution to the regions that were presently being exercised by the ministries and/or national agencies had to be transferred in an organic rather than piecemeal fashion, (2) the remaining administrative functions that had not been passed down in 1972 had to be decentralized, (3) all state expenditures that directly or indirectly were attributable to the regions had to be eliminated as a block and not through piecemeal legislation, (4) all agencies and functions in areas of regional responsibility that bridged more than one region had to be transferred, and (5) the regions had to have full administrative and legislative powers within the limitations of national legislation and EC directives.[16]

In contrast to the 1970 laws, 382/1975 provided for a number of reviews – one on the part of the regions and two on the part of the Interparliamentary Commission – before the decrees could be transformed into law. In this manner the regions would not be left at the mercy of the state bureaucracy. The steps provided for by the law were: (1) draft of the decrees prepared by the government, (2) opinion on the draft presented by the regions within 60 days, (3) observations of the Interparliamentary Commission within the subsequent 60 days, (4) second government draft of the decrees, (5) a second review by the Interparliamentary Commission, and (6) the final definitive decree by 25 July 1977. To these six steps were added another two: one prior to the formulation of the first government draft with a report by the Giannini Commission and another with the creation of a working group composed of three politicians and three jurists who negotiated the final version of the decrees.[17]

The first draft of the decrees was presented to the regions on 18 February 1977. After three weeks of studying the proposal the regions informed Parliament that the decrees were unacceptable in either quantitative or qualitative terms and not in adherence with the objectives of law 382: 'What is necessary therefore is more organic rather than sectoral powers, sustained by an adequate source of funding in order to launch a serious planning process in the areas of regional responsibility.'[18]

The first governmental version of the decrees represented an attempt to abort the maximalist approach to the regional reform that had characterized law 382 and the recommendations of the Giannini Commission. One Christian Democratic regional councillor observed that the proposed decrees 'do adhere to neither the letter nor the spirit of law 382'.[19] The reductionist orientation of the first version was evident in the government's forecast of having to transfer 93 billion lire to the regions as a result of the devolution of powers. The Giannini Commission had foreseen a transfer of 120 billion lire and the regions in their subsequent evaluation came up with a figure of 200 billion. As a result, several members of the Interparliamentary Commission agreed with the view expressed by the regions and undertook to rewrite a good part of the decrees, and the Commission's draft provided the basis of the version that was finally promulgated – in fact, four-fifths of it.

Added weight was given to the work of the Commission by the agreement stipulated on 25 June 1977 by all of the parties supporting the Andreotti government that the version of the decrees supplied by the Interparliamentary Commission would be accepted by all concerned.

This accord was not completely respected as the government sat down on 8 July 1977 to consider its response to the Commission's new draft. The Minister of Agriculture, Giovanni Marcora, was particularly incensed by the massive transfer of powers in the agricultural sector. In his opinion, the regions were in no way prepared to manage such a large set of new powers effectively.

The text that returned to the Interparliamentary Commission modified some of the Commission's proposals, especially in the area of social assistance where the Church had expressed major concern about provisions restricting public support of religious organizations. On this matter, the Socialists insisted that local governments be given exclusive control of public funds destined for social assistance programmes. A compromise was reached in the Commission.

After 30 years of waiting, a major form of regional devolution was achieved substantially on the basis of a DC, PSI, and PCI accord – that is, the parties that had collaborated in the founding of the Italian Republic. Guido Fanti, president of the Interparliamentary Commission for the Regions, noted the difficulties of trying to maintain harmony within the Commission so that the objectives of the reform would not be lost in the sometimes bitter exchanges between Commission members.

The decrees, DPR 616, went into effect on 1 January 1978. In making some of the final touches, the government attempted to postpone the decentralization of a few national agencies until there was an explicit law covering the subject, but the overall impact of the decrees was not diminished. In financial terms the decrees gave the regions control of approximately 25 per cent of the entire national budget with some estimates running as high as one-third; 20,000 offices were abolished or transferred to the regions, and 15 general directorates and a large number of divisions within the ministries were abolished. Another innovation inserted in the decrees was the stipulation that deadlines were set for the passage of a whole series of reforms, from the reform of the university system to public health, local government, and local finance.

The 1977 decrees were unique in a number of ways, not only in the way they were formulated but also in the way that they defined regional powers. They implemented a creative interpretation of article 117 of the Constitution and reflected modern conceptions of socio-economic policy-making that group together organic sectors expressing interrelated social needs and therefore institutional functions. The weak point of this revolutionary re-definition of regional responsibilities was that there was little echo of the change at the national level – that is, there was no parallel radical change in the central government's structure or mode of behaviour. There was no paring down of the central administrative apparatus, change in the legislative process to take into account the regions' primary responsibility in a number of policy areas, or provisions for the consultation of the regions during the deliberations of national decision-making centres such as the Council of Ministers or Parliament.

The government was still in a position to interpret the implications of the regional reform for national policy-making processes and structures. For example, in 1978 the Pandolfi plan ignored the existence of the regions and Article 34 of its own financial legislation (468/1978) stipulating consultations with the regions in formulating the national budget. Even worse was the government's budgetary proposal for 1979 which foresaw, once again, a cut in allocations to the regions and an increase to those ministries – for example, transportation and public works – severely affected by the regional devolution of power. In addition, the government postponed the crucial reform of local governmental bodies until a full 13 years later.[20]

Parliament, on its part, also did not demonstrate a full understanding of the new distribution of powers in its formulation of national legislation. To overcome the regions' prerogatives in the areas of policy-making, Parliament authorized the setting up of state–regional commissions for the co-determination of policies. By the early 1980s, there were 99 such commissions. Nor was there any attempt to change parliamentary procedures so that standing committee deliberations could solicit regional views when policies involving the regions were under consideration or requiring a 'consultative' opinion on the part of the Interparliamentary Commission on the Regions.

In the period between the end of the 1970s and the beginning of the 1980s, the regions were faced with the problem of the economic crisis which increasingly exercised pressure to reduce public spending at the regional level at a time when the regions were called upon to assume new responsibilities. In 1978 the ministers for the Treasury and Budget imposed a reduction in regional and local spending.

In response to these measures the regions concentrated on three objectives in redefining their relations with the national government: (1) 'penetrating' into the center of national decision-making – that is, Council of Ministers – with the institutionalization of a direct political dialogue with the national representatives and placing the stress on the political nature of the dialogue and abandoning the alternative of administrative relations that had proven so conflict ridden and which had for so long dominated centre–regional relations; (2) emphasizing the reform of local government that would allow the regions to resolve the problem of the 'intermediate' level of government that was crucial for the implementation of a planning approach to policy-making at the regional level; and (3) insisting with parallel resolve on the restructuring of local government financing that would permit sub-national levels of government to know in advance how much to expect in income and therefore be in a position to finalize investment programs.

In 1980 the Interparliamentary Commission suggested the creation of a 'state-region conference' that would bring together on a regular basis the 20 regional presidents, the prime minister and the ministers for the Treasury, Regions, and Budget. It also suggested that the institutional site for the conference be the Council of Ministers. The institutionalization of a permanent presence of the regions at the centre was seen by the regionalist forces as an absolute necessity in stopping attempts by the state through the power of the purse to weaken the regional reform. In 1983 Franco Bassanini observed that:

> We are passing through a period of increasingly limited resources in relation to the services and public policies that the society demands. If today we were to conserve a strict separation between the regions and the central organs of the state, the regions may have the formal appearance of autonomy but in fact will find themselves only capable of administering the cuts in spending imposed by the state. Therefore, either we guarantee the regions' and other local governments' participation in the process where resources are distributed or else the regional reform will be emptied of its content.[21]

The creation of the Conference of Regional Presidents was the last major innovation that was implemented as part of the second, post-1972 innovative thrust that consolidated the role of the regions in the Italian policy-making and political process. The calling of the first meeting of the Conference on 12 October 1983 signified the adoption of a model of state-regional relations that emphasized co-participation in decision-making and interdependence in the administration of policies at the two levels of government. This model was qualitatively different from the one that emphasized the separation of sectoral responsibilities that was dominant during the first ten years of the regional reform, and it foreshadowed the evolution of an inter-governmental process based on institutionalized inter-regional linkages that would become important in the latter half of the 1980s. In the Italian case the holding of regular meetings between the political leaders of the regions (presidents of regional giuntas) and the national government (PM and his ministers) would serve as the basis for the 'partnership' and 'subsidiarity' principles in regional policies that were to be required by the Community Support Frameworks and the Integrated Mediterranean Programmes.

IV. THE UNRESOLVED PROBLEMS OF ITALIAN REGIONALISM

During the second half of the 1980s the initiative for regional reform was removed from the national political arena and transferred to the Community level. No other reforms were seriously debated or passed. Government in Italy was, in fact, conducting a rearguard action against granting any further powers to the regions and taking back what it could. This was particular evident in the areas of policy-making where the regions had assumed early initiatives – such as in environmental and territorial planning, small and medium-sized enterprises, transport, and social services.

The last five years of the 1980s were also characterized by the lack of central government reform in the areas of economic development, infrastructure planning, and subsidies for the southern regions. In 1986 the Agency for the South was refinanced with the expectation that it would adopt a more technocratic approach to the implementation of projects and undertake serious forms of evaluation of the impact of nationally managed and funded projects. However, the reality proved to be considerably different. What planning and rationalization that took place of the diverse and conspicuous sources of funding flowing to the southern Italian regions came on the heels of the implementation of the Community Support Frameworks (CSFs) requiring regions to *submit* and *respect* objectives, projects and schedules underwritten by regional and national officials.

Research in Sicily has shown that the implementation of the CSFs at the beginning of the 1990s represented the first time that regional planning was seriously undertaken in the South as an exercise in bringing into line budgetary allocations, government programmes, and administrative efficiency.[22] Prior to the CSFs, regional plans and commitments to a rational planning approach had never been seriously required or expected by the national government as a condition for resource allocation in the South or in other parts of the country. In addition, monitoring of the pace of development of regions receiving special funding from national and Community sources was undertaken as a product of EC pressure rather than as a normal part of the evaluation process instituted by the national government. In summary, the central government ceased to function in the later part of the 1980s as a focus for debate and experimentation. That role had been allocated to the European Community.

The reluctance of the national government to discuss the regional issue, of course, did not make the problem go away. Regionalism continued to be a point of debate among scholars, politicians, and the general public. The new elements that emerged in that debate in the late 1980s and early 1990s were:

(1) how the regions could interact more effectively with Brussels and establish themselves as a significant interlocutor with the Community. Early experiments in this regard were undertaken in the 1980s with the first IDO programme in Naples and in a tangential manner with regard to the Social and Agricultural Funds. However, the first concrete step forward was the opportunity on the part of the Italian regions (15 of them) to participate in the Integrated Mediterranean Programmes (IMPs). The IMPs introduced the discipline of regional planning as a policy requirement outside of the confines of intra-regional activities. Prior to the IMP experience various regional governments had engaged in some form of regional planning but it had never been required (aside from multi-annual budgetary allocations) by the national government as a means of spending money. In fact, it readily became apparent that those regional governments which had experimented with regional planning as an approach to policy-making and implementation had no difficulty in implementing the IMPs (Umbria, Emilia-Romagna, Tuscany, Veneto, Friuli-Venezia Giulia, Marche, and Lazio.). However, those regions (for example, Sicily, Campania, and Calabria) which had not had an extensive experience with planning and intra-regional networking by bringing into the policy-making process regional interest groups, voluntary groups, and other levels of government ran into serious problems in meeting the EC criteria for the disbursement of funds. In these cases, the IMPs proved to be highly unsuccessful, but nevertheless they served as an introduction to the approach that the EC would later implement with the Community Support Frameworks;

(2) the need to alleviate the region's dependence on funds as exclusively derived from the national government. The request for taxation powers found increasing favour among the general public and regional officials, but the national government was very reluctant to loose its monopoly. This situation tended to exacerbate relations between the regions and the centre and, in the final analysis, served to fuel smoldering resentment against an over-bearing state that was unwilling to relinquish any of its power over the purse. In the late 1980s this resentment expressed itself in the growing demand voiced by the regional leagues (Leghe) to stop continuously financing through transfer payments and unproductive investments the maintenance of political clienteles, high levels of consumption, unemployment, and corruption in the South in the name of national unity and solidarity. That demand found full expression in the 1992 national

parliamentary elections when the Lega Nord became the fourth largest party in Italy with over eight per cent of the vote thereby placing on the future political agenda the issue of transition to a full federal structure in Italy; and

(3) the reinforcement of regional autonomy through a two-pronged approach. On the one hand, initiate referenda whose aim was to cut out redundant ministries and governmental agencies. Since the government was unwilling to reduce the size of the national government and duplication with the regions, the regional authorities and citizens had to take the initiative through direct action. On the other, there were demands for a constitutional change that would place a barrier on further central government meddling in regional affairs. One proposal was to move towards a full-fledged federal system (Federalist Movement) while the more radical proposal of the regional leagues was to cut the country into three republics: the Republic of the North, the Republic of the Centre and the Republic of the South. Such a move was designed to dismember the Italian state and to put an end to Italian unity and obligations that at times seemed to draw its aspirations from the recent Yugoslav experience.

The debate has not yet reached any form of consensus, the aftermath of the results of the 1992 parliamentary elections having still to ripple through the system. However, it is clear that the Italian regional reform has not yet been completed. It still has to achieve the full objectives outlined by the Constitution and supported by the general public. That criteria can only be satisfied with a full restructuring and paring down of the central government and the realization of full decision-making, implementation, and financial autonomy of the regions from central government tutelage.

V. SURVEY RESPONSES TO THE SINGLE MARKET QUESTIONNAIRE

What was expressed in political terms in the 1992 elections by the Italian public had already been expressed clearly in the 1989 survey of politicians, interest group leaders, and citizens on the need to strengthen the regional reform and make the transition at the Community-level to a federal form of state system in a position to manage public policy in the post-1992 setting.[23] The creation of the single market poses the basic question of: who governs the market? It is already clear that the unified market will need to be governed by new organs and procedures that have still to be fully decided.

One of the central characteristics of Italian society during the last two decades has been its sustained level and pace of change. Economic and institutional performance has been maintained at levels that place the Italian regions among the more dynamic realities in Western Europe.[24] When we asked respondents located within the regional institution (that is, councillors (N = 215)) and 'external' elite groups (that is, the 'observers' (N = 133)) and ordinary citizens (N = 2,000) to evaluate the state of the region in light of the challenges posed by 1992, we found a uniform set of responses among all three sample groups that significantly distinguished respondents in the Centre and North from those living and working in the South.

Table 1 demonstrates the serious division in attitudes in all three samples between respondents in the South and those in the North. Opinions tend to vary more between the educated elites represented in the councillor and observer samples, but their views are consistent on a comparative basis with those expressed by citizens. The only items where a majority of the southern elites feel that their regions are well prepared for 1992 are with regard to the road and university systems. Ordinary citizens seem to be less critical concerning the shortcomings of the South in other areas, but their level of satisfaction is lower than those expressed by citizens in the North. These survey data provide a parallel source of information that corroborates the data presented in the conclusions suggesting that the North is ready and able to take advantage of the challenges offered by the single European market. During the last two decades it has developed the social and economic structure that will allow it to compete with other industrialized and developed parts of Europe. Data concerning other areas of the regional structure – such as its institutional development and political culture – provide additional information that the North is already an integral part of Europe and will face few obstacles in operating within an open European context.

After having asked respondents in our three samples to evaluate the state of the regional economy and society, we solicited their opinions on the perceived impact that the creation of the European market would have on three sectors: the economy, social services, and regional institutions.[25]

Table 2 shows that respondents in the North expect the unified market to have a significant, positive impact on the regional economy in the form of access to new markets, stimulation of technological innovation, more competition, access to new financial resources, restructuring of the commercial distribution network, reconversion of agricultural production, and concentration of industry. Respondents in the South, instead, are much more conscious of the potential negative impacts of the single

TABLE 1

STATE OF REGIONAL ECONOMY IN VIEW OF 1992 IN THE OPINION OF REGIONAL COUNCILLORS, OBSERVERS, AND CITIZENS

	(%responding "adequate" or "good")					
	Regional councillors		Observers		Citizens	
	North	South	North	South	North	South
Structural elements:						
Structure of small and medium-sized industry	79	35	65	43	73	51
Port system	35	20	40	16	NR	NR
Air Communications	39	32	40	33	62	55
Road network	33	66	46	79	72	62
Railway network	20	24	31	27	62	54
Structure of agricultural enterprises	56	25	35	42	62	54
Network of social services	60	15	42	11	43	30
Health services	64	11	46	13	NR	NR
University system	67	56	67	65	62	55
Level of associationalism	77	47	71	46	NR	NR
Skill level of workforce	73	40	73	37	68	51
Technological innovation in industry	81	40	81	45	79	52
Industry restructuring	78	31	75	45	NR	NR
Functionality of urban areas	12	7	13	10	NR	NR
Utilization of historical-environmental resources	33	18	38	29	67	50
Structure of commercial network	55	35	56	48	77	56

'What is your assessment of this region's economic and social condition in preparing for 1992? For *each* of the following sectors please indicate your opinion.'

Responses: good, adequate, inadequate.

TABLE 2

IMPACT OF THE SINGLE EUROPEAN MARKET ON THE REGIONS ON THE OPINIONS OF REGIONAL COUNCILLORS, OBSERVERS, AND CITIZENS

	(%responding "will have an impact")					
	Regional councillors		Observors		Citizens	
	North	South	North	South	North	South
Impact:						
-Access to new markets	86	80	81	80	83	78
-Stimulate technological innovation	96	81	100	88	82	79
-More competition	97	96	94	95	91	82
-Provide access to new financial resources	83	86	85	83	NR	NR
-Increase the cost of production	21	36	32	34	50	54
-Concentration of industry	86	78	83	71	NR	NR
-Increase unemployment	25	46	27	45	NR	NR
-Restructure commercial distribution networks	94	88	88	90	76	72
-Stimulate reconversion of agricultural production	79	78	77	79	64	65
-Worse situation in under-developed areas	56	77	66	74	56	52
-Improvement in public services	56	36	53	42	57	60
-Raising standards in social services	49	63	73	64	NR	NR
-Stimulate adoption of new environmental standards	89	84	90	76	64	66
-Stimulate institutional renewal	84	81	83	76	NR	NR
-Modernization of regional administration	50	53	56	56	64	66
-Confusion of functions	45	57	39	46	NR	NR
-Slow-down decision making process	40	44	40	47	NR	NR
-Loss of regional identity	8	20	9	18	27	36

'In 1992 the unified European market will be created. For *each* of the following areas do you believe that the unified market will have or not have an impact on your region?

market in stimulating an increase in the costs of production, increased unemployment, and worsening of economic conditions in the less developed parts of the country. Nevertheless, most of the respondents expect the creation of the new European market to have, in general, a beneficial rather than negative impact on the region.

When it comes to social services, residents of the North see less of an impact originating from the consequences of the unified market. Half or less of the respondents believe that the Community will help improve social standards or the quality of public services, though a good portion across the board see the impact of the Community being more important in the establishment of new environmental standards. A similar pattern is evident with regard to attitudes toward the impact of the Community on regional institutions and identity. Few believe that the creation of the single market will cause a loss of regional identity, and large majorities are of the view that it will have a significant role in stimulating institutional innovation. However, close to half of the elite respondents believe that the effect of greater European integration will slow down the regional decision-making process, lead to greater confusion in the allocation of policy-making and administrative functions, but at the same time stimulate the modernization of administrative structures.

As part of the analysis of the linkage between Italian regions and European integration, we asked our elite respondents their views on whether the functions of the European Community should change in light of the creation of the unified market. Table 3 presents the data on the responses of regional councillors and observers on twelve possible areas where change might take place after 1992. In asking the questions, we wanted to find out whether the respondents wanted an increased, the same, or a decreased presence of the Community. Data in the table show that northern respondents are overwhelmingly favourable toward an increase in Community responsibilities in the area of providing a European perspective to scientific research, promotion of technological innovation, and promotion in the integration of non-Community emigrants. They tend to be at the same level as their counterparts elsewhere when it comes to favouring an increase in the Community's role in controlling the application of urban and environmental standards (high across the board), financing of development projects for depressed areas, monitoring of financial markets, providing direction for vocational education, monitoring of labour markets, and co-ordination of foreign trade. There is, in general, less enthusiasm when it comes to the control of migratory flows of workers from non-EC countries or the financing of a European defence system. In contrast to the responses reported in the previous two tables, southern politicians are here more favourable in ten out of the 12 items toward an increase in the functions of the European Community while among the observers those in the South are slightly less favourable than their counterparts in the North. The southern political elite is, thus, highly favourable toward a growing level of European initiatives.

The generally favourable attitude of the South toward the Community is increasingly marked when we consider the responses to the question of what institutions or agencies should be created to aid the functioning of the European market. Table 4 shows that the equipping of the European Community with the agencies that characterize large federal systems – such as those that exist in the United States, Canada, and Australia –

TABLE 3

FUNCTIONS OF THE EUROPEAN COMMUNITY AFTE 1992: OPINIONS OF REGIONAL COUNCILLORS AND OBSERVERS

	(%responding "increases")			
	Regional Councillors		Observers	
	North	South	North	South
<u>Function</u>:				
Control of the enforcement of environmental and urban planning standards	74	89	87	87
Evaluation of regional investment projects	64	75	66	76
Financing of projects for underdeveloped areas	89	95	87	91
Monitoring of financial markets	79	85	89	81
European perspective for scientific research	89	93	94	89
Financing of European defence policies	33	34	26	28
Promotion of technological innovation	94	96	98	90
Formulating guidelines for professional education	79	90	90	84
Monitoring of labour markets	79	91	83	85
Control of immigration from non-EEC countries	54	64	62	53
Promotion of integration of emigrants	87	91	89	80
Coordination of foreign trade	91	91	92	88

'After the implementation of the European market, how in your opinion should the role of the Community change? For *each* of the following functions please indicate your preference.'

Responses: increases, stays the same, decreases.

TABLE 4

INSTITUTIONS NECESSARY FOR THE COMMUNITY AFTER 1992, IN THE OPINION OF REGIONAL COUNCILLORS AND OBSERVERS

	(%responding "indispensable" or "necessary") Regional Councillors North	South	Observers North	South
Operational instruments:				
Federal European Bank	97	100	96	98
European Environmental Agency	99	100	98	100
EEC Europrogrammes for sectoral intervention	100	99	98	94
Interregional Euroconsortia for the planning of services and public infrastructure	89	86	72	91
Euroagencies for interregional co-operation for the management of services and infrastructure	81	87	72	87
University postgraduate Eurodiplomas in sciences	83	94	78	89
European Administrative Court	88	88	86	83
European Agency to monitor labour markets	99	100	94	96
European Securities and Exchange Commission	95	99	92	85
European Conference for regional Presidents	91	93	74	77
European-level representation of regional councils	90	91	61	73
Regional offices in Brussels	83	92	65	72
European telecommunications agency	98	99	87	96

'After the implementation of the unified European market, in your opinion what operative instruments should the Community create in order to meet the challenges of the post-1992 period? Please express your opinion of whether you think that the Community needs to or does not create *each* of the following policy instruments.' For *each* of the following functions please indicate your preference.'

Responses: indispensable, necessary, not advisable.

TABLE 5
TRANS-REGIONAL CO-OPERATION AFTER 1992, OPINIONS OF REGIONAL COUNCILLORS AND OBSERVERS (1988–89)

	(%responding "indispensable" or "opportune") Regional Councillors North	South	Observers North	South
Common initiatives:				
Lobby the EEC Commission	48	61	40	52
Formulating development programmes	99	98	91	97
Cultural/turistic exchange programmes	98	100	96	100
Plans for applied research	100	98	98	99
Policy to protect the environment	100	99	98	97
Activity to promote products/services	93	96	96	97
Strenthening regional airline service	84	90	96	93
Preparation of administrative personnel	97	99	98	92
Promotion of joint-ventures between enterprises	88	93	94	95
Integrated programmes for contiguous border regions	97	96	94	93

'After the implementation of the European unified market in your opinion what are the common initiatives that should be created among regions located in different European countries? For *each* of the following possibilities please express your opinion '
Responses: indispensable, opportune, not necessary.

enjoy widespread favour among councillors and observers in the North as well as in the South.

A similar pattern of responses can be noted when the question of inter-regional co-operation was posed (see Table 5) in terms of promoting common initiatives among regions in various European states; the level of adherence in almost all cases close to or above 90 per cent. The only exception is the question of 'lobbying' the European Commission. Responses to this question may reflect much more the negative connotations of the work 'lobby' in Italian rather than a rejection of the act itself. It is well documented in the literature on pressure groups and governmental institutions that lobbying in Italy has a long and successful tradition.

VI. CONCLUSIONS

Overall, then, it is clear that the prospect for a more integrated Europe after 1992 is not a source of preoccupation for regional elites and citizens in Italy. Both levels of opinion feel that the regions are well endowed with the economic and social resources and structures that will permit them to compete successfully in an open market. Respondents also supported further steps in the integration process in the form of allocating additional functions, creating European level agencies to oversee important sectors that must be rationalized at the European level, and promoting trans-regional cooperation to pool resources and formulate common solutions to problems. Such forms of co-operation are seen as necessary and even indispensable elements in a post-1992 Europe.

The above analysis shows that the regional institution enjoys widespread support in developing the institutional mechanisms that will make possible its activities in a potentially revised institutional framework after 1992. The creation of a Council of Regions by the provisions of the Maastricht Treaty is a sign that the moment for the institutionalization of the regions' role in European Community affairs has finally arrived.

To operate at the European level the region must have the policy making initiative to flag and analyse problems as they crop-up in the regional environment and be willing to co-operate with other regions in developing innovative schemes and policies in resolving problems. Given the broader range of resources that can be mobilized and brought to bear on issues, the regions have to hone their capacity to interpret and translate existing Community programmes into specific policy alternatives that can be implemented at the regional level. Finally, they must be discriminating in their choice of policies and seek intra-Community alliances in pursuit of solutions. After 1992 the regions will not be able to undertake policies to protect the local models of development. They must, instead, transport them to the European level and make the model of diffused enterprise a part of a European system of small and medium-sized enterprise. In this manner the regions will be able to co-ordinate their strategies with other sub-national levels of government managing similar industrial and entrepreneurial realities – that is, in Italy and the Community. The challenge is to bring the industrial district model of enterprise based on the partnership between private and public interests to the European level and provide it the infrastructure to allow it to compete with large, multinational corporations.

Having identified the problem of the institutional model that should govern the creation of linkage networks after 1992, what are the prospects for its realization? The answer to this question is not only in the hands of the Italian regional elites to determine. It is, in effect, the fundamental issue that is now being debated and experimented with at all levels of the Community. The economic logic of the post-1992 model is self-evident. It makes little sense to abolish all barriers to economic interaction among member states while at the same time maintaining restrictions on sub-national levels of government from interacting across national boundaries.

NOTES

1. M. Monaco *La regione* (Rome: Edizioni Cinque Lune, 1957), pp. 20–21.
2. C. Pavone *Amministrazione centrale e amministrazione periferica da Rattazzi a Ricasoli (1859–1866)* (Milan: Giuffré, 1964), p. 5.
3. R. Grew *A Sterner Plan for Italian Unity* (Princeton, NJ: Princeton University Press, 1963).
4. Monaco, op. cit., p. 11.
5. See A. Agnelli and S. Bartole *La regione Friuli-Venezia Giulia* (Bologna: Il Mulino, 1987).
6. See R. Leonardi and D. Wertman, *Italian Christian Democracy: The Politics of Dominance* (London: Macmillan, 1989).
7. P. Calamadrei *Dieci anni dopo, 1945–1955: Saggi sulla vita democratica italiana* (Bari: Laterza, 1955).
8. The Italian experience with the creation of the regions reflects, to a certain extent, the debate taking place in Portugal today. See the contribution by Walter C. Oppello, Jr. in this volume.
9. A. Barbera *Le istituzioni del pluralismo* (Bari: De Donato, 1977).
10. G. Falcon 'Corte Costituzionale e Regioni', *Guida per le autonomie locali '78* (1978), p. 192.
11. P.A. Allum, *Italy: Republic Without Government* (New York: Norton, 1973), p. 236.
12. See A. Bagnasco, *Tre Italie: La problematica territoriale dello sviluppo italiano* (Bologna: Il Mulino, 1977) and *La costruzione sociale del mercato: Studi sullo sviluppo di piccola impresa in Italia* (Bologna: Il Mulino, 1988); M. Piore and C. Sabel *The Second Industrial Divide: Possibilities for Prosperity* (New York: Basic Books, 1983); and R. Leonardi, R.D. Putnam, and R.Y. Nanetti, *Il caso Basilicata: L'effetto regione dal 1970 al 1986* (Bologna: Il Mulino, 1986).
13. It should be added that the trade union movement and private economic interests were also members of this regionalist front.
14. In fact, the Senate version of the bill treated the special regions on the same basis with the regular regions. Based on an explicit request by the five special regions, they were excluded from subsequent reformulations of the bill in the Chamber of Deputies. The feeling of the five was that if they were placed on the same plane with the other 15 they would lose their privileged relationship with the centre.
15. M.S. Giannini 'Del lavare la testa all'asino', in A. Barbera and F. Bassanini (eds.), *I nuovi poteri delle regioni e degli enti locali* (Bologna: Il Mulino, 1978), p. 10.
16. E. Modica and R., *Triva Dizionario delle autonomie locali* (Rome: Editori Riuniti, 1977), pp. 815–21.
17. The time period allowed for this procedure was one year, but before the year was up, a governmental crisis in January 1976 brought on new parliamentary elections in the summer of 1976. Thus, formulation of the regional decrees was postponed until 25 July 1977 with the passage of law 894/1976.
18. Camera dei Deputati, *L'attuazione della '382'* (Rome: Camera dei Deputati-Servizio per i rapporti con le regioni, 1977), p. 23.

19. Ibid, p. 4.
20. For a discussion of the 1990 local government law, see Luciano Vandelli, 'The New Local Government Law' in R. Leonardi and F. Anderlini (eds.), *Italian Politics, A Review*, Vol. 6 (London: Pinter Pulishers, 1992), pp. 25–40.
21. F. Bassanini, 'Bisogna partecipare alle scelte economiche', *L'Italia delle regioni*, 26 (Oct.–Nov. 1983), pp. 6–7.
22. See Raffaella Y. Nanetti 'Coordination in Development Planning: An Evaluation of the Initial Implementation of the Community Support Framework', Commission of the European Community, Brussels, 15 May 1992.
23. The interviews with Italian regional councillors and interest group leaders took place in 1989 based on a questionnaire that had been developed during the course of a 20–year study of the institutionalization of Italian regional government. In this chapter we will report the results of the responses concerning EC issues while the reader can find the results of the other questions reported in R.D. Putnam, R. Leonardi, and R.Y. Nanetti, *Governance and the Civic Community* (Princeton, NJ: Princeton University Press, 1992). The total number of interviews conducted in 1989 was 179 with regional councillors and 198 with regional observers. The mass survey covered a sample of 2,000 citizens spread over the entire nation. The interviews with politicians and observers covered the regions of Lombardy, Veneto, Lazio, Puglia, Abruzzo, and Sicily. Thus, the sample was divided between three Objective 1 (Puglia, Abruzzo and Sicily) and three non-Objective 1 regions (Lombardy, Veneto, and Lazio).
24. See the concluding contribution to this volume for a comparison of Italian *vis-à-vis* other countries' regional performance between 1970 and 1988.
25. In the questionnaire the areas of impact were scattered randomly. The aggregation of potential impacts on the three groups is the product of analysis.

Conclusions: Sub-National Elites and the European Community

ROBERT LEONARDI and SHARI GARMISE

The previous nine contributions have provided an analysis of the changes in the structure of sub-national governments in the Community's Objective 1 areas as well as a clear indication of how elite opinion is distributed on the issues involving the creation of the single market and the opportunities and dangers that the 1992 programme presents for regional economies and societies. In this article we will attempt to draw some general conclusions on the impact of regionalism on the European Community and the role that the regions will be able (and will want) to play in the post-1992 Europe.

The last two major revisions of the original Rome Treaty (the Single European Act and the Maastricht Treaty) identified the regions as key actors in a stronger and more integrated European Community, but the question remains whether regionalism and the institutionalization of regional government are really in the best interest of Europe. The argument has repeatedly been made that regionalism helps to promote democracy, administrative efficiency, sense of political efficacy, and participation in the policy process of regional and local level interests.[1] However, little attention has been given to the issue of whether regionalism and institutionalization of regional government helps to achieve the promotion of economic and social development. The growing literature on flexible specialization and the networking approach to economic restructuring[2] place a significant emphasis on the role of decentralized governmental institutions (governments, development agencies, research centres, etc.) in stimulating the growth and development of the structure, but little has been written concerning the key role of decentralized governments in stimulating the growth of these alternative forms of production processes. In the second section of this article we will look at the possible connection between regional government and economic growth by analysing the comparative economic performance of 168 regions in the European Community during the past decade and try to draw some conclusions on the role that viable regional institutions can play in helping to achieve economic growth and development. The article will conclude with an analysis of the implications of the provisions of the

Maastricht Treaty for the regions, and how these provisions – tied to those already put in place by the Single European Act – serve to identify an increasingly important role for the regions in European Community affairs.

I. REGIONAL ELITE ATTITUDES TOWARD THE SINGLE MARKET

Taken together, the interviews conducted in 1989 provide a unique basis for comparing the views of regional elites in Objective 1 areas toward a number of key issues concerning the operation of the single market. In addition to gauging elite opinion on the costs and benefits tied to the entry of their regions into the single market, the respondents were asked to provide their views on two sets of issues: (1) the areas where the Community will have to take preventive measures to counteract the negative ramifications of the single market; and (2) the areas in which the Community can build alternative policy-making and implementation structures in order to take advantage of the opportunities presented by the changes in the post-1992 market and institutional configurations.

As was discussed above, the Community is presently composed of nation-states possessing significantly different sub-national institutional structures. Four out of the five 'big' states – Germany, France, Italy, and Spain – have extensive regional or federal intermediate government bodies positioned between the national and local levels. The UK, on the other hand, has effectively abolished regional planning and administrative bodies and metropolitan governments, and the current government announced prior to the 1992 parliamentary elections that it would 'restructure' the remaining pillar of local government in the UK, the county councils. Among the smaller countries, the example of Belgium points to a strong affirmation of regional government during the last two decades. Portugal and Greece have constitutional provisions that provide for the creation of regional governments, but they have as yet to be fully implemented.

These differences in institutional structures need to be kept in mind in interpreting the answers to the question concerning the creation of the single market in 1993.[3] The implications of a lack of homogeneity in sub-national institutional structures are twofold. In centralized governmental systems policy issues concerning regional economic and social development remain a national concern. Secondly, local government officials and interest group leaders do not have the opportunity of accumulating experience in dealing with and having responsibility for the implementation of economic and social development policies. As a result, the 'relevance' of the questions – that is, the experience from which information is drawn to decide on a issue – varies from one group of respondents to another.

For those with regional government experience, the questions on the role of the regions in the post-1992 setting proposed concrete issues of immediate relevance. For the others, the questions tended to be more abstract in nature. However, the responses of both sets of respondents – those operating within regional institutions and those without them – are important in that they reveal the state of opinion among sub-national elites on vital issues concerning national as well as EC institutional arrangements as the Community moves toward further integration.

The presentation of the surveys of regional and local political elites in the five member states covers those countries – that is, Greece, Italy, Spain, Portugal, and Ireland – where a nation-wide survey was conducted and completed with regional politicians and interest group leaders. The more limited regional surveys conducted in Northern Ireland and Corsica were too fragmentary and small to be used in a comparative perspective.[4]

The first concern in the interviews was to gauge political elite opinion on the state of the regional economy in light of the challenges presented by the creation of the single market. Table 1 shows that there is a consistent feeling among sub-national political elites in Objective 1 areas that their regions are not adequately prepared for the rendezvous with Europe after 1992, especially in the case of regional economic infrastructure – for example, port system, air communications, road systems, and railroad networks. One of the few exceptions to this general conclusion can be found in the opinions expressed by regional political elites toward the state of air links in Spain and Ireland and the road network in Italy.

The Greek respondents were particularly dissatisfied with local transport and community infrastructure, reflecting the physical isolation in which the country finds itself. Greece is the only member state in the Community that does not share a common border with another EC member, and the resolution of its transport problems are not dependent on entirely EC decisions. The current civil disorder in Yugoslavia, contrasts with the Republic of Macedonia, its varying relationship with Bulgaria and Albania, and its outright hostility versus Turkey stress even more than before the linkage problems that Greece has with the Community. Rail and road links can be compromised by civil disorder in other states, and the definition of its borders and national interests are constantly called into question by the actions of its neighbours. Secure transport links between Greece and the Community have to be based on the strengthening of Greece's sea and air links with other member states rather than depending on surface road or rail links. While Greece has a

TABLE 1

STATE OF THE REGIONAL ECONOMY IN VIEW OF 1992 IN THE OPINION OF SUB-NATIONAL POLITICIANS

Structural elements	IT	GR	SP	PO	IR	Total
Structure of small and medium-sized enterprises	58.9	8.4	97.3	8.5	37.1	48.4
Port system	29.1	32.8	46.9	42.5	39.0	37.3
Air communications	36.8	27.2	60.1	30.4	63.8	44.0
Road network	54.7	27.3	42.4	34.0	18.9	38.4
Railway network	22.8	9.3	37.5	7.4	39.6	25.7
Structure of agricultural enterprises	43.2	17.9	11.5	4.3	57.7	27.4
Network of social services	41.1	32.9	45.5	39.4	66.0	43.4
Health services	34.1	43.9	32.1	43.6	63.8	41.0
University system	63.1	22.8	29.3	52.2	72.6	47.1
Level of associationalism	65.4	38.1	51.1	24.5	-	48.8
Skill level of workforce	59.6	12.9	44.5	12.8	78.3	43.1
Technological innovation in industry	61.9	5.3	48.9	9.6	55.7	39.9
Industrial restructuring	54.9	6.0	34.8	6.4	42.5	32.3
Functionality of urban areas	14.0	20.6	62.4	28.7	35.6	31.9
Utilization of historical-environmental resources	27.7	22.7	35.7	36.6	35.6	30.8
Structure of commercial network	44.3	34.0	59.9	24.7	53.3	44.8

'What is your assessment of this region's economic and social condition in preparing for 1992? For *each* of the following sectors please indicate your opinion.'

Responses: good, adequate, inadequate. The table presents the percentage of respondents stating that the structural elements of the region's economic and social structures are 'good' or 'adequate'.

robust shipping industry, its air links and quality of its airport infrastructure are not up to EC standards. One of the priorities for Greece should be the strengthening of its air links and airport infrastructure. In a similar vein, Greece's telecommunication links with the outside Community need to be reinforced and brought up to modern technological standards.

A more differentiated situation existed when the respondents were asked to comment on the state of industrial and agricultural enterprises. Italian respondents, in general, were much more sanguine in their expectations that their regional economies will be ready to meet the competitive challenges of 1992. However, the differences with their colleagues in other countries disappear when the respondents operating in Objective 1 (depressed) are separated from those living in non-Objective 1 (non-depressed) regions.[5] Elites in southern Italian regions are much less satisfied with the structure of their small and medium-sized enterprises, level of associationalism, skill level of workforce, technological innovation in industry, contribution to industry from the university system, and level of industrial reconversion than are their colleagues in the North. The same generalization holds with regard to the system of social service and commercial networks. Thus, in Italy northerners feel that they have an adequate public infrastructures, private associations, and level of interaction between the public and private sector that will permit them to meet the challenges of the single market.

In the South, the lack of adequate public infrastructure, presence of a culture of social solidarity and associationalism, combined with an ephemeral private industrial sector reduce the chances for mounting a credible response to potential competitors from other Community regions. The surveys illustrate that the accelerated and extensive funding programme initiated by the Italian national government and then reinforced by contributions from the European Community to create economic infrastructures (roads, aqueducts, dams, electrical lines, natural gas pipeline, etc.) has not served to reinforce the sense of efficacy of southern elites. Despite the aid, the South still feels that it is operating in a less than competitive framework and that the provision of economic infrastructure is not sufficient to fill the competitive void that exists between the South and the North.

Two countries where the elites share the pessimistic views of their southern Italian colleagues are Greece and Portugal. Both feel that they are particularly exposed to and unprepared for the increased competition from the rest of Europe. The views of the respondents reflect the opinion that the regional economies of Greece and Portugal are afflicted with two shortcomings that place into question their future under open competition rules. First of all, their peripherality increases the costs of competition due to the greater role played by transport costs in bringing their goods to mass markets, and secondly, the level of 'maturity' of their industrial and service sectors, plus the relative low level of their technology place them at a competitive disadvantage.

Ireland, on the other hand, presents a mixed view on its state of competitiveness. On one hand, Irish respondents feel that Ireland is better off than Portugal and Greece when it comes to its service sector, institutions of higher education, and the skill level of its work force. On the other hand, Ireland feels that it is at a disadvantage with regard to the rest of Europe when it comes to the state of its industrial structure (weak and highly dependent on large external firms) and transportation and communications links with the other eleven member states. The major transport projects being carried out in the Community (Channel Tunnel and TGV high speed train network) offer little opportunity for Ireland to reduce its isolation. Thus, Ireland needs to strengthen its ties to Europe through alternative networks. Telecommunications is seen as the main alternative for the reduction of the impact of its physical peripheral position.

Despite the fears concerning the competitive position of their regional economies, Table 2 shows that sub-national political elites in the five countries share highly positive views toward opportunities for growth and development associated with the creation of the single market and see the 1992 programme as a golden opportunity for overcoming existing levels of underdevelopment. In general, the impact or 'market shock' of the creation of the single market is considered to be a positive factor for regional economies in most Objective 1 regions. An overwhelming majority of elites believe that the single market will have a *positive* impact on their own individual regions by providing access to new markets, stimulating technological innovation, providing more competition, encouraging the reconversion of agricultural production, and restructuring the commercial distribution network.

In contrast, opinion is divided on the more negative aspects of the potential impact of the single market on, for example, the increase in production costs, increase in unemployment, and worsening the condition of underdeveloped areas. The reason for the significant lack of pessimism in evaluating the impact of the single market is due to the fact that the regional elites do not see the single market as a zero sum game. Even though they are ready to acknowledge that some might gain more than others, the basic orientation is that the single market programme does not represent a zero sum game. It is generally viewed as a positive sum game where everyone will gain something. In addition, most of the

TABLE 2
IMPACT OF THE SINGLE MARKET ON REGIONS IN THE COMMUNITY,*
POLITICIANS

Impact	IT	GR	SP	PO	IR	Total
Access to new markets	83.5	88.2	96.5	80.6	90.6	88.5
Stimulate technological innovation	88.8	88.4	93.9	89.2	77.1	88.5
More competition	96.7	94.8	94.9	92.6	96.2	95.3
Provide access to new financial resources	83.9	90.8	91.5	85.1	83.7	87.4
Increase the cost of production	28.4	36.2	42.3	65.6	33.0	38.9
Concentration of industry	82.1	59.5	82.9	47.8	72.1	72.4
Increase unemployment	35.3	56.6	23.0	42.6	40.4	38.0
Restructure commercial distribution network	92.0	90.1	96.8	90.2	80.6	90.2
Stimulate reconversion of agricultural production	78.5	92.2	89.3	90.2	81.0	85.8
Worsen situation in underdeveloped areas	67.1	47.1	44.2	63.0	52.8	54.7
Improvement in public services	44.3	79.9	67.9	72.8	-	63.8
Raising standards in social services	55.3	77.8	85.3	80.4	52.9	70.5
Stimulate adoption of new environmental standards	85.5	94.1	90.3	91.5	93.2	90.3
Stimulate institutional renewal	80.5	91.5	75.0	96.8	72.4	82.2
Modernization of regional administration	48.3	90.3	66.5	91.5	67.3	69.5
Confusion of functions	50.7	53.6	58.4	40.9	54.4	52.6
Slow-down decision-making process	40.5	38.1	49.2	64.9	48.1	46.5
Loss of regional identity	13.6	35.5	19.7	16.1	37.7	23.2

'In 1992 the unified European market will be created. For each of the following areas do you believe that the unified market will have or will not have an impact on your region?' The table presents the percentage of respondents stating that the single market 'will' have an impact on the particular item listed.

respondents report a commitment to make the most out of the 1992 programme because it does provide hope for lifting their localities out of underdevelopment and continuing the allocation of development funds that flow into the Community's Objective 1 regions.

In a similar fashion, a majority of respondents willingly acknowledge the positive impact that the single market will have in raising social standards and services in the Community as a whole (that is, stimulate the adoption of new environmental standards, raise wages and levels of well-being, improvement in public services, and stimulate institutional renewal). This might explain, in part, the willingness of the less developed countries such as Greece, Portugal, Ireland, and Spain to sign up for the 'Social Chapter' in Maastricht. It may increase at the margins the burden on the economy, but the rise in social standards is one of the great expectations that the common citizen residing in the peripheral countries of the EC nurtures in relation to the European Community. The EC and the 1992 programme are not merely the realization of a 'free market' design, but they represent a social and economic goal involving better living and working conditions for the citizens of Community member states.

When it comes to evaluating the impact of the single market on regional institutional structures, there is much less unanimity. Respondents display a general feeling that the single market will stimulate institutional renewal and modernize the regional administration, especially in the two countries (Greece and Portugal) lacking a long tradition of local government autonomy. Much less credence is given to the potential negative impact of the Community on the loss of regional identity, slowing down the decision-making process, or adding to the confusion of policy and administrative functions. Thu,s taking all three sectors, regional political elites judge the impact of the single market to be generally positive, and they display strong support for the growth of a regional dimension at the Community level.

The desire for a greater Community role in the regulation of regional and national affairs is immediately evident in the responses to the question of how the role of the Community should change after 1992. In Table 3 we can see that there is general support in all of the countries for an increased economic and social policy role on the part of the European Community. Those interviews generally reported that respondents wanted the EC to control the enforcement of environmental and urban planning standards, to continue financing projects for underdeveloped areas, to provide a European perspective for scientific research, etc.. But, there was much less support for the assumption of a greater European role in the financing of defence policies and control of immigration from non-EC countries.[6]

TABLE 3

OPINIONS ON THE *INCREASED* FUNCTIONS OF THE EUROPEAN COMMUNITY AFTER 1992, POLITICIANS

Function	IT	GR	SP	PO	IR	Total
Control of the enforcement of environmental and urban planning standards	82.3	95.5	80.5	75.5	67.9	81.7
Evaluation of regional investment projects	71.0	89.6	83.2	45.2	73.3	75.1
Financing of projects for underdeveloped areas	91.6	98.7	96.0	92.6	93.4	94.5
Monitoring of financial markets	81.8	90.1	57.2	67.4	70.5	73.8
European perspective for scientific research	91.9	94.7	82.7	81.5	79.2	87.0
Financing of European defence policies	35.2	35.1	34.8	-	26.5	33.7
Promotion of technological innovation	95.3	98.7	93.9	89.2	90.5	94.2
Formulating guidelines for professional education	84.5	86.5	82.7	64.9	69.5	79.9
Monitoring of labour market	84.5	86.4	80.2	63.0	77.1	80.2
Control of immigration from non-EC countries	58.9	70.4	44.2	20.7	44.8	50.8
Promotion of integration of emigrants	89.6	47.0	72.6	78.7	42.3	68.3
Coordination of foreign trade	90.7	87.3	76.8	55.6	76.2	80.2

'After the implementation of the unified European market, how in your opinion should the role of the Community change? For each of the following functions please indicate your preference.'

Responses: increases, stays the same, decreases.

TABLE 4

INSTITUTIONS NECESSARY OR INDISPENSABLE FOR THE COMMUNITY AFTER 1992, POLITICIANS

Operational instrument	IT	GR	SP	PO	IR	Total
Federal European Bank	98.1	89.3	95.5	88.0	94.3	93.9
European Environmental Agency	99.1	99.4	99.0	97.9	97.2	98.7
EC Europrogrammes for sectoral intervention	98.6	89.5	95.3	95.7	90.5	94.4
Interregional Euroconsortia for the planning of services and public infrastructure	32.9	84.3	34.4	-	25.7	44.0
Euroagencies for interregional cooperation for the management of services and infrastructure	83.0	82.8	90.4	90.4	90.4	86.8
University postgraduate Eurodiplomas in sciences	90.9	92.7	94.3	80.9	92.4	91.1
European administrative court	87.9	62.3	89.7	86.0	71.2	80.6
European agency to monitor labour market	99.1	90.8	98.0	88.3	94.3	95.1
European Securities and Exchange Commission	96.0	88.4	-	78.7	92.2	92.2
European Conference for regional presidents	89.5	94.1	91.9	90.4	-	91.4
European-level representation of regional councils	44.1	92.9	69.1	-	36.8	60.6
Regional offices in Brussels	85.2	86.8	90.9	84.0	85.7	86.9
European telecommunications agency	97.6	89.9	98.4	95.7	94.3	95.6

'After the implementation of the unified European market, in your opinion what operative instruments should the Community create in order to meet the challenges of the post-1992 period? Please express your opinion of whether you think that the Community needs to or does not need to create each of the following policy instruments.'

Responses: indispensable, necessary, not advisable.

TABLE 5
TRANS-REGIONAL CO-OPERATION AFTER 1992, POLITICIANS
(% responding 'indispensable' or 'opportune')

Common initiatives	IT	GR	SP	PO	IR	Total
Lobby the EC Commission	49.0	78.4	69.0	80.0	98.1	70.9
Formulating development programmes	98.6	93.5	98.4	94.6	100.0	97.2
Cultural/touristic exchange programmes	98.6	95.5	99.5	100.0	96.2	98.0
Plans for applied research	98.6	95.4	98.9	98.9	92.5	97.2
Policy to protect the environment	99.5	96.7	99.5	100.0	99.0	98.9
Activity to promote products/services	94.2	90.8	96.2	91.2	96.2	93.9
Strengthening regional airline services	87.4	92.8	95.1	95.7	97.2	92.8
Preparation of administrative personnel	98.1	94.1	94.5	92.5	91.5	94.8
Promotion of joint ventures between enterprises	90.9	90.7	97.2	96.8	91.5	93.2

'After the implementation of the European unified market in your opinion what are the common initiatives that should be created among regions located in different European countries? For each of the following possibilities please express your opinion.'

Responses: indispensable, opportune, not necessary.

As demonstrated in Table 4, regional elites are strongly supportive of creating European institutions to govern the single market and a system of extensive trans-regional co-operation that can take advantage of the fall of state borders as impediments to the natural flow of goods and services across national frontiers (Table 5). Thus, there is a strong desire to participate in trans-regional networking schemes under the auspices of the European Community that were effectively initiated one year later by the Commission.

Over four-fifths of the respondents are in favour of a wide variety of 'federal' agencies such as a European Central Bank, European Securities and Exchange Commission, and European Telecommunications Agency that are common in federal systems and which are slowly emerging as component parts of a new European institutional architecture. They also support the strengthening of regional policy linkages across regions straddling the northern Mediterranean coastline and Europe's western Atlantic rim in line with the programmes launched by the Community that gave substance to Article 10 of regulation 1042/1988 and trans-regional networks initiated under the auspices of the Structural Funds.[7]

The data presented above demonstrate that the ongoing European integration process has established deep roots in the local body politic. During the past 20 years the structure and function of sub-national government have changed significantly. Nevertheless, regional governments are still prevented from operating fully at the Community level by legal and political barriers imposed by the nation-state.[8]

The analysis of the responses presented above points to the existence of four major areas of concern that still have to be resolved as part of the preparation for and implementation of the single market. These areas of concern are: (1) the compensation for the lack of regional policy-making entities in centralized member states; (2) the establishment of direct EC-regional linkages in the implementation of Community policies; (3) the development prospects of the less developed regions in the context of the financing of the Structural Funds and sectoral policies of the European Community; and (4) the significance of a 'Europe of the Regions' for the institutional architecture of a 'new and closer union'. A number of these issues have already been covered by some of the preceding articles on a national basis, but what needs to be done now is to analyse what has taken place in economic terms at the regional level during the past decade: have regions within strong centralized states grown faster than their counterparts in federal or regionalized system or has the institutionalization of regional government in decentralized states provided a boost for economic and social development?

II. REGIONAL ECONOMIC PERFORMANCE DURING THE LAST TWO DECADES

In moving from the analysis of institutional structures and administrative issues to the evaluation of the outcomes of regional reforms on the local economy, a number of issues arise. What is the link between institutional change and economic performance? Can regional governments play a role in encouraging or discouraging economic activity in their regions? Are regional governments as economic actors relevant in a context where regional and national economies are increasingly becoming internationalized?[9]

Answers to these questions will be sought in a comparison of regional economic performances during the 1970s and 1980s and an extrapolation of the significance of the results for Community and regional government policies. The data-base used for the analysis consists of the results produced by an analysis of GDP per capita scores expressed in ECU at market prices and exchange rates and GDP per capita translated into purchasing power standards (PPS) used by the EC to measure levels of consumption and well-being.[10] The data were drawn from the European Community's regional data set (REGIO) and analysed by the authors using the raw data for each region covering the years included in the analysis.

To assess the regions' potential to adapt to changes in the international economy and develop indigenous resources to the highest degree possible, the EC's *First Periodic Report on the Regions* chose GDP per head measured at current market prices and exchange rates as the key indicator because it demonstrated the income generating capacity of an economic unit in the international arena. The assumption underpinning the logic was that integration was succeeding if all firms took the levels and changes of international prices as a reference point. This was particularly relevant, it was argued, because the EC faced increasing challenges from the international economy and, even if an area was not directly involved in international markets, international prices affected regional producers through inter-regional linkages.[11]

The *Fourth Report* alternatively applied purchasing power standards as its key indicator for income disparities. Purchasing power standards (PPS) compares prices for the same basket of goods and services in the different member states.[12] Income is expressed in terms of its ability to purchase that basket. PPS is, then, an indicator of the standard of living because it examines the internal purchasing power of a region's residents. The *First Report* argues that it is not an adequate indicator for comparing economic performance and potential. However, it may be a better indicator of development, especially if the objective of the Community is a convergence of living standards and not just income.[13] The analysis used here will employ both in order to draw a more complete picture of trends in regional economic performance.

Using the REGIO database as the source, both GDP per head according to market prices and PPS were used to classify the regions. The rankings were compared over the years to spot the upwardly mobile regions (those that improved) and the downwardly mobile ones (those that declined). The rank of one (1) indicates the strongest region and 167 the weakest region in our dataset. There are 170 regions in the REGIO dataset, but the data for Corsica, the Azores and Madeira were unavailable for the period of time analysed. Before 1981, the data for Spain, Greece and Portugal were also not available.[14]

The core of the comparison will be based on data for the 1980s, complemented by references to several years in the 1970s for the EC nine member states (UK, France, Italy, Germany, Belgium, Luxembourg, Netherlands, Denmark, and Ireland). Including these earlier years will help to distinguish between absolute and relative changes given that during the 1980s the member states of Greece, Portugal and Spain contained the bulk of the weaker regions. The comparison between regional rankings during the 1970s and 1980s is important because the addition of the later three Mediterranean countries pulled down the overall EC mean and made the original weaker regions (for example, Calabria, Basilicata, Sicily, etc.) rise in the ranking. The years examined – 1970, 1977, 1981, 1984, 1986, and 1987 – were chosen on the basis of data availability.

The first step to be taken in the analysis will be to briefly review the changes in the top 25 and bottom 25 regions in the rankings. The top regions remained more or less stable over time. The only clear change was the entry of Italian regions into the ranking. Italy's presence went from zero regions in 1970 to two regions, Val D'Aosta and Liguria, in 1987. Luxembourg dropped out of the top 25 ranking in 1981 and France went from four regions in 1970 to one in 1987. The rest remained rather stable on the average. As for the bottom 25, once Spain, Greece and Portugal entered in 1981, they comprised the bottom tier with an Italian region or two for company. In the 1970s the Italian Mezzogiorno dominated the group of bottom 25 regions. While these regions left the bottom of the rankings in the 1980s due to enlargement, they continued to register index scores substantially below the EC average.

Contrasting the rates of growth of the EC and the top and bottom 25 regions in the eighties, the evidence is not promising. Table 6 shows that between 1981 and 1984 and 1984 and 1986, the strongest regions had a higher growth rate than the rest. From 1986-87, the distance between the two closed with the growth rate of the stronger 25 only 0.2 per cent higher than the weaker 25. Notably, the weaker 25's growth rate between 1986-87 was higher than the Community average. Convergence, as noted earlier, depends upon the weaker regions having the faster rate of growth than the Community mean.

Looking at GDP according to PPS standards, again we see the same degree of stability for both the highest and lowest 25 regions since 1981. What is interesting, however, is the number of Italian regions – six or seven – that have entered the group of top 25 regions. They represent the second highest number of regions for one country (Germany had the largest number). Comparing PPS to market prices, we see that the Italian regions are replacing the German regions in the top positions; the regions in other countries are more or less stable.

Turning to growth rates (see Table 6) the distance between the strongest and weakest 25 is much closer than when the PPS indicator was used. In all cases, for the weaker 25 the average growth rate was higher than the EC average which suggests that some convergence of living

TABLE 6

GROWTH RATES IN THE 1980s ACCORDING TO GDP AT MARKET PRICES (ECU) AND PURCHASING POWER STANDARDS (PPS) PER INHABITANT

(in per cent)

YEAR	1981-1984		1984-1986		1986-1987	
UNIT	ECU	PPS	ECU	PPS	ECU	PPS
MEAN						
EC(12)	25.0	33.4	13.1	17.0	4.9	6.6
TOP 25	26.6	35.4	16.4	18.2	5.6	6.0
BOTTOM 25	22.8	33.6	8.6	17.2	5.4	6.7

TABLE 7

PERCENTAGE OF REGIONS ABOVE THE MEAN ACCORDING TO GDP AT MARKET PRICES (ECU) AND PPS

(per cent)

1970		1977		1981		1984		1986		1987	
ECU	PPS	ECU	PPS	ECU	PPS	ECU	PPS	ECU	PPS	ECU	PPS
43	37	58	NA	48	38	47	39	43	40	42	39

standards in the EC 12 took place over the period being considered. In 1986-87, the growth rate for the weaker regions was higher than for the strongest 25, although only by 0.7 per cent. Significantly, the average of the top 25 was lower than both the EC and bottom 25 means. This underscores the conclusion that convergence is being achieved.

To finish up this brief look at convergence or divergence of the Community as a whole, one more set of statistics needs to be examined – the number of regions above the mean. Looking at GDP at market prices, a disturbing trend is immediately evident – the percent of regions above the Community mean is decreasing. In 1981, 48 per cent or 83 regions had incomes above the mean. In 1987, 42 per cent or 71 regions were above. Table 7 shows a steady downward trend in the 1980s. This would suggest that the wealthier regions are getting wealthier and pulling up the mean. Looking at PPS, the number of regions above the mean remains fairly stable, if anything it increases going from 38 per cent in 1981 to 39 per cent in 1987. Although every year there are fewer regions above the mean according to this indicator, it is here that we are witnessing a stronger trend towards convergence.

Many Italian and British regions have experienced marked changes in ranks. It should be noted that both Italy and Britain endured vast economic and political upheaval during the 1970s and 1980s, more so than most of the other Community member states. This makes the success of the Italian regions especially deserving of notice. We will first examine

TABLE 8

LIST OF REGIONAL RANKING AND PERCENTAGE OF EC MEAN (EC=100) FOR ITALY'S UPWARDLY MOBILE REGIONS

	1981		1987		Change		EC--48% S25-55% W25-40%
	rank	% of mean	rank	% of mean	in rank	in %	
Liguria	65	104	23	129	+42	83%	
Lombardy	58	109	26	128	+32	75%	
Piedmont	69	102	37	121	+32	75%	
Emilia-Romagna	63	96	31	126	+32	77%	
Friuli-V-G	95	95	44	117	+51	75%	
Lazio	121	86	61	106	+60	81%	
Tuscany	106	93	46	114	+60	78%	
Veneto	119	87	68	102	+51	74%	
Trentino-A.-A.	107	93	52	110	+56	76%	
Umbria	122	85	74	99	+48	71%	
Marche	124	81	81	96	+43	71%	

GDP at market prices. Table 8 presents a list of Italian upwardly mobile regions which have risen steadily in position in the 1980s.

The growth of these Italian regions is impressive. All have growth rates well above the EC mean and the average of the top 25 regions. Six regions have moved above the mean and two others right up to it in a period when the number of regions above the mean is decreasing. The regions in the *Mezzogiorno*, however, still remain at the bottom of the rankings.

Many French regions remained more or less stable in terms of relative rank. However, France did have a notable number of downwardly mobile regions. Like their British counterparts, all these regions have growth rates below the EC, top 25 and bottom 25 averages. Lorraine and Nord-Pas-de-Calais were also ranked much higher in 1970 – 34th and 38th respectively – which makes their fall even more severe.

The German regions, which make up a major fraction of the strongest regions, held their positions. Several of them which had been initially located at relatively low levels did improve noticeably. All had growth rates above the EC mean and the mean for the top 25 but below the growth rates of the Italian regions which averaged 76 per cent growth.

We will examine the rest of the countries together because only a few regions moved significantly. These can be examined from 1970 until 1987. In Belgium, Liège, West Flanders, Hainault, and Namur Province all underwent fairly serious decline moving from 36th to 71st, 41st to 64th, 60th to 108th, and 62nd to 104th respectively. The movement of Hainault and Namur Province to well below the mean in the 1980s is disturbing because they both hugged the mean in the 1970s and the mere addition of

TABLE 9

RANKING OF TOP TWELVE ITALIAN REGIONS ON PPS

Region	1970	1977	1981	1987	Improvement in rank '87-'70
Lombardy	25	38	10	10	+15
Val d'Aosta	26	6	5	5	+21
Liguria	18	44	13	9	+9
Emilia-Romagna	55	53	11	13	+42
Piedmont	33	51	14	16	+17
Friuli-V.-G.	62	67	22	22	+40
Toscana	70	81	28	25	+45
Trentino-A.-A.	85	64	29	27	+58
Lazio	69	95	42	35	+34
Umbria	98	96	52	56	+42
Veneto	80	90	40	41	+39
Marche	96	97	55	66	+30

Greece, Spain and Portugal in the accounting should have moved them up. This result demonstrates that these regions underwent absolute and not just relative decline. Two Dutch regions also suffered such decline between the 1970s and 1980s. Gelderland fell from 68th to 100th and South Holland went from 30th to 51st. One Dutch region showed marked improvement; Drenthe rose from 91st in 1970 to 48th in 1987. However, earlier in the 1980s, it was actually ranked at 34th so it has been experiencing some fluctuation.

One last region deserves mention: Balearic Islands in Spain. Whereas its improvement has not been remarkable, from 130th or 72 per cent of the EC mean in 1981 to 112th or 80 per cent of the mean in 1987, it is the only region in any of the three later countries – Greece, Spain and Portugal – which has demonstrated steady improvement. Its growth rate is 66 per cent which is above both the EC and top 25 means.

Let us now look at the regions which have changed positions using GDP per head at purchasing power standards from 1981 to 1987. One encouraging finding is that the rate of growth of the bottom 25 between 1981 and 1987 which was 70 per cent is higher than both the EC rate (66 per cent) and the mean for the strongest 25 regions (67 per cent). As noted previously, this variable indicates increasing convergence of living standards.

Looking now at the data in Table 9, the top 25 and bottom 25 regions show a high degree of stability. Italy represents a large and very stable percentage of the top 25-30 regions in the decade of the 1980s. Improvement can be noted if we compare the positions from 1970 to 1987. At the beginning of the analysis (1970), Italy had one region (Lombardy) in the top 25 regions. By 1987 that number had increased to seven. Lombardy had been joined by Val d'Aosta, Emilia-Romagna, Piedmont, Liguria,

TABLE 10
RANKING OF BOTTOM TEN ITALIAN REGIONS IN PPS

	1981	1987	Change in ranking '87-'81
Abruzzo	120	120	0
Molise	133	133	0
Sardegna	137	138	-1
Basilicata	138	139	-1
Puglia	140	140	0
Campania	141	143	-2
Sicily	142	144	-2
Calabria	146	150	-4

Friuli-Venezia Giulia, and Toscana. Four other regions (Lazio, Trentino-Alto Adige, Umbria, and Veneto) also underwent significant improvements in rank but did not succeed in breaking into the top 25. However, these 12 regions of the North improved on the average 33 positions on the EC ranking over the 17-year period, which represents by far the best performance of any group of regions in the European Community.

The radical shift upward of the top 12 Italian regions contrasted quite significantly from what happened to the ranking of the other eight regions that represent the South. Given the entry after 1980 of the three countries (Greece, Portugal, and Spain) of the southern periphery, the comparison between the regional rankings in the 1970s *vis-à-vis* those in the 1980s for those regions at the bottom of the ranking would not be valid. In the previous period, the eight southern regions occupied the last eight spots in the ranking. Therefore, it is more appropriate to look at how the southern regions fared in the shorter 1981-87 period.

Table 10 shows that the eight southern regions had dismal showings when compared to their northern neighbours. Three failed to make any progress in their rankings and the other five even lost further ground to a few Spanish and even to one Portuguese region: Lisbon-Val de Tejo. The contrasting performance of the central/northern regions versus their southern neighbours argues against the search for an explanation of their change in ranking in the overall increased performance of Italy *vis-à-vis* the other eleven countries in the EC. On the contrary, if Italy's relative rank did improve it was due to the activity of the 12 central and northern regions rather than the eight southern ones. Thus, the analysis at the national level would mask the tremendous differences and different trajectories that characterize two parts of the same country.[15]

Some striking differences emerge when we compare this indicator and GDP in market prices. First, many of the British regions which declined using the first indicator improved according to purchasing power standards. Second, the top 25 positions were shared in the 1980s by Germany and Italy when PPS was employed. Instead, when GDP at market prices was used German regions became clearly dominant. Third, there were many more German regions below the mean, and some Spanish regions were at the mean or even above (Balearics). Denmark's regions were placed lower, and more French and Dutch regions showed decline where they had demonstrated stability using GDP at market prices. What these discrepancies suggest is that growth and development are not synonymous concepts.

Economic growth, which is actually measured with GDP at market prices, is not always equivalent to real development. Growth is solely an economic notion. For instance, both Groningen (NL) and Grampian (UK) have extremely high regional outputs but in both cases it comes from the extraction of natural resources: gas (Groningen) and oil (Grampian). They may be wealthy regions, but they are not necessarily developed. Development is a multi-dimensional process which centres as much on changes in structures and institutions as on economic growth and output.

By re-examining the results, we can see that there is some evidence for arguing that regional development may be strongly promoted by regional government activity. First, the strongest regions – found in Germany – have the most developed regional institutions with the most widespread powers. Second, the weakest regions – found in Portugal, Ireland and Greece – have regional bodies in name only. Third, the most dynamic regions, found in Italy, have had regional governments growing in institutional capability over the past two decades and demonstrating a higher level of governmental performance.[16] Here, economic and political development appear to be growing in a parallel and mutually reinforcing fashion. Fourth, the strongest regions in Spain, which was the fastest growing country of the weakest group in the mid- and late 1980s, have the greatest degree of autonomous powers in the Spanish context.[17] Fifth, the regions showing an alarming decline of output, the British areas, also experienced during the same period a centralization of power towards the national government away from the sub-national institutions. France may be experiencing a similar pull of resources toward the centre which may explain why many regions experienced decay. Although France regionalized in 1985, there is still some question as to whether the decision-making authority has actually been decentralized when it comes to regional planning or decisions regarding regional economic and social development.

The analysis of the economic data suggests that centralized nation-states have been less successful in mobilizing resources in the pursuit of economic and social development than their more decentralized counterparts in Europe. In the past, these nations have been considered underdeveloped because of their peripheral location. The hypothesis advanced here is that, keeping all other factors – capital, labour skills, infrastructures, entrepreneurship – constant, the existence of decentralized forms of policy-making and administrative structure helps countries to accelerate their rates of development *vis-à-vis* centralized states. The implications of the hypothesis are that decentralized and productive forms of sub-national governments (for example, regional governments) capable of operating in the field of economic and social planning and development constitute a necessary but not sufficient condition for economic development within the context of the European Community. Why is this so?

The answer can be sought in the work that has begun to focus on the 'endogenous development' and 'networking' approaches to the organization of production in the field of regional development analysis. Endogenous development is related to the changes taking place in production and transportation technologies that lead to a greater spatial diffusion in both industrial and service activities. A spate of studies have recently concentrated on the development of small firms in specialized industrial districts and emphasized the role of firm organization, agglomeration economies, transaction costs, innovation diffusion, technological poles and research parks, and regional policies that emphasize the role of customized policies responding to the local mix of economic needs in promoting local opportunities for economic growth and spurring the local capacity to engage in innovation.[18]

The endogenous approach differs greatly from previous theories that emphasized the role of relocating productive forces from developed to underdeveloped regions, thus placing the emphasis on transferring productive capabilities from outside of underdeveloped regions to them on the basis of economic and financial incentives. Traditional policies placed much less emphasis on the development of endogenous resources within the regions.

What is important in the endogenous approach to regional development strategies is the role of a common structure in providing input into the determination of firm organization, management, production, and distribution of goods and services – that is, an emphasis on shared service and manufacturing facilities – at the regional level. Shared services systems provide firms with similar needs through common access to technologies, manufacturing facilities, marketing services, research and development, credit, management systems, etc. These services are made available to entrepreneurs in the immediate vicinity by structures –

industrial parks, research and marketing centres, vocational education programmes, fairs, joint decision-making processes, etc. – promoted and sustained by regional and local governments operating in co-operation with the interested firms and social groups.

A shared manufacturing system constitutes a shared strategic alliance among manufacturers in a specific region that meets specific entrepreneurial needs. In this system of shared services and manufacturing facilities, the role of viable regional and local government institutions is central because the local government bodies are in a position to assume a 'strategic' role within the system by: (1) allocating public resources (grants, loans, joint funding programmes, etc.) to make them available to entrepreneurial groups; (2) engaging in strategic planning to assess and prioritize the region's needs in formulating a common strategy; and (3) networking at higher levels in the institutional structure to gain access to additional funding (Community and national government funds) and formulate strategic alliances.

In the past, low levels of economic development, weak administrative capacity, and a lack of constitutional authority on the part of sub-national units to engage in economic and social policy-making were used to justify the intervention of national administrative authorities, but experience has shown that national administrations are not in a position to fine tune their intervention policies to the needs of the local economy and customize them for the local area. In addition, the role of the national administrations prevents sub-national administrations from improving their level of efficiency and ability to react to local exigencies. The emphasis on national initiatives tends to produce a cycle of dependency on the part of local administration. The monopolization of decisions by the centre leads to the nurturing of a dependence syndrome where the initiative and resources provided by national level institutions leads to the emphasis of top–down linkages and eventually to a growth in the size and actions of the national bureaucratic machinery. The impact of these policies has been to create a state of mind that emphasizes the role of national assistance and initiative in alleviating depressed local conditions. The supply of national assistance may ease severe economic conditions in the short run, but it also creates a dependency syndrome. As a result, local economic behaviour is distorted, and incentives are created for local government to seek external aid as the answer to local needs rather than promoting the creation of self-sustaining development process.

A case in point of the shortcomings of central control of local economic development is provided by the illustrations from two cases – Greece and France – that seem on the surface to be poles apart but which in reality are highly similar in developing a dependency mentality in the pursuit of economic development. Greece's national administrative structure is centralized but 'weak' from an organizational and professional perspective while France has a very 'strong' administrative structure manned by highly qualified professionals.

Greece's administrative structure is weak because (1) it has inadequate linkages with the local population and institutions, (2) its bureaucratic personnel are not sufficiently qualified for tackling the increasing activities allocated to national administrations, (3) administrative job retention and promotion are heavily dependent upon political connections, (4) alternative institutions do not exist (the administrative regions are national creations and continue to exist as parts of the national administrative structure) and alternative institutions have not been put into place, (5) the national bureaucracy is over burdened with responsibilities and the lack of viable sub-national institutions do not permit it to off-load responsibilities, and (6) the centre is incapable of operating in an effective manner in the peripheral and island areas of the country. The lack of a viable administrative infrastructure at the sub-national level also makes itself felt in the inability of Greece to apply for and use European Investment Bank (EIB) funds for the stimulation and sustenance of entrepreneurship. Greece continues to apply and spend most of its EIB money for infrastructure projects which the national administrative structure is capable of managing. Industrial development, the creation of technological parks, and the formation of policy networks on a small scale seem to be beyond the ability and interest of the national authorities to tackle in a successful manner.

France offers an example of a centralized but strong national administration that still has difficulty in promoting regional development. This was particularly evident in the formation of the IMP projects. The French Integrated Mediterranean Programmes (IMPs) were grafted on to the existing national administrative structure rather than to a fully autonomous regional administrative system. Thus, the French IMP programmes represented elaborations of existing national regional development programmes. In comparative terms the continuation of central control of regional development planning and policies well into the 1980s seems to have translated itself into a slow down of development in the French periphery. French central control has not been able to adequately stimulate the growth of southern French regions to the same extent as their neighbours in Italy and Spain; nor has national policy-making enabled the traditional industrial areas of France to adequately handle the industrial restructuring process.

The region which has prospered, however, under central guidance of the planning and development has been the Ile-de-France, the Paris region, which has remained on the top of European rankings throughout the last two decades and has not followed the downward spiral in the ranking that has affected the other French regions. Central control, therefore, helps the central area to the detriment of the peripheral areas as a whole, and this may help to explain why central areas and central political figures are so reluctant to give up control of the decision-making process to the benefit of non-central areas – that is, the periphery. In this light arguments of bureaucratic efficiency and control mask, in fact, the need to make sure that central areas remain the main beneficiaries of development policies targeted toward a change in the balance between centre and periphery. Under centralization, the relative winner in the struggle between centre and periphery is the central area where decision-making and responsibilities for administration lie. However, with decentralization not only is decision-making devolved but so is the responsibility for implementation. Thus, under decentralization, the periphery gains *vis-à-vis* the centre.

The ability of central governments to remain the main interlocutor for regional development has been eroded during the last two decades due to the introduction of regional governments in a number of formally centralized states such as Italy, Belgium, France and Spain. Further erosion in the state's role has been introduced by the evolution of the Community's role in regional planning and development as a product of the creation of the ERDF, experimentation with the co-ordinated approached during the 1980s, and the initiation of the Community Support Frameworks (CSFs) in the late 1980s. These changes made the Community an important source of funding for regional development and decision-making in the allocation of resources. We should also keep in mind that in the first instance with the IMPs and then in the second instance with the CSF the Community introduced the concept of 'partnership' which recognized the existence of a regional role (even in cases where regions as such did not exit) in the determination of development priorities and in the implementation of programmes.

Significant changes have also taken place in the Community's right to co-ordinate and supervise regional policies. The Single European Act introduced, as stated above, the principle of partnership – sharing of responsibility among levels of government – and 'subsidiarity' – allocating decisions to the appropriate level of territorial responsibility – in the regional policy-making process, thereby giving the Community a pre-eminent role in the field of regional policy and forcing previously highly centralized nation-states to recognize the role of sub-national forces in the planning and implementation process. Further changes have been introduced by the Maastricht Treaty.

III. THE REGIONS AFTER MAASTRICHT

The provisions of the Maastricht Treaty promise to move the role of the Community in regional affairs one step further. If before 1992 the Community provided for itself the legal right and the ability to intervene in regional policy, from 1992 onwards it will have the political will to do so. Maastricht represents an important step along the road toward institutionalizing the role of regions in the governing of the Community and in expanding the policy reach of the Community into regional and social affairs.

The creation of a Committee of the Regions in Article 198 places the region at the same level as interest groups which have had for a long time representation through the Economic and Social Committee. Article 198c specifies that 'where it considers that specific regional interests are involved, the Committee for the Regions may submit an opinion on the matter'.

It might be observed that giving the regions an advisory role is not tantamount to making them a central institution in Community decision-making, but it should be remembered that up to now the regions have had no recognition, outside of the creation in 1988 of the Assembly of Regions and Local Authorities as an advisory body within DG XVI, as representatives of sub-national interests. The Assembly has operated since 1988 as a weak body and more as a channel for information from the Community to the regions and local authorities rather than as a channel for regional demands to be funnelled up to the Community. The present institution created by the Maastricht Treaty will operate to channel information and opinions from the bottom up. As stated in the last provision of Article 198c: 'The opinion of the Committee, together with a record of the proceedings, shall be forwarded to the Council and to the Commission.'

Article 198a states that the members of the Committee will consist of 'representatives of regional and local authorities', and it divides the 189 members among the twelve member states. Thus, even though the Committee was named after the regions, room has been left for the Council to nominate members representing local authorities as well as the regions.

The members of the Committee of the Regions will 'be appointed by the Council acting unanimously on proposals from the respective Member States for four years'. How this provision will be implemented will probably vary widely from one member state to another. Where regional and Länder authorities are powerful, they will most likely gain the lion's share of the representation. However, where regional authorities are

completely missing the bulk of the representatives will most likely be chosen from the local authorities. The instructions provided for the members of the Committee of the Regions make it clear that once nominated the representatives cannot be limited in their activity by 'any mandatory instructions'. The last paragraph of Article 198a stipulates that 'They shall be completely independent in the performance of their duties, in the general interest of the Community'.

Building on the impetus provided by the realization of the 1992 programme in the Single European Act, the Maastricht Treaty gives the Community in Article 2 the task of establishing economic and monetary union and implementing the common policies listed in Article 3. This article lists 22 activities for the Community, ranging from the elimination of customs duties and quantitative restrictions to a common agriculture and fisheries policy to measures in the sphere of tourism. What is of interest in the list is how the number of policy areas for which the Community assumes a direct responsibility continues to grow over time. The Community is becoming increasingly the central actor in a broad range of policy areas dealing with regional planning, the Structural Funds, trans-European networking, and economic and social cohesion, and these areas are regulated by qualified majority voting on proposals originating from the Commission and after an Opinion of the European Parliament.

Changes in Article 189 foresee that the European Parliament will now be recognized as having co-decision making powers along with the Council in the making of regulations and issuance of directives. The December 1991 agreement in Maastricht was criticized in some quarters for not having given enough powers to the Parliament, but it did make a breakthrough in awarding the Parliament a veto in the legislative process that has been dominated for such a long time by the Council. These changes will undoubtedly enhance the Parliament's powers in policy making in general but particularly in the areas of policies applying to economic and social cohesion, a code word for policies dealing with economic and social matters that are of importance to sub-national governmental bodies and to peripheral member states.

Rather than weakening the commitment of the member states to reducing regional disparities, Maastricht signalled an acceleration in the provision of funds from the Community budget for regional development as accounted for by the Structural Funds and the new Cohesion Fund. Structural Fund allocations have not been reduced and they will be increased even more in the Delors II budget proposal. In addition, extra money will be provided through the Cohesion Fund designed to finance projects in Spain, Portugal, Ireland, and Greece in the areas of the environment and transportation. As a consequence, the final allocation of the Community budget earmarked for the regions might well constitute a watershed that will significantly contribute to the convergences of peripheral regional economies with the levels of those of the more core regions. Indications from recent studies are that even before the Community doubled its contributions to the Structural Funds in 1988 a significant impact was being made on the potential, as well as the reality, of peripheral regional economies in closing the gap with those of the core regions.[19] All of what we have seen in the Maastricht Treaty bodes well for the continuation of this process throughout the 1990s.

By the publication of the next Periodic Report on the regions, we might see that the regions with institutionalized regional governments have succeeded in making more strides in producing policies that meet local exigencies and make maximum use of the potential for growth demonstrated by their regional economies and encourage other countries which persist in maintaining centralized states in finally moving towards more decentralized administrative and political structures. Such a policy shift is essential if Objective 1 areas are expected to evolve towards forms of structural growth and development that will bring them closer to the European Community mean and full partnership in the development process.

NOTES

1. See the book edited by V. Wright and Y. Mény, *Centre–Periphery Relations in Western Europe* (London: Allen & Unwin, 1985) and Raffaella Y. Nanetti, *Growth and Territorial Policies: The Italian Model of Social Capitalism* (London: Pinter Publishers, 1988).
2. See the contributions by R. Camagni (ed.), *Innovation Networks: A Spatial Perspective* (London, Belhaven, 1991); P. Bianchi and R. Cappellin, 'The European Internal Market and the Internationalization of Small and Medium Sized Enterprises', *Built Environment*, Vol. 16, No. 1, 1990; P. Bianchi, *Antitrust e gruppi industriali* (Bologna: Il Mulino, 1988); G. Becattini (ed.), *Mercato e forze locali: il distretto industriale* (Bologna: Il Mulino, 1987); G. Fua' and C. Zacchia (eds.), *Industrializzazione senza fratture* (Bologna: Il Mulino, 1983); M. Piore and C. Sabel, *The Second Industrial Divide: Possibilities for Prosperity* (New York: Basic Books, 1983).
3. The same could be said for the creation of a consultative Regional Council provided by the Maastricht Treaty. For countries with existing regional governments, the representatives of the regions will effectively represent viable policy-making structures. In those countries where they do not exist, it is uncertain exactly what they will be representing.
4. The two surveys ran into serious organizational problems due to the conflict present in the two regions. In Northern Ireland the survey of regional politicians' attitudes was not possible due to the lack of an institutionalized setting for the identification of regional political elites such as the former Stormont or regional assembly; nor was it possible to interview the administrative elites responsible for the management of policies. The

questionnaire was considered to be 'too political' despite of its focus on the European Community. The fieldwork in Corsica was also interrupted by a prolonged strike of regional civil servants and civil strife that broke out on the island during the spring and summer of 1989.

5. For purpose of building into the dataset a control factor to distinguish between Italian-specific and Objective 1-specific attitudes, the Italian interviews were divided between three Objective 1 regions (Abruzzi, Puglia, and Sicily) and three non-Objective 1 regions (Lombardy, Veneto, and Lazio).
6. It is interesting to note that these two items were of major concern to the representatives of the member states at the 9-10 December 1991 European Council meeting. The change in views may be a product of the experience with the war against Iraq and the collapse of the Soviet sphere of influence in the East that have set of fears that the Community would be inundated by hordes off Eastern Europeans and Russians trying to escape hunger and a bleak economic future.
7. For a detailed discussion of these programmes, see Robert Leonardi 'The Implications of Economic and Social Cohesion on the Community's Institutional Architecture after the Creation of the Single Market: The Role of Transregional Networks', Dec. 1991, Department of Government, London School of Economics.
8. Since the interviews were completed, there has been a de facto loosening of the restrictions imposed on regional governments from being present at the European level. See the model of post-1992 linkages in the European Community presented by Robert Leonardi and Raffaella Nanetti in 'Introduction', *The Regions and European Integration: The Case of Emilia-Romagna* (London: Pinter Publishers, 1990), pp. 1-8.
9. For an argument that in order to succeed local economic development efforts have to be in line with world economic trends, see Ash Amin, *Journal of Urban and Regional Research*.
10. For a detailed discussion of these measures, see *The Regions of Europe: First Periodic Report on the Social and Economic Situation of the Regions of the Community* (Luxembourg: Office of Official Publications, 1981).
11. There are certain problems noted by the Commission reports regarding this indicator. First, short run exchange rate variations may draw a skewed picture of real economic activity. Second, this indicator cannot account for internal price differentials, especially of services and goods not traded on the international market.
12. See CEC, *The Regions in the 1990s - Fourth Periodic Report*, Brussels, COM(90) 609, 1991.
13. The Third Periodic Report ranked the regions according to a synthetic index of the intensity of regional problems they devised. The index was comprised of several variables including GDP and employment rates. Why it was not repeated in the Fourth Report is not known.
14. Additionally, the classification of British regions was re-categorized for the decade of the eighties, thus making comparisons with the seventies somewhat awkward. In 1970 and 1977, using the older, larger classifications, there was not a single UK region above the European mean. In 1981, after the re-categorization, there were two in the top 25 and eleven above the mean, which is a change not entirely attributable to the entry of Greece, Portugal, and Spain.
15. A case in point is the performance of the Abruzzo and Molise regions which performed at a higher level than their neighboring southern regions. For a detailed analysis of Abruzzo, see Robert Leonardi, 'Riflessi della riduzione del sostegno comunitario sull'economia regionale, con particolare riguardo al sistema industriale', Presidenza della Giunta Regionale, Nov. 1991.
16. See R. Putnam, R. Leonardi and R.Y. Nanetti, *La pianta e le radici: Il radicamento dell'istituto regionale nel sistema politico Italiano* (Bologna: Il Mulino, 1985).
17. At the end of the 1980s and beginning of the 1990s, the highest growth rate is in fact registered by Portugal.
18. See S. Illeris, *Services and Regions in Europe* (Aldershot: Avebury, 1980); R. Cappellin and P. Nijkamp (eds.), *The Spatial Context of Technological Change* (Aldershot:

Avebury-Gower, 1990); E. Malecki 'R&D and Technological Transfer in Economic Development: The Role of Regional Technology Capability', in R. Cappellin and P. Nijkamp (eds.), 1990; A.J. Scott and M. Storper 'Regional Development Reconsidered', *Working Paper No. 1, Lewis Center for Regional Policy Studies*, University of California, Los Angeles, Dec. 1990; W. Stoehr, *Global Challenge and Local Response: Local Initiatives for Economic Regeneration in Contemporary Europe* (London: Mansell Publishing, 1990); D. Cleland, S. Dharwadkar and B. Bidanda (eds.), *Shared Manufacturing: The Strategic Choice* (University of Pittsburgh, School of Engineering, 1992); G. Garofoli and F. Latella (eds.), *Endogenous Development in Southern Europe* (Aldershot: Avebury, 1992); and M. Tykkylainen (ed.), *Development Issues and Strategies in the New Europe* (Aldershot: Avebury, 1992).

19. See the report by the author on 'The State of Social and Economic Cohesion in the Community Prior to the Creation of the Single Market: The View from the Bottom Up' to be published by the Community in the near future.